Preface

History, sir, will tell lies as usual.
—GENERAL BURGOYNE IN
GEORGE BERNARD SHAW'S *The Devil's Disciple* (1897)

She was not a humiliated woman.
—HORACE, *Ode* 1.37.32 (20S B.C.)

IN 34 B.C. A REMARKABLE CEREMONY took place in the Gymnasium of Alexandria. Cleopatra VII, 35 years of age, ruler of Egypt for the past 17 years and a Roman citizen, legally confirmed that her Ptolemaic kingdom—established 270 years previously by Ptolemy I, her ancestor and a companion of Alexander the Great—had been restored to its former territorial glory. It now extended from Cyrene in North Africa through Egypt proper, well up the Nile, and around the eastern perimeter of the Mediterranean, including Cyprus and parts of Crete, to the edge of the Aegean. Cleopatra's four children participated in the ceremony, as they were to continue the kingdom and to create a network of allied monarchies that would extend as far as Armenia and Parthia (the modern Iranian plateau). Because Cleopatra was allied with the Roman Republic, these arrangements were by necessity approved by the senior Roman official in the region, the triumvir Marcus Antonius (Mark Antony), also present at the ceremony. If all had gone to plan, most of the eastern Mediterranean would have been under Ptolemaic rule, with Rome and a few small kingdoms reduced to scattered territories.

Yet in four years Cleopatra was dead and her possessions annexed by Rome and other monarchs. Things had gone badly wrong. Simply put, her vision of the future was actually one of the past. She was the last of the true Hellenistic rulers, and her dream of creating a new order and a new concept of monarchy fell victim to the overwhelming power of Rome. Technically a failure in her ambitions, ironically she was instrumental in creating the Roman Empire, although she never was to know this.

Today Cleopatra is best known through her extensive afterlife, especially of the last 500 years, pervasive in drama, visual and performing arts, and film. It is hard to escape any view of the queen that is not dominated by these popular conceptions. Yet it is the purpose of this book to create a portrait of Cleopatra based solely on information from the ancient world. To produce as complete an account as possible, one must draw upon everything available, not only Greek and Latin literature, but Egyptian art, architecture, and official documents, and Greco-Roman art and coin portraits. The picture remains frustrating because of the sheer lack of evidence. The information that is available can be badly tainted by the victor's point of view, which pervades the relevant classical literature. There are several gaps in the record, most notably the three years from late 40 to late 37 B.C., when there is simply nothing. Yet it is nonetheless possible to put together a fascinating picture of this most dynamic of women, who in her 39 years became one of the most remarkable people in world history. What follows is an attempt to use all the evidence and to learn as much as possible about the queen and her world.

The writing of this book draws on the author's previous experience with the environment of the last century B.C. and the phenomenon of the friendly or allied king (in this case a queen), the monarch who ruled an independent kingdom but was closely tied to Rome. Cleopatra is not usually considered in this category because she predated the Roman Empire (Herod the Great and Juba II of Mauretania, both previously treated, are often considered better examples), but nevertheless she fits all the criteria of an allied monarch—even receiving official Roman recognition as such—and is a transitional figure between the Roman Republic and the empire.

The author first and foremost would like to thank Ronnie Ancona and Sarah Pomeroy for their original commission to write this biography and to include it in their series Women in Antiquity, as well as for the faith in the author's abilities that such an offer represented, and their many helpful comments. Although most of the writing was done in the author's study in Santa Fe with its inspiring views, the library research

CLEOPATRA

WOMEN IN ANTIQUITY

Series Editors: Ronnie Ancona and Sarah B. Pomeroy

This book series provides compact and accessible introductions to the life and historical times of women from the ancient world. Approaching ancient history and culture broadly, the series selects figures from the earliest of times to late antiquity.

Cleopatra
A Biography
Duane W. Roller

Clodia Metelli
The Tribune's Sister
Marilyn B. Skinner

Galla Placidia
The Last Roman Empress
Hagith Sivan

CLEOPATRA

A BIOGRAPHY

Duane W. Roller

OXFORD
UNIVERSITY PRESS

OXFORD
UNIVERSITY PRESS

Oxford University Press, Inc., publishes works that further
Oxford University's objective of excellence
in research, scholarship, and education.

Oxford   New York
Auckland   Cape Town   Dar es Salaam   Hong Kong   Karachi
Kuala Lumpur   Madrid   Melbourne   Mexico City   Nairobi
New Delhi   Shanghai   Taipei   Toronto

With offices in
Argentina   Austria   Brazil   Chile   Czech Republic   France   Greece
Guatemala   Hungary   Italy   Japan   Poland   Portugal   Singapore
South Korea   Switzerland   Thailand   Turkey   Ukraine   Vietnam

First published by Oxford University Press, Inc., 2010
198 Madison Avenue, New York, New York 10016
www.oup.com

First issued as an Oxford University Press paperback, 2011

Library of Congress Cataloging-in-Publication Data
Roller, Duane W.
Cleopatra : a biography / Duane W. Roller.
p.   cm. — (Women in antiquity)
Includes bibliographical references and index.
ISBN 978-0-19-536553-5; 978-0-19-982996-5 (pbk.)
1. Cleopatra, Queen of Egypt, d. 30 B.C.
2. Queens—Egypt—Biography.
3. Egypt—Kings and rulers—Biography.
4. Egypt—History—332–30 B.C. I. Title.
DT92.7.R65 2010
932'.021092—dc22   [B] 2009024061

1 3 5 7 9 8 6 4 2

Printed in the United States of America
on acid-free paper

Contents

Illustrations

was largely performed in the Harvard College Library, the Ohio State University Library (with the special assistance of its interlibrary loan staff), and the Institut für Archäologie, Karl-Franzens Universität, Graz, Austria. The author would like to thank those institutions and their staff for their support. Further thanks go to Sally-Ann Ashton, Malcolm Chisholm, Erich S. Gruen, Kathryn Gutzwiller, Pietro Giovanni Guzzo and Domenico Esposito of the Soprintendenza Archeologica di Pompei, George L. Irby-Massie, Diana E. E. Kleiner, Christa Landwehr, William M. Murray, Nancy Leonard and the Rosicrucian Museum in San Jose, Josephine Crawley Quinn, Letitia K. Roller, John Scarborough, Elena Stolyarik and the American Numismatic Society, Stefan Vranka and many others at Oxford University Press, Susan Walker, and Wendy Watkins and the Center for Epigraphical and Paleographical Studies at the Ohio State University.

CLEOPATRA

Introduction

FEW PERSONALITIES FROM CLASSICAL ANTIQUITY are more familiar yet more poorly grasped than Cleopatra VII (69–30 B.C.), queen of Egypt. The subject of a vast repertory of post-antique popular culture and also a significant figure in literature, art, and music, Cleopatra herself is surprisingly little known and generally misunderstood. Even in the years immediately after her death her memory was condemned by those who had defeated her, thus tainting the ancient sources.

Cleopatra VII was an accomplished diplomat, naval commander, administrator, linguist, and author, who skillfully managed her kingdom in the face of a deteriorating political situation and increasing Roman involvement. That she ultimately lost does not diminish her abilities. Yet her persona in popular culture and the arts often overrides her real self, and even scholarly accounts of her career may rely on information from early modern drama and art or the movies, which are interesting and significant in their own right but of no relevance in understanding the queen herself. Although she is the subject of an extensive bibliography, she can be unfairly represented as a person whose physical needs determined her political decisions. Some of the most unbiased evidence from her own era, the art and coinage produced while she was alive, is too frequently ignored.

Like all women, she suffers from male-dominated historiography in both ancient and modern times and was often seen merely as an appendage of the men in her life or was stereotyped into typical chauvinistic female roles such as seductress or sorceress, one whose primary accomplishment was ruining the men that she was involved with. In this view, she was nothing more than the "Egyptian mate"[1] of Antonius and played little role in the policy decisions of her own world. Even into the twentieth century she could still be seen as a remarkably insignificant figure in Greco-Roman history. In the 1930s the great Roman historian Ronald Syme—without whom so much less would be known about the ancient world—astonishingly wrote: "Cleopatra was of no moment whatsoever in the policy of Caesar the Dictator, but merely a brief chapter in his amours," and "the propaganda of Octavianus magnified Cleopatra beyond all measure and decency."[2]

Yet she was the only woman in all classical antiquity to rule independently—not merely as a successor to a dead husband—and she desperately tried to salvage and keep alive a dying kingdom in the face of overwhelming Roman pressure. Descended from at least two companions of Alexander the Great, she had more stature than the Romans whom she opposed. As a woman, her dynastic survival required personal decisions unnecessary to men. Depicted evermore as the greatest of seductresses, who drove men to their doom, she had only two known relationships in 18 years, hardly a sign of promiscuity. Furthermore, these connections—to the two most important Romans of the period—demonstrated that her choice of partners was a carefully crafted state policy, the only way that she could ensure the procreation of successors who would be worthy of the distinguished history of her dynasty.

Role models for Cleopatra were limited but dynamic. First there was the most famous of Egyptian queens, Hatshepsut (ruled ca. 1479/3–1458/7 B.C.), who succeeded upon the death of her husband, Thutmosis II. She saw herself as the one who liberated Egypt from years of Hyksos rule and was patroness of a remarkable building program, still conspicuously visible. She also extended the boundaries of the Egyptian state: like Cleopatra, she was especially concerned with creating a presence in the Levant. Another inspiration for Cleopatra was Artemisia, queen of Halikarnassos in 480 B.C. Although little is known about her, she is remembered for commanding her own fleet and playing a crucial (if somewhat enigmatic) role in the Battle of Salamis, the great concluding event in the war between the Greek states and Persia. And finally there was the first major Ptolemaic queen, Arsinoë II (ca. 316–270 B.C.), daughter of Ptolemy I, who defined the characteristics of female royalty within the dynasty. Although she never ruled on her own, her status in Egypt was equal to that of her brother-husband, Ptolemy II. She established the concept of sibling marriage—an essential dynastic tool—among the Ptolemies and was also married to two Macedonian kings. Like Cleopatra, she carefully chose her partners to enhance her own status.

All three of these queens had qualities that molded Cleopatra VII. There were many other influences, including Alexander the Great, Mithradates VI the Great of Pontos, and her male Ptolemaic ancestors, as well as the dynamic women of Greek mythology, such as Penelope, who, although married, ruled a kingdom alone for 20 years. Even the aristocratic Roman women who were her competitors, such as Fulvia, Octavia, and Livia, were models, resulting in a cross-fertilization between the role of the Hellenistic queen and that of the Roman matron.

Because there are no certain portraits of Cleopatra except the two dimensional-shorthand on her coinage, little can be said about her physical appearance. The coins show a prominent nose (a family trait) and chin, with an intensity of gaze and hair inevitably drawn back into a bun. That she was short is explicitly stated in one source and perhaps implied in the famous bedsack tale.[3] A notice by Plutarch is often misquoted to imply that she was not particularly beautiful,[4] but what was actually written is that the force of her personality far outweighed any physical attractiveness. Sources agree that her charm was outstanding and her presence remarkable, something still noticeable even a few days before her death.[5] As a proper royal personage she was skilled in horseback riding and hunting;[6] in fact more than once she was described as male in Egyptian records.

Cleopatra VII was born around the beginning of 69 B.C.; she was the last of the Ptolemaic dynasty, rulers of Egypt for 250 years. She was the second oldest of five siblings, children of Ptolemy XII, who had become increasingly entangled in the politics of the emergent Roman state. When Ptolemy XII fled to Rome in 58 B.C. to escape the anger of his people in the face of declining economic conditions and a feeling that he was too beholden to the Romans, Cleopatra may have joined him. He was restored three years later, with significant Roman help, including the efforts of the young cavalry officer Marcus Antonius. Ptolemy's eldest daughter, Berenike IV, who had seized the throne in her father's absence, was executed at this time, putting Cleopatra in line for the succession. Ptolemy XII died in 51 B.C. and Cleopatra did become queen, but jointly with her younger brother Ptolemy XIII, as there was significant opposition to a woman's ruling alone. In fact this coalesced into a faction, and civil war broke out between the siblings. The war was still under way when Julius Caesar arrived in 48 B.C. and invoked long-standing legal grounds for Roman involvement in Egyptian politics.

Caesar spent the winter of 48–47 B.C. settling the war—Ptolemy XIII was a casualty—and left in the spring after placing Cleopatra alone on the throne. That summer she bore a son, whom she named Caesarion, and claimed that he was Caesar's. With her rule secure, she devoted herself to stabilizing the kingdom: her father's debts, economic problems, and the looming Roman presence made her task difficult, but it was manageable. To assert her position in the ever-changing Roman political scene, she journeyed to Rome in 46 B.C. and received legal recognition as an allied monarch. A second trip in 44 B.C. put her in the city when Caesar was assassinated, and she remained there for several weeks afterward in an unsuccessful attempt to have her son accepted as Caesar's heir.

As the Roman triumvirate of Antonius, Octavian (Caesar's grand-nephew and heir), and Lepidus moved to take vengeance against Caesar's assassins, Cleopatra was approached by both sides and temporized, but she eventually cast her fortunes against the tyran-nicides and with the avengers, sending her fleet under her own command to Greece. After the defeat of Brutus and Cassius at Philippi in 42 B.C., Antonius was left in command of the East. The following year he summoned Cleopatra to his headquarters at Tarsos. At first she refused to go, not recognizing his authority, but eventually, in one of the famous events of her career, she sailed up the Kydnos to the city. Antonius well recognized that in these turbulent times Cleopatra's Ptolemaic Empire was the strongest hope for stability in the East, although he supported her as part of a network of several allied monarchs. Yet he steadily moved to restore her kingdom to the greatest previous extent of Ptolemaic territory, and he began a policy of expanding her possessions in the Levant, Asia Minor, and toward the Aegean. He also came to Egypt for a personal vacation with the queen in the winter of 41–40 B.C. When he returned to Rome in the spring, Cleopatra was pregnant again, and she soon bore twins. Yet in Italy Antonius married Octavia, the sister of his fellow triumvir Octavian, and presumably the personal relationship between Antonius and Cleopatra was over.

Little is known about Cleopatra's activities during the next three years: presumably she was devoted to running her kingdom and raising her three children. In 37 B.C. Antonius returned to the East in preparation for a Parthian expedition, a long-standing need of Roman foreign policy. Before long he summoned Cleopatra to his current headquarters, Antioch, and, in his continuing reorganization of the East, further enhanced her territory, especially at the expense of another allied king, Herod the Great, better known to moderns through the Christian nativity story. But all the territories given to Cleopatra had been historically Ptolemaic, and Antonius's donations were fully within his powers as triumvir.

The Parthian expedition, largely funded by Cleopatra, set forth in 36 B.C. She returned home pregnant again and soon bore her fourth and last child. The expedition was a total disaster, and Antonius returned to the Mediterranean coast and requested that Cleopatra send money and supplies. Feeling totally disgraced, he probably believed that he could not go back to Rome (in fact he never did), and returned to Alexandria with the queen. Further attempts at a Parthian expedition over the next two years got nowhere.

In 34 B.C. Cleopatra and Antonius formalized, in a ceremony in Alexandria, the territorial adjustments that he had bestowed on her, and they designated her children as rulers of much of the region. This did not go over well in Rome, and Antonius's fellow triumvir Octavian, now the sole power in Italy and the west, began to see him as a rival. The fact that Antonius had sent Octavia home and was living permanently with Cleopatra turned the political disputes into a family quarrel. A fierce propaganda war, largely centered on who was the true heir of Julius Caesar, erupted between the two triumvirs. Cleopatra was embroiled in this, and all the Roman prejudices against foreigners and barbarian women came forward; most of the popular tales about her personality and lifestyle date from this period. Events drifted toward war, which Octavian declared on Cleopatra in 32 B.C. The

Ptolemaic fleet, again commanded by her, accompanied by the land forces under Antonius's control, moved to the west coast of Greece to prevent any possible attack on Egypt by Octavian. An engagement took place off the promontory of Actium in September of 31 B.C.; Cleopatra, realizing that the defense of Egypt was threatened, removed her ships from the battle and returned home, carrying Antonius along with her.

Back in Egypt she understood that her position was desperate and made attempts to flee to India and to ensure that her son Caesarion was placed on the throne. Antonius, on the other hand, was suicidal and withdrawn for much of the rest of his life. Protracted negotiations between Octavian and the couple failed to resolve anything, and in the summer of 30 B.C. Octavian invoked the military option, invading Egypt. Cleopatra, finding Antonius dispensable and hoping that she or her kingdom might survive without him, tricked him into suicide, but when she found that she herself was being saved to be exhibited in Octavian's triumph in Rome, she also killed herself. In August of 30 B.C. the Ptolemaic kingdom came to an end.

The bibliography on Cleopatra VII is enormous, running to thousands of entries. Yet because the queen is a figure in popular culture and indeed world history, many of these works are not relevant to the classical scholar or, indeed, to those who wish to know about the queen herself and her role in the history of the first century B.C. For obvious reasons a wide variety of scholars have their own interest in Cleopatra, from students of Renaissance drama to art historians, musicologists, and filmographers. Study of Cleopatra from these points of view is totally legitimate, but this approaches the queen as a constructed icon of cultural history, not an historical personality of the late Hellenistic period. The recension of the myth of Cleopatra is not the concern of the present volume, and indeed however interesting has nothing to do with the queen herself besides demonstrating the power of her reputation. Yet the strength of her afterlife is so great that not even the best classical scholars can be free of it, and they often fall into the trap of an apt quotation from drama or a discussion of a nineteenth century work of art. Certainly there is nothing wrong with this, and the modern evolution of the classical tradition is an inevitable part of classical studies. But in the case of Cleopatra it can be dangerous for the simple fact that the post-antique material so greatly overwhelms the extant information from the classical world, that it is thus possible—more than with anyone else from antiquity—to lose sight of Cleopatra as she becomes tangled up in the encumbrance of her reputation. In fact, some of the most familiar episodes of her career simply did not happen. She did not approach Caesar wrapped in a carpet, she was not a seductress, she did not use her charm to persuade the men in her life to lose their judgment, and she did not die by the bite of an asp. She may not even have borne a child of Caesar's. Yet other important elements of her career have been bypassed in the post-antique recension: she was a skilled naval commander, a published medical authority, and an expert royal administrator who was met with adulation throughout the eastern Mediterranean, perhaps even seen by some as a messianic figure, the hope for a future eastern Mediterranean free of Roman domination.

A Note on Sources

Even though Cleopatra is probably the most famous woman from classical antiquity, the literary accounts of her life and career are sparse. This is attributable largely to the limited information about women, even famous ones, that pervades Greek and Roman literature and to the effects of the destruction of her reputation in the propaganda wars of the latter 30s B.C. Nearly 50 ancient authors mention the queen, but the bulk of these are brief repetitive notices about the Battle of Actium, her suicide, or the alleged deficiencies of her character. The most thorough date from a century or more after her death, when her Augustan recension had become well established. It thus became difficult for any later author to provide a balanced portrait.

The most complete source is Plutarch's *Life of Antonius*, written in the latter first century A.D. It is not a biography of Cleopatra, but about the most important man in her life, yet the queen pervades the work. Although Plutarch was remote from events, he often used sources from her era, such as Philotas of Amphissa, a friend of Plutarch's family who had access to the royal palace; Plutarch's great-grandfather Nikarchos, who was in Athens when Octavian arrived after the Battle of Actium; Cleopatra's personal physician Olympos; and, most of all,

Quintus Dellius, the confidant of Cleopatra, Antonius, and Herod the Great. Plutarch was not free from the traditional views of the queen that had become canonized by his day, yet his insights were astute, he used a number of eyewitness reports, and his contact with sources outside the Augustan viewpoint provides a somewhat more balanced view.

Next in importance is the *Roman History* of Cassius Dio, written in the early third century A.D., and thus much later than the events that he described. Dio was a public official in a world where the convulsions of the collapse of the Roman Republic and the environment of the Hellenistic kingdoms were no longer relevant and hardly understood. He thus often lacked subtlety and comprehension of the complexities of the first century B.C., yet he remains the only surviving continuous history of the era of Cleopatra and thus is of great significance. The third source for Cleopatra is Josephus, a contemporary of Plutarch's, whose works focus narrowly on the Jews and Judaea, but thus provide the only information for an important phase of Cleopatra's life, her relationship with Herod the Great and her policies toward the southern Levant. Josephus relied heavily on two authors who had agendas of their own but both knew Cleopatra, Herod himself, through his memoirs, and Nikolaos of Damascus, tutor to Cleopatra's children who moved on to Herod's court and became a major advisor and chronicler of his reign. As Herod's apologist, Nikolaos was extremely negative toward Cleopatra, despite their earlier relationship, but nevertheless as a source he is extremely valuable.

Other authors add details. Despite the existence of Julius Caesar's own memoirs and those written by his unknown staff officer under the title *de bello alexandrino* (*On the Alexandrian War*), the queen is hardly mentioned. Yet Cicero, who also knew her, provided a starkly negative portrait. The familiar authors of the Augustan period— Vergil, Horace, Propertius, and Ovid—lie fully within the politically correct view of the era and are eloquent in their condemnation, although Horace showed a certain admiration. Other authors, from the Augustan period and later, such as Strabo, Velleius, Valerius Maximus, Pliny the Elder, and Appian, provided occasional details not known elsewhere. There are faint hints of a pro-Cleopatra tradition preserved outside the Augustan version of events, in the remnants of the historical work of Sokrates of Rhodes, probably a member of her court, and the *Libyka* of her son-in-law Juba II of Mauretania. As always, inscriptions and coins and—because the area of interest is Egypt—papyri offer a significant amount of valuable evidence, all from the queen's point of view. But the preponderance of the literary material comes from Plutarch, Josephus, and Dio. Yet much of the modern popular image of Cleopatra is based on the post-antique elaboration of her career, especially in drama, rather than any information from her era.

Personal and Geographical Names

The matter of handling personal and place names from antiquity is difficult and admits of no obvious resolution. Transmission of proper names from one language to another, and also from one form of writing to another, causes numerous problems. This is a difficulty anywhere in classical studies, but it is worse with Cleopatra than in many cases because the heavy modern overlay has created popular forms such as "Antony" (for Antonius) or "Pompey" (for Pompeius) that have no authority from antiquity and are probably no earlier than the sixteenth century. There is the further problem of indigenous names passing through Greek into Latin and then English, often inaccurately. Moreover, the late Hellenistic eastern Mediterranean was a region of intense linguistic diversity—one need only remember that Cleopatra herself knew many languages—and names moved through several forms. Malchos, the king of Nabataea, may have his name also represented as Malchus, Malichos, or Malichus, dependent on the language and orthography of the written source, all versions of the original Maliku (*mlkw* or *mnkw*). Egyptian names can be even more confusing, transliterated according to a variety of competing schemes.

With a certain amount of reluctance, the present author has used popular English spellings of well-known ancient names (Cleopatra, Ptolemy, Herod) rather than direct transliterations from the original (Kleopatra, Ptolemaios, Herodes). Less common names that may not have an accepted English form are directly transliterated insofar as this is possible. But any system is full of difficulties and inconsistencies, and it is recognized that modern constructs may be more useful than precise accuracy.

It should also be noted that Octavian, the grandnephew and heir of Julius Caesar, and Cleopatra's Roman opponent, took the name Augustus in 27 B.C. Although most of the references to him are before that date, those afterward use the latter name.

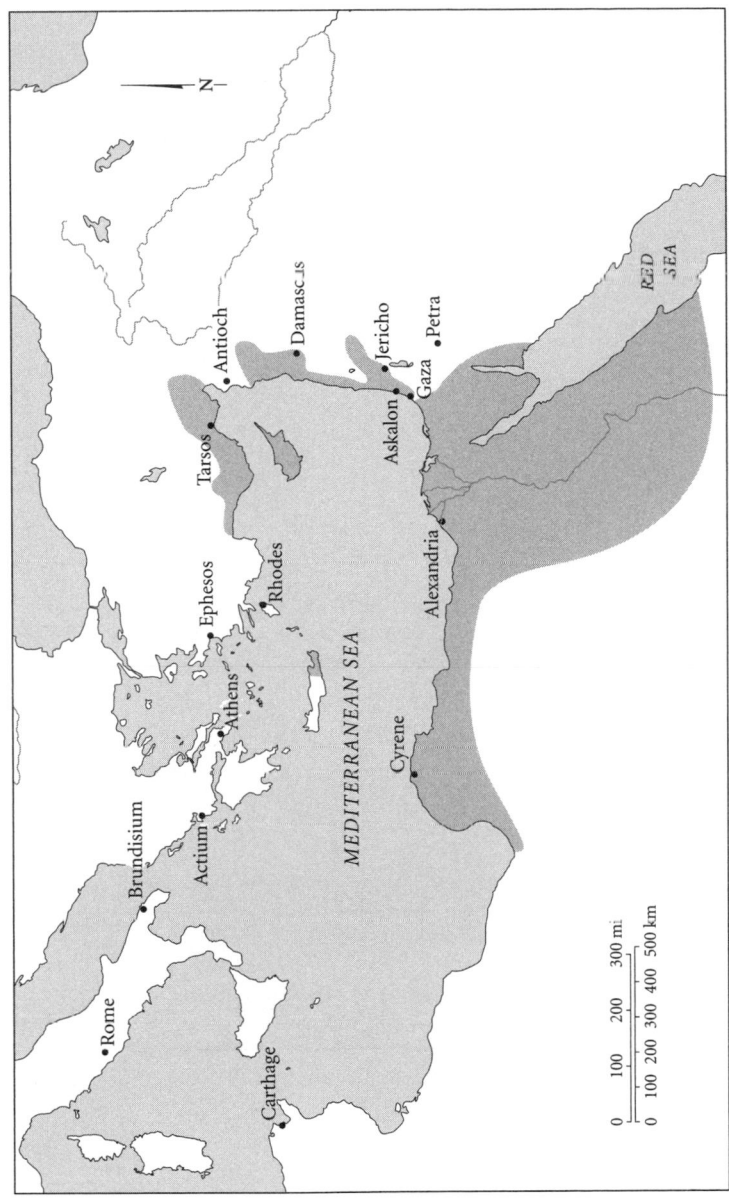

MAP 1. Cleopatra's kingdom at its greatest extent. Drawn by Bill Nelson for Oxford University Press.

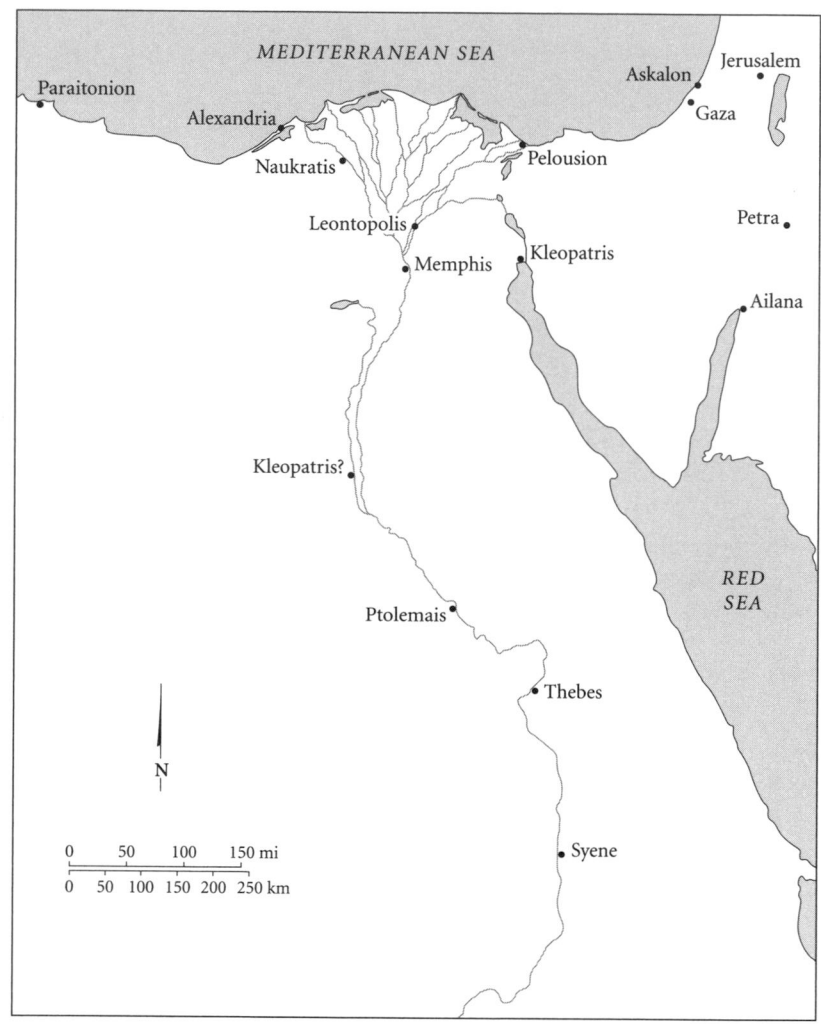

MAP 2. Egypt in the time of Cleopatra. Drawn by Bill Nelson for Oxford University Press.

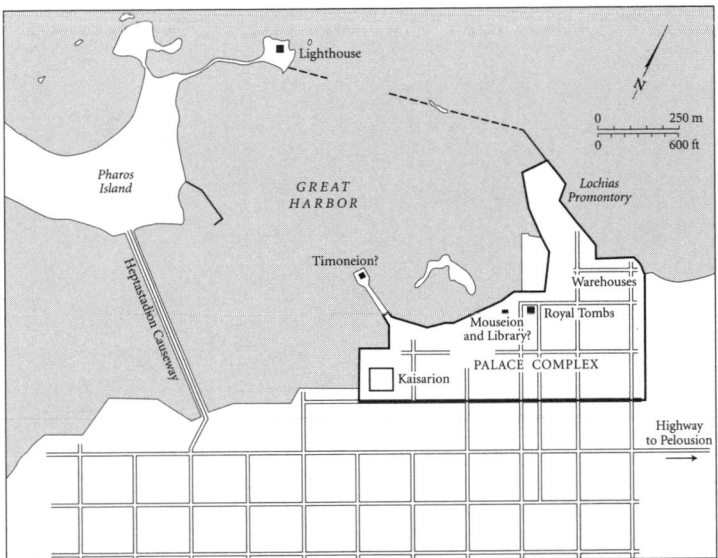

MAP 3. Alexandria in the time of Cleopatra. Drawn by Bill Nelson for Oxford University Press.

CHAPTER ONE

Cleopatra's Ancestry and Background

CLEOPATRA VII, THE LAST MACEDONIAN Greek queen of Egypt, was born around the beginning of 69 B.C., descendant of a long line of Ptolemaic kings.[1] Her father was Ptolemy XII, known derisively and perhaps slanderously as the "Flute Player," or even as a charlatan.[2] He had been on the throne for a decade when Cleopatra, the second of his three daughters, was born. The identity of her mother is uncertain, but she probably was a member of the Egyptian priestly family of Ptah, yet also with some Macedonian ancestry herself.[3]

Cleopatra VII, then, was perhaps three-quarters Macedonian and one-quarter Egyptian, and it was probably her half-Egyptian mother who instilled in her the knowledge and respect for Egyptian culture and civilization that had eluded her predecessor Ptolemies, including an ability to speak the Egyptian language. Yet it was her Ptolemaic heritage that Cleopatra valued the most, inherited through both her parents, a tradition steeped in Greek culture. She could trace her ancestry back to at least two companions of Alexander the Great. She was a direct descendent of the first Ptolemy, her great-great-great-great-great-great-grandfather, a childhood friend of Alexander's who was one of his major advisors and a military commander throughout the eastern campaign.[4] In the contentious days after Alexander's death in 323 B.C., Ptolemy was given Egypt as his province, and in time he skillfully assured his position by absconding with Alexander's body and eventually bringing it to the new city of Alexandria. Surviving until 283 B.C., he wrote the definitive history of Alexander's career. Nearly a century later his great-great-grandson Ptolemy V married another descendant of one of Alexander's companions, Cleopatra I, who could trace her lineage back to her own great-great-grandfather, Seleukos I.[5] Seleukos was also a childhood friend of Alexander's who played a prominent military role in the eastern campaign. After the leader's death he eventually established himself in coastal Syria and in 300 B.C. founded the famous city of Antioch, named after his father, creating the other great dynasty of the Hellenistic world, the Seleukid, which at its peak controlled territory as far as India. In the 190s B.C. the Ptolemies and Seleukids were joined by the marriage of Ptolemy V and Cleopatra I.[6]

The Seleukids thus brought to the Ptolemies the distinguished name Cleopatra, which would pass through five royal descendants before reaching the last Egyptian Cleopatra.[7] The name came from Alexander's own family, especially his sister, an important player in the complexities of her brother's world: it was at her wedding that their father Philip II was assassinated.[8] The name even went back to the mythological period, most notably Cleopatra the wife of Meleagros, the protagonist of the great Kalydonian Boar Hunt. Cleopatra VII would have grown up hearing the tales of these illustrious namesakes, whether historical or mythological. If she were also a descendant of the priests of Ptah, this would have added even more distinction to her ancestry. The ancient god had been associated with the Greek rulers of Egypt since the time of Alexander, and in fact this connection was a source of the Ptolemies' legitimacy.[9]

Four siblings of Cleopatra VII are known.[10] Her two sisters were Berenike IV and Arsinoë IV: thus the three daughters possessed the dominant female names of the dynasty. Berenike, the eldest child and probably the sole daughter of Cleopatra VI, the official wife of Ptolemy XII, was named queen by a faction when her father went into exile in the 50s B.C., but she was killed by him on his return. Arsinoë, younger than Cleopatra VII, was made queen of Cyprus by Julius Caesar in 47 B.C.—a position that she never actually held—and, becoming the focus of opposition to Cleopatra, was soon exiled to Ephesos, where she was killed by Antonius at Cleopatra's request in 41 B.C. Cleopatra's two brothers, Ptolemy XIII (born 61 B.C.) and Ptolemy XIV (born 59 B.C.), both fell victim to Cleopatra's dynastic needs. Although they both ruled with her for short periods, she effected their deaths in the 40s B.C. None of Ptolemy XII's five children died naturally. Cleopatra lived in difficult times. The Ptolemaic Empire was collapsing, and Rome was ascending, although it too had serious problems. As a child she would not know that her father would be the last significant male ruler of his line or that dynastic realities would cause her to be responsible for the death of three of her four siblings. She would produce four heirs, but none of them would reign as her successor.

Her father was born in the last years of the second century B.C., a turbulent era when Roman intervention in Ptolemaic politics was becoming more intense.[11] He did not succeed his father, Ptolemy IX, directly, for there was a complex dynastic struggle that lasted for nearly a year, something hardly unusual in the Ptolemaic world. Ptolemy IX died in late 81 B.C., to be succeeded by his daughter (Ptolemy XII's half-sister), Cleopatra Berenike III, but by the following summer opposition to rule by a queen alone had reached the point that her 19-year-old cousin and stepson, Ptolemy XI, was given joint rule, which included the expected marriage. Bringing this about was the Roman dictator L. Cornelius Sulla, who was at the peak of his power at the time: Ptolemy XI had been living in the city as his protégé.[12] Sulla had had many dealings with indigenous royalty, most notably in North Africa and Asia Minor, and was one of the first Romans to consider systematically the destiny of the various kingdoms that bordered Rome. Yet Ptolemy XI's marriage to his 36-year-old stepmother was not particularly pleasing, for within a month king had murdered queen. He was killed in the ensuing riot.

The death of three rulers within a few months left a power vacuum that the Romans were only too anxious to fill. In fact, Rome had legal support for intervention, since either Ptolemy XI or, more probably, his father Ptolemy X—who had reigned until expelled in 88 B.C. and died shortly thereafter as he tried to regain his throne—had willed the kingdom to Rome as collateral for loans.[13] It was conceivable that Rome might invoke the will and take over Egypt, as by 80 B.C. there were few Ptolemies available to carry on the dynasty. Ptolemy XI had no children. Ptolemy IX had two sons, but neither was legitimate. Like Cleopatra VII's mother, their mother was unknown, and it is possible that she also came from the priestly elite, but the evidence is even more obscure than in the later case. One son was given Cyprus, where he ruled for 25 years as Ptolemy of Cyprus. The other, Ptolemy XII, Cleopatra's father, became king of Egypt. Unlike her, his parentage was questioned for the rest of his life, and he was regularly called *nothos*, or "bastard," which may mean nothing more than that, like Cleopatra, he had Egyptian blood.[14] He also received the epithet "Auletes," or "Flute Player," because of his adoption of the title "New Dionysos" and his alleged performance in the

Dionysiac festivals.[15] He married his sister Cleopatra VI and probably had a relationship with at least one woman from the family that held the hereditary priesthood of Ptah, producing his five children, Berenike IV, Cleopatra VII, Ptolemy XIII, Ptolemy XIV, and Arsinoë IV. As children of the New Dionysos, they could be considered offspring of a god,[16] yet there is no solid evidence that any of them was deified during their lifetimes, although Cleopatra was always afforded the veneration appropriate to a goddess.[17] The new king was young when he came to the throne, about 20, and tales of his indolence and life of luxury soon circulated, perhaps reflecting his genuine distaste for rule and involvement in global politics, as well as the knowledge that he had become king essentially by default. He may have taken his priestly duties more seriously, and his portraits show a certain dignity. The coin portraits, especially, are strikingly similar to those of his daughter Cleopatra VII.[18]

The first years of his reign, which includes the period of the birth of Cleopatra VII, were quiet. But the king had inherited a dangerous situation. The population of Alexandria—with various factions supporting other potential rulers, dead or alive, Egyptian interests, and Roman involvement (or distaste for it)—had shown its willingness to intervene violently in the matter of the rule. The ever-looming presence of Rome, which had financial as well as political aspects, was ominous. There was increasing disenchantment with the Ptolemies as a whole. Ptolemy's

FIGURE 1. Marble head of Ptolemy XII, reworked from an earlier portrait, in the Louvre (Ma 3449). Photography by Hervé Lewandowski, courtesy of the Réunion des Museés Nationaux and Art Resource, New York (ART151975).

persona as the diffident bastard flute player, even if more slander than reality, was no help.

In late 69 B.C. Ptolemy's legal wife Cleopatra VI fell out of favor. The details are obscure: she is missing from documents and inscriptions after that time and does not reappear for more than a decade.[19] She vanished a few months after Cleopatra VII was born from another mother, although it is not known whether Ptolemy's liaisons played any role in his wife's fortunes. Whatever happened, this is a further indication of instability, and although there are no details about Ptolemy's personal relationships in the years immediately following, his three younger children were born during the queen's absence.

By this time Egypt had become a regular topic in Rome. It is difficult to summarize with any brevity the contemporary situation there and how it affected Egypt.[20] Since Rome's final defeat of Carthage 80 years previously, the city had become a world power, with territory stretching across the Mediterranean. Yet there had been no resulting significant constitutional changes: Rome still operated as a central Italian city-state, in much the way that it had for hundreds of years, and it was not equipped to function as a global power. Her broad reach meant contacts with many other states, especially the Greek kingdoms that had come into existence after the time of Alexander the Great. In the western Mediterranean there were other indigenous kingdoms, not Greek, but often heavily influenced by Greek ways. Since the second century B.C. all had looked to Rome as the emergent power of the Mediterranean. Kings had sent their children to Rome to be educated, had sought Rome themselves as a refuge in times of trouble, and had even willed their kingdoms to Rome as a way of convincing their families that usurpation was futile.[21]

For its part, Rome's interest was not only a matter of global politics but one of finances, since the resources available to the kings far exceeded Rome's income. Ever since the legacy of Attalos III of Pergamon had been accepted in 130 B.C., bringing Rome not only territory but immense revenue that was of great assistance in the difficult years after the Carthaginian wars, the city had regarded the kingdoms with covetous eyes. But its antiquated government had no effective way of implementing its needs. The ancient system of short-term elected magistracies did not operate efficiently in a state whose territory extended from one end of the Mediterranean to the other. Officials sent to the perimeters had little time to acquaint themselves with issues before their term was over, and few funds were available for their duties unless local sources were acquired. In fact, service in a province came to be a significant way of gaining wealth, legally or otherwise, that could be used to advance one's career. A magistrate stationed at the edge of Roman territory would look avidly at a rich adjoining kingdom, and perhaps wonder how much of its resources could be obtained for Rome and for himself. The kings would be caught in an inescapable bind: Rome was a source of protection and stability but could destroy them and their kingdoms. The erratic nature of internal Roman politics also played a role, since a political leader prominent one year could be ostracized the next, and he might effectively be exiled to a remote province where extortion of his neighbors would be the only way of gaining funding to reinstate himself, which he might use to mobilize a private army to assist in his restoration. As leaders rotated in and out of favor, so did those who supported them: someone newly discredited might have once offered protection or support to a king, which would make the king fair game for his opponents. Ironically, all the monarchs who sought Roman assistance to stabilize and preserve their kingdoms began a process, often lasting several generations, of destroying them.

Inevitably, the first century B.C. saw the rise of powerful Roman political leaders who sought to operate within the faulty system for personal and political gain. Many of these are familiar, including Gnaeus Pompeius the Great, M. Tullius Cicero, Julius Caesar, and Marcus Antonius. Most of them at one time or another concerned themselves with the matter of Egypt. In 65 B.C. the censor M. Licinius Crassus suggested that Egypt come under direct Roman control, perhaps using the existing Ptolemaic will as a pretext.[22] The dominant reason for the proposal was financial gain, for Egypt represented a great potential source of wealth. Yet Cicero saw Crassus's proposal merely as greed and argued that it was hardly advisable for the Romans to become involved in the unstable world of Egypt. His eloquence was a major factor in the dropping of the matter. As king of Egypt, Ptolemy XII realized the implicit threat, and resorted to the only option available to him, financial remuneration of prominent Romans, a long-standing policy for barbarian kings in his position, but one that quickly would put him into debt despite his wealth. He reached out to one Roman in particular, his acquaintance Gnaeus Pompeius the Great, who was at the peak of his short and brilliant career. He had risen to prominence during campaigns in Africa and Spain and had become consul at an early age in 70 B.C. (with Crassus as his colleague); in 66 B.C. he had been sent to settle Rome's festering war with Mithradates the Great of Pontos in northern Asia Minor, who had been causing difficulty for many years. Early in this campaign, or just before it, he may have visited Egypt and been entertained lavishly by Ptolemy.[23] After succeeding in neutralizing Mithradates, Pompeius moved into Syria, where he dissolved the Seleukid kingdom and annexed its remnants. He was in Damascus, conveniently close to Egypt, in 63 B.C. when envoys arrived from Ptolemy bearing a valuable gold crown, a symbol indicating that he recognized Pompeius's authority. There was also an offer to finance his next endeavor, an operation in Judaea.[24] Pompeius was further invited to continue on to Egypt to put down local agitation, but he declined.

Yet Ptolemy's lavishness cost him dearly, with both internal instability and Roman concern increasing. There are scattered notices of disturbances in Egypt all through the 60s B.C.[25] The historian Diodoros, who visited Egypt about this time, witnessed a riot and lynching that occurred when someone accidentally committed the sacrilege of killing a cat, an incident that was notable for the failure of government officials sent to the scene to intervene.[26] Taxes were increased, resulting in strikes by farmers in the villages: as was usual in times of financial excess and overseas adventures, the poor suffered the most. It was said that money to pay the king's debts was exacted by force. Even the gold sarcophagus of Alexander the Great was melted down.[27] Civil disturbances reached such a point that in 63 B.C. Ptolemy had to issue an order that unauthorized persons could not enter temple treasuries. His expenditures soon reached a point that he went into debt, borrowing from the famous Roman banker C. Rabirius Postumus.[28]

Despite his financial straits, the king continued to spread money around Rome. After Pompeius, his next target was Julius Caesar, consul for 59 B.C., which eased the way for Ptolemy to be legally confirmed as a friend and ally of the Romans. As customary, the agreement was registered on the Capitol as an official treaty.[29] Roman citizenship, if not already held by the Ptolemies, may also have been conferred. This was an important benefit that gave its holders certain privileges, such as access to the Roman legal system, and created a useful bond between those in power on the fringes of Roman territory and the government in Rome. Ptolemy may have believed that his problems were now solved, but he underestimated the complexities of the political world in which he had become involved. Soon the Romans annexed Cyprus, ruled by his brother Ptolemy of Cyprus and part of the Ptolemaic kingdom since its earliest days. As usual, money was a primary reason: M. Porcius Cato was appointed to effect the operation and given instructions to acquire the royal treasury. Ptolemy XII was strangely silent as his brother went to his downfall. Ptolemy of Cyprus was offered internal exile as a priest of Apollo at Paphos, but he chose suicide instead, and Cyprus became Roman territory.[30]

The Cyprus incident used up the last of Ptolemy XII's credibility at home. Discontent and opposition to his rule, especially his failure to hold traditional Ptolemaic territory and to keep it from the Romans, as well as his financial policies, resulted either in his expulsion or, more likely, voluntary departure from Egypt in the summer of 58 B.C. He may have been encouraged to do this by Pompeius, who was then accused of creating a power vacuum in Egypt that would give him a new command and further career advancement.[31] The king borrowed more money from Rabirius Postumus to be able to travel in the accustomed royal style, and he headed first for Rhodes, the headquarters of Cato, who lectured him on his mistake in becoming so entangled in Roman politics and abandoning his kingdom. Egypt would be drained by Rome, Cato insisted. Ptolemy was convinced and resolved to return to Egypt but was dissuaded by his advisors, although later he would find Cato's words prophetic. He then went to Athens, which had had close relations with the Ptolemies since early times, including a festival called the Ptolemaia.[32] Here he dedicated a monument to his father and half-sister Ptolemy IX and Cleopatra Berenike III.[33] His 11-year-old daughter, Cleopatra VII, may have accompanied him on at least this part of the journey, if she is the "Libyan princess" whose servant was memorialized in a grave inscription of the period.[34] She may have continued with her father to Rome, thus being exposed at an early age to that dynamic environment which would be so important to her future career.[35] When Ptolemy arrived in the city, he took up residence in Pompeius's villa in the Alban hills, near the great sanctuary of Fortuna Primigenia at Praeneste, and he lived there for nearly a year. Soon he had to borrow even more money from Rabirius Postumus.

With the expulsion or self-exile of Ptolemy in 58 B.C., his sister-wife Cleopatra VI, whose whereabouts for the last decade are unknown, emerged from obscurity, perhaps to represent her husband and to oppose their daughter, Berenike IV, who made her own attempt for the throne. The circumstances are unclear, but Berenike was the only child of Ptolemy XII close to adulthood, and she was perhaps put forward by the faction opposing the king. It is possible that mother and daughter ruled jointly for a while, since a papyrus refers to "the queens" (and incidentally gives an insight to the chaotic conditions of the era, as it records a public demonstration demanding royal intervention against corrupt officials).[36] The queens may have started as colleagues and ended up as rivals. How much longer Cleopatra VI survived is uncertain. She may have lived until early 55 B.C., shortly before her husband's return, although the evidence is disputed.[37] Her death, however, left Berenike as sole ruler, only the second time that a queen ruled alone in the Ptolemaic dynasty. If Cleopatra VII had returned to the court, she would have seen all this happening around her.

Meanwhile the Romans were debating what to do about Ptolemy, comfortably residing with Pompeius. For kings to flee to Rome at times of difficulty was nothing new: Ptolemy's grandfather Ptolemy VIII had made several trips to the city, as had the famous Numidian king Jugurtha. Herod the Great was to do the same 20 years later. The indebtedness of Ptolemy XII to Roman bankers meant that his political survival was more than an idle question in Rome, since the best way to ensure that the debts would be paid would be to implement his restoration and thus give him renewed access to the Egyptian treasury. The Senate was at first inclined to support this, and in fact the consul of 57 B.C., P. Lentulus Spinther, was given the task as part of his proconsular command of the following year, although Ptolemy let it be known that he would have preferred Pompeius. But the king seriously weakened his standing in the city when his assassins disposed of an embassy sent from Alexandria to speak against him. The leader of the embassy, the philosopher Dion, survived and was summoned to the Senate, but Ptolemy, through the agency of Pompeius, was able to keep him from speaking and eventually had him killed. The whole matter was hushed up, as Ptolemy still had the support of powerful Romans.[38]

Portents were also being used by both sides. A thunderbolt struck the statue of Jupiter in the Alban hills, followed by a conveniently produced Sibylline oracle—promulgated by Cato—that enjoined the Romans to offer friendship but no military assistance. Interpretation of it threw the Senate into confusion, and it was suggested that Lentulus Spinther restore Ptolemy without the use of an army, or that he merely be sent home with a minuscule Roman escort. Ptolemy realized that he was getting nowhere and asked for the latter, but when even this was denied he quietly left Rome, probably at the end of 57 B.C., and sought sanctuary in the famous Temple of Artemis at Ephesos.

In Alexandria the death of Cleopatra VI during her husband's exile created an awkward situation, as the surviving queen Berenike IV had no husband. As had happened with her aunt Cleopatra Berenike III, one had to be found. A comical series of events ensued: one candidate died, another was detained by Aulus Gabinius, the Roman governor of Syria, and a third was so unacceptable to Berenike that she had him killed. A fourth, a certain Archelaos, was finally successful. His background is contradictorily described in the sources, but he claimed to have been a descendant of Mithradates the Great and happened to be a protégé of Pompeius.[39]

The Romans were not finished with Ptolemy XII, however. Although Archelaos and Berenike seemed firmly in control in Egypt with Archelaos now accepted as king, the Roman bankers, led by Rabirius Postumus, knew that restoration of Ptolemy was their only means of salvation. Yet discussions about whether to restore the king led to rioting in Rome, less out of concern about Ptolemy's future than the machinations of those in power, whose interests included the future of Egypt.[40] Lentulus Spinther, established in his proconsular command in Kilikia (southeastern Asia Minor), despite his instructions and intense urging from Cicero, avoided involving himself. Pompeius, however, persuaded Gabinius, the governor of Syria, to bring about the restoration, and his willingness to comply was eased by 10,000 talents provided by Ptolemy. Gabinius prepared for an invasion of Egypt, an illegal act that would involve him in serious difficulties in Rome.[41]

The expedition set forth in the spring of 55 B.C. On Gabinius's staff was young Marcus Antonius as cavalry commander and in his first provincial post. As the expedition passed through Judaea, it received the support of the high priest Hyrkanos II, who instructed the wealthy Antipatros of Askalon to provide supplies, which he did in a lavish way.[42] Antipatros was an important figure in the regional politics of the era, but he is best remembered today as the father of Herod the Great, who was 15 years of age and certainly a curious onlooker as the Romans passed by, if not actively involved. Like Cleopatra, he was observing events that determined his future policies.

When the expedition reached Egypt, Antonius distinguished himself in the two battles that resulted and prevented Ptolemy from massacring the inhabitants of Pelousion. King Archelaos was killed in the second battle. Antonius saved his body from desecration and ensured him a royal burial, an ironic harbinger of events of 25 years later. By April Ptolemy XII was restored to his throne and to his family, including 14-year-old Cleopatra, who may have been more impressed by the Roman officers whom she saw, especially Antonius, who so quickly had won such favor with the Egyptians. In later years Antonius claimed to have fallen in love with her at this time.[43]

Although Antonius was at the beginning of his career and his relationship with Egypt, Gabinius paid dearly for his actions. On his return to Rome he was indicted both for exceeding his authority and accepting bribes. The trials were violent and prolonged, with a defense based on the unsuitability of Archelaos to be king of Egypt, claiming that the Sibylline oracle—which seemed quite explicit—had actually referred to some other king, and blaming Pompeius for everything. The first trial, for exceeding his authority, resulted in acquittal, but the second, for bribery, with Cicero defending him, led to conviction.[44] It was rumored that Gabinius bribed the jury, perhaps an unwise move under the circumstances. Obviously the trials were only a small part of the larger political activities of the era, and Gabinius may have understood the conditions in the East more astutely than either those in Rome or the hostile sources that recorded his trials.[45] He went into exile until recalled seven years later by Caesar. His successor in Syria, none other than Crassus, who in many ways had started the entire Egyptian issue by proposing annexation a decade previously, had Egypt added to his provincial command, although continuing instability in Rome and Crassus's death shortly thereafter in his misbegotten Parthian expedition meant that this was more a legal technicality than reality. Yet it demonstrated the inevitable course of events.[46]

Whatever joyous reunion Ptolemy might have had with his family did not extend to his daughter Berenike, who had opposed both him and his wife, and she was promptly executed along with many of her wealthiest supporters, one way for the king to gain revenue. Other indignities followed. Gabinius had left a Roman garrison to prop up Ptolemy's rule, which was not only insulting to the locals but caused other problems, as its members tended to disappear into the streets of Alexandria, assaulting women and thus creating a Roman ethnic component in this multicultural city.[47] In fact, perhaps like any major port city, Alexandria seems to have attracted low characters from throughout the Mediterranean, including pirates, brigands, and fugitive slaves, and this added to a general perception of lawlessness. For Ptolemy, money continued to be an issue, as the king remained heavily in debt. His ingenious solution to this was to make none other than the Roman banker Rabirius Postumus his chief financial officer, ironically giving someone from a state that was a novice on the global scene control of the world's oldest financial administration. None of this endeared Ptolemy to the Egyptians.[48]

Rabirius seems to have been given a free hand to drain the kingdom of its resources, yet the debts were so enormous that they were never paid off in Ptolemy's lifetime and were passed on to his successors.[49] Rabirius offended everyone so effectively that within a year he was placed in protective custody by the king and sent back to Rome, where he became the second person to stand trial over the matter of the restoration of Ptolemy XII. Cicero again defended and attempted to portray Rabirius as a hostage of Ptolemy who had made the best of an impossible situation. The outcome of the trial is unknown, but Rabirius too had powerful friends and was in the service of Caesar in Sicily eight years later.[50]

There were no further disasters in the three years remaining to Ptolemy. His primary concern now was the royal succession. Having already eliminated his one legitimate child, Berenike, by necessity he turned toward the four remaining, the two girls, Cleopatra and Arsinoë, and the two boys, Ptolemy XIII and XIV. Of these only Cleopatra was close to adulthood, about 14 when her father was restored. The boys were six and four, and Arsinoë was also a child.[51] Hence it was obvious that Cleopatra would be the primary heir.

Thus, shortly after his reinstatement, Ptolemy wrote his will. He listed his eldest surviving daughter (Cleopatra) and eldest son (Ptolemy XIII) as joint heirs: inclusion of the boy would in theory avoid the difficulties the two Berenikes had found when they became sole rulers without a male consort.[52] Most important, the will asked that the Roman people be the guardian of the two children. Exactly what this meant is uncertain, but it provided the legal excuse for the extensive Roman intervention of the following years. Ptolemy also invoked all the gods and all his treaties with Rome as encouragement to carry out his instructions. Envoys took a copy of the will to Rome to be deposited in the state treasury, but not unexpectedly it ended up in the hands of Pompeius,[53] who was now the most powerful man in the city and, of course, Ptolemy's primary Roman benefactor. Pompeius believed that the document might be useful to him in the future.

Writing such a will shows unexpected political incisiveness on the part of a king whose reign does not seem to have been especially distinguished. But the stories of his frivolity that pervade literature may have been exaggerated: like his daughter, he had particularly articulate Roman opponents. Although remembered as a bastard flute player, this may not have affected his ability at rule. Most analyses of his character are from Roman sources, and they had little patience for the luxuriant lifestyle of eastern royalty, as Cleopatra and Antonius were soon to learn. Despite his exile and treatment of his eldest daughter Berenike, his reign was more peaceful than many of the previous ones, and he took serious steps to avoid the protracted succession struggles that had become commonplace among the Ptolemies, although this was futile. His legal recognition by Rome, which Cleopatra would profit from, brought him into the mainstream of world politics, inevitably hastening the end of his dynasty as rulers of Egypt, although he was hardly aware of this. He seemed to have been greatly disliked by the Alexandrian elite, yet by and large he administered the state fairly well, except perhaps for the unfortunate incident of Rabirius, whom Ptolemy himself removed from power. Although the loss of Cyprus was a major blow to Ptolemaic foreign policy, the empire still had access to the wealth of India and East Africa. A certain Kallimachos, an important official who would continue into the reign of Cleopatra VII, was "Overseer of the Erythraian and Indian Seas" in 62 B.C.[54] Documents also testify to Ptolemy's steady involvement in the internal workings of Egypt. He completed the Temple of Edfu, which had been under way since the time of Ptolemy III, and, probably transferring the workmen downriver to the new site, began construction at Dendera.[55] He paid special care to his religious duties, traveling throughout the country.[56] Most important, he died of natural causes, an increasingly rare phenomenon among the Ptolemies.

In the spring of 52 B.C. he gave his two heirs the titles of "new gods" and "loving siblings" (Theoi Neoi Philadelphoi).[57] The former was an ancient formula and honorific, the latter a vain hope for the future. Cleopatra seems to have become regent at about the same time, assuring a smooth transition since her coheir was still a child. Her legal status is represented in the crypt of the Temple of Hathor at Dendera, her first appearance in the historical record, sometime in 52 B.C. Ptolemy XII died early the following year.

CHAPTER TWO

The Ptolemaic Heritage and the Involvement with Rome

MORE THAN 250 YEARS BEFORE Cleopatra VII's birth, her ancestor Ptolemy I established himself in Egypt, fulfilling a long-standing Greek interest in the country that went back to prehistoric times. Egyptian objects have been found in Mycenaean tombs on the Greek mainland,[1] and by Homer's day Egypt was well known to the Greek world. Achilles understood that it was a place of great wealth, and Menelaos was detained there after the Trojan War. Odysseus used travel to Egypt as a subterfuge to hide his identity, claiming to have stayed there seven years, becoming wealthy.[2] Egypt came to be seen not only as a source for riches but for all knowledge, as early Greek intellectuals such as Thales were said to have learned their ideas from Egyptian sources.[3] A Greek trading post at Naukratis, established in the seventh century B.C., became an island of Greek culture.[4] By the Classical period there was a steady stream of Greek visitors to the country, of which Herodotos was the most famous. Egyptian institutions became respected in Greece: the Athenian political leader Kimon consulted the famous oracle of Ammon at the Siwa Oasis. There was even political intervention, beginning with the Athenian invasion in 459 B.C.[5]

So it is perhaps no surprise that Alexander the Great, accompanied by two of Cleopatra's ancestors, would invade Egypt. After difficulties working his way down the Levantine coast in 332 B.C., including a seven-month siege of Tyre, the king reached Egypt late in the year, remaining there until spring. Like Kimon, he visited the oracle of Ammon. But perhaps more significant for the future was Alexander's assumption of the religious titles and honors of the Egyptian king, especially upholding the kingship's linkage to the god Ptah,[6] which ensured the lasting support of his priesthood, a significant factor that continued into the time of Cleopatra. Moreover, as the creator god of Memphis, Ptah gave Alexander connections to that most historic Egyptian city, long the seat of royalty. Thus Alexander and his successors were more easily able to see themselves continuing the historic lineage of the indigenous Egyptian royalty. Association with Egyptian cult and royalty also gave Alexander access to the concept of deification of the ruler, something alien to the Greek world (although similar to the cults of dead heroes). Greek leaders had long been bestowed with quasi-divine honors in recognition of their services, but Alexander, a unique personality, became essentially a god. This concept of divine monarchy would continue into Cleopatra's day and affect the self-image of the Roman emperors.

Another significant accomplishment of Alexander's took place at Rhakotis, on a spit of land just west of the Kanobic mouth of the Nile, where he began laying out a new city, to be named Alexandria, one of many such foundations that he would make.[7] He designated the grid for the city himself and located its major building sites, and Alexandria was formally founded on 7 April 331 B.C. Recording the events was his close companion and Cleopatra's ancestor, Ptolemy I.

Eight years later, at the end of 323 B.C., Ptolemy was back in Egypt. Alexander had died at Babylon in the summer, leaving no provisions for governance of his realm, and the 40-year-long struggle of his Successors was under way. In the assignment of territory after Alexander's death, Ptolemy had received Egypt as his satrapy—the Persian administrative model was still in use—but soon he began to act as if he were an independent ruler. Within a year he had intervened in the politics of the ancient Greek city of Cyrene, west of Egypt.[8] Shortly thereafter he engineered the major coup of his career, bringing the body of Alexander to Egypt and eventually enshrining it in a monumental tomb at Alexandria, creating a royal burial precinct that would be part of the palace compound. As the successor to Alexander, Ptolemy could acquire his divine attributes for himself, both those connected to the personality of his predecessor and those obtained through ancient Egyptian ruler cult. Ptolemy thus had a status that none of the other Successors could ever claim, and this passed to his descendants. By 305 B.C. he was calling himself king and in the following year was crowned as Egyptian pharoah.[9]

Monarchy, which had lost favor in the Greek world in the sixth century B.C., had been rejuvenated through the personality of Alexander.

The failure of the Classical city-states to create stable governments had discredited the more broadly based systems such as democracy, and from at least the time of Plato political theorists had seen monarchy, of a proper sort, as the best form of government. Alexander's personal charisma had restored faith in monarchy—assisted, perhaps, by his association with the outstanding political theorist of his era, Aristotle— and after Alexander's death many of the Successors adopted the title of "king," although at first more as a personal honorific than a legal term for a ruler of a specific territory. Ptolemy, in Egypt, had further reason to be sympathetic to monarchy, since when Egypt had been handed over, Alexander had followed the standard procedure for accession of a new pharaoh. As Alexander's designated successor in Egypt, Ptolemy himself could assume the role of pharaoh, providing additional linkage to his illustrious predecessor and his adopted country, both important sources of his power. From Ptolemy's inauguration as king of Egypt until the death of Cleopatra VII 275 years later, this amalgamation of the historic religious and cultural role of the pharaoh with the concept of Alexander-inspired Greek kingship was Egypt's form of government.[10]

Unlike Alexander's other Successors, Ptolemy ruled an established state with a long history and a defined territory. The royal administration in Egypt had existed for thousands of years. Egypt had been a state since long before the rise of the Greek world. This did not mean that the Ptolemies were immune to territorial expansionism, as is demonstrated by events from Ptolemy I's invasion of Cyrene in 332 B.C. to Cleopatra VII's acquisition of Levantine regions 300 years later. At its greatest extent the Ptolemaic kingdom spread from the shores of Greece to the interior of Africa. But at the heart of the kingdom there was always Egypt, and from the beginning Ptolemy respected as much as possible its historical prestige. Egypt was already multicultural, and an increasing number of Greeks flocked to Alexandria and other Greek cities such as Naukratis. There were other groups of foreigners, especially a significant Jewish contingent that had existed for hundreds of years. Persians, Africans, and eventually Romans became part of Alexandria, and a distinction developed between the mixed population of the city and the ancient unchanged countryside. Although Ptolemy I and his descendants made use of the ancient Egyptian royal administration, at the same time they lived in isolation from Egypt as monarchs ruling in Greek fashion in a Greek city: it was said that none of the Ptolemies before Cleopatra VII even learned the Egyptian language.[11]

The history of the Ptolemaic dynasty is essential to understanding the life of Cleopatra VII as she was the inheritor of nearly 250 years of its policies. These determined the nature of her rule and her relationship with her subjects, of whatever ethnicity, as well as her own political stance. Ptolemy I, as founder of the dynasty, established the concept of Ptolemaic kingship: Cleopatra would be influenced by many of his ideas. The first half of his reign, when he still used the title "satrap" rather than "king," was concerned with establishing his position in the chaotic era of Alexander's Successors, the struggle that created the political nature of the Hellenistic world. Ptolemy's position was by no means secure, and he had to repel a number of external threats. He acquired the Cyrenaica in 332 B.C.; in 301 B.C. he occupied the coastal Levant as far north as Byblos and soon took control of Cyprus and Lykia on the southern coast of Anatolia, creating a Ptolemaic empire that extended from the borders of Greece proper to the frontier of Carthage, excepting only portions of Syria and the southern Levant.[12] Although the boundaries of the Ptolemaic state remained in flux throughout its history, Cyprus and the Cyrenaica would, with minor exceptions, always be Ptolemaic possessions, and there would be regular attempts to acquire Syria and the southern Levant. Until Rome became a significant player, the only state that could rival the Ptolemies was the Seleukid Empire, founded by Seleukos I, another companion and fellow traveler of Alexander and ancestor of Cleopatra VII. After 300 B.C. the Seleukids would be centered at the new city of Antioch in Syria; their dynasty would survive until the Roman dissolution of their empire in 64 B.C. The Seleukids and the Ptolemies would be in constant contention for the Levant: Cleopatra's interest in the kingdom of Herod the Great was a continuation of a long-standing Ptolemaic policy.

Egypt was the most ancient state in the world. In recognition of its traditions, Ptolemy I had made Memphis his original residence, following not only Egyptian practice but Alexander's precedent, who, in honoring the city, upheld venerable Egyptian customs, since it was associated with Menes, the founder of the Egyptian state. Moreover, at Memphis Alexander had shown his respect for the priesthood and cult of Ptah, which would remain an essential component of Ptolemaic royal power. Yet by 311 B.C., and perhaps several years earlier, even before Ptolemy took the title of king, he moved his royal seat to the new city of Alexandria.[13] In part this may mean that the city, under construction for a number of years, was now suitable to receive his residence.

But at the same time the move created the duality that was to characterize Ptolemaic rule. Kings and queens continued to be crowned at Memphis by priests of Ptah, and the priesthood became closely intertwined with the Ptolemaic dynasty. But by making a new Greek city his capital, Ptolemy established the concept of the Hellenistic royal city that remained a pattern well into Roman times. Antioch and Pergamon would be founded a few years later, and even as late as the first century B.C. Romanized kings such as Herod the Great and Juba II of Mauretania would follow the precedent of Alexandria with their own royal capitals.

Placing himself and his royal administration at Alexandria situated Ptolemy firmly within the mainstream of Greek culture. As a coastal city, Alexandria would be connected with the rest of the world, unlike Memphis, which was 300 miles upriver. Alexandria quickly developed into the world's greatest city. It lay where a number of promontories and islands created a natural series of harbors, which were enhanced by breakwaters and causeways. Most prominent was the island of Pharos, known to Greeks since Homeric times. A promontory to the east, called Lochias, was the location of the palace, which also extended to the southwest into the heart of the city. The street grid, some of which is still visible, covered several square miles south of the palace.[14]

Most notable was the emergence of the city as an intellectual center, with the creation of the Mouseion and its Library, the concept, at least, of Ptolemy I, although his son and successor Ptolemy II probably implemented the plans.[15] Aristotle's student Theophrastos was involved in the project, and Ptolemy I himself presumably had the inclination to conceive of such an idea.[16] Nothing is known specifically about the king's studies, although as a published historian, who wrote a definitive account of Alexander's career, he was an educated man.[17] Given that he was a childhood friend of Alexander's, he may have been raised at the Macedonian royal court; if so, he probably met Aristotle and Theophrastos when they came to the court in the 340s B.C. Ptolemy developed a personal relationship with the latter, who eventually encouraged him to create a Mouseion in Alexandria.[18] A Mouseion was literally a place inspired by the Muses, and thus associated with the arts or intellectual culture, a locale for scholarly and artistic activities. It came to be a component of the great philosophical schools of Athens such as Plato's Academy.[19] Theophrastos established a Mouseion on his estate at Stageira in northern Greece: his will lists the scholars who would be allowed to study there, the nucleus of its intellectual community.[20] Ptolemy invited

Theophrastos to Egypt, perhaps with similar ideas in mind, but he declined the invitation, and his most famous student, Demetrios of Phaleron, accepted the offer. He was available after 307 B.C. because he had been expelled by the Athenians, whom he had ruled for a number of years.[21] A rare example of an intellectual and scholar who was also politically experienced, Demetrios provided the advice, both scholarly and political, that Ptolemy needed in order to turn Alexandria into a cultural center, including establishment of the Mouseion and Library. Eventually the personal libraries of Aristotle and Theophrastos became the core of the collections.[22] Demetrios himself would give luster to the court, as he was one of the most prolific scholars of the era and thus the first major intellectual to receive Ptolemaic patronage. He probably also encouraged the original contingent of scholars to come to Alexandria, of which the most famous was the mathematician Euclid,[23] thereby establishing the city as the new cultural center of the emergent Hellenistic world. It is difficult to imagine that, 250 years later, Cleopatra did not frequent the Library and attend events at the Mouseion—it was part of the royal palace complex[24]—a place where, if nothing else, she could have learned the many languages in which she became fluent.

Ptolemy I, in addition to creating an ideal Greek state at Alexandria, also had to contend with the indigenous Egyptian population. He had to be accepted by them as king while retaining his identity as a Greek monarch in the tradition of Plato and Alexander. Transferring his capital to Alexandria assisted with the latter; making as few changes as possible in the age-old Egyptian administration and cultivating the priestly elite ensured the former. Yet there was a steady influx of Greeks to Alexandria and the few other Greek cities within Egypt. Naukratis, founded as a Greek trading outpost in the seventh century B.C. 35 miles up the Kanobic Nile from where Alexandria would be built, underwent a renaissance. Inscriptions show that Ptolemy I and II favored it with new buildings.[25] Like Alexandria, it was constituted as a quasi-independent Greek city and had its own coinage. Far upriver was a third city, Ptolemais Hermiou, the first of many Ptolemaic city foundations,[26] located in the ancient Thebaid and conveniently providing a Greek southern anchor to the historic territory of Egypt. It too was organized as a Greek city. These three were the core of the Greek presence, but the remaining territory, the vast bulk of Egypt, was in many ways unchanged by the new administration. Ptolemy I did not find it necessary to learn Egyptian.

A final concern for the king had nothing to do with Egypt but was of vital interest to his descendants and would become an obsessive matter for Cleopatra. For the dynasty to survive, heirs had to be carefully produced. Ptolemy was married four times and had at least 10 children. Although his first two marriages were obscure and seem to have been childless, the third and fourth represented a careful choosing of partners who were of sufficient status to produce heirs, a tradition that would continue to the end of the dynasty. Ptolemy's third wife was Eurydike, the daughter of Antipatros, a powerful associate of Alexander's father Philip II who was responsible for ensuring the succession for Alexander and was left in command in Greece during the eastern expedition.[27] Although two of the children of Ptolemy and Eurydike became kings of Macedonia, it was Ptolemy's fourth wife, Berenike I (the first use of that famous name in the dynasty), who produced the heir, Ptolemy II. She was also related to Antipatros and had joined her cousin Eurydike when the latter went to Egypt to marry Ptolemy around 320 B.C. Berenike eventually supplanted Eurydike as his wife[28] and became the mother of not only Ptolemy II but his sister-wife Arsinoë II. From its very beginning, the Ptolemaic dynasty was known for its complex family relationships.

When Ptolemy I died in the winter of 283–282 B.C., arrangements had already been made for Ptolemy II to succeed him, ensuring that the Ptolemaic Empire would be a hereditary dynasty. The father was in his eighties and was one of the last surviving who had known Alexander; the son was in his mid-twenties. Allegedly, he had been regent for two years, although there is some evidence that this was a fabrication created in the succession struggle that erupted,[29] which essentially pitted Eurydike's children against Berenike's. Two of Ptolemy II's brothers were executed, although only one is known by name, Argaios, probably the eldest son of Ptolemy I. Another member of the family, Ptolemy II's half-brother Magas (a son of Berenike by her first husband), who was governor of Cyrene, declared himself king of that city. Ptolemy II expected that he would attack Egypt, but this never happened, and Magas ruled largely unchallenged until his death 30 years later.[30] A casualty of this succession struggle was Demetrios of Phaleron, who supported the children of Eurydike and was expelled from Alexandria to die at his country estate by the bite of an asp. This interesting other case of death by asp in Ptolemaic Egypt is first mentioned in extant literature by Cicero in his defense of Rabirius Postumus.[31] It is hard to imagine that Cleopatra VII, who would familiarize herself with the documents of her father's administration, had not read the transcript of the trial of his most notorious Roman confidant.

When Ptolemy II was finally firmly on the throne, many of the characteristics of Ptolemaic rule that Cleopatra was to inherit had been established, including the relative isolation of the Greek enclaves of Egypt, the dynastic support of intellectual culture and the arts, the lack of interference in traditional Egyptian ways, the closeness between rulers and the ancient priesthoods, and the careful choice of partners to produce dynastic heirs. It was already seen, however, that regardless of such heirs, succession struggles were an essential part of the Ptolemaic world, as Cleopatra herself would find out.

Lacking, however, in the reign of Ptolemy I was one of the most notorious characteristics of the dynasty, brother-sister marriage. This was to appear in the early years of Ptolemy II and, although scandalous at the time, would become normal by the time of Cleopatra VII. There were ancient Egyptian royal precedents,[32] but the actual perpetrator was Ptolemy II's sister, Arsinoë II, the first significant woman among the Ptolemies.[33] She was originally married to Lysimachos, the king of Macedonia. Upon his death in 281 B.C., Arsinoë maintained her position as queen of Macedonia by marrying her half-brother, Ptolemy Keraunos, who was the son of Ptolemy I and Eurydike, and who was at the court of Lysimachos when he died, thus being able to seize control of Macedonia. But soon Ptolemy Keraunos and Arsinoë were estranged, not unexpectedly as he killed her existing children, since they had a more legitimate claim to the throne. She fled to her brother in Egypt, eventually engineering her marriage to him, becoming queen for the third time. The marriage produced no issue, and it was not until the marriage of Ptolemy IV to his sister Arsinoë III that a ruling heir (Ptolemy V) was produced from a brother-sister marriage.

Despite the fact that brother-sister marriage became normal among the Ptolemies, the relationship of Ptolemy II and Arsinoë II caused a great scandal. Incest was seen as an Egyptian, not Greek, practice.[34] It existed in Egypt as early as the Fourth Dynasty, and more than half the known incestuous royal marriages from antiquity were Egyptian.[35] Yet it was still not considered acceptable in the Greek world (at least among mortals), although few dared point this out at the time. One who did draw attention to the questionable propriety of the marriage of Ptolemy II and Arsinoë II was a poet named Sotades, who wrote explicit lines outlining physical details about how the royal couple implemented their incestuous practices. He was forced to flee from Alexandria, and he was eventually tracked to a remote Greek island by a Ptolemaic agent and killed by being sealed in a lead container and dropped into the sea.[36]

Incest thus began among the Ptolemies seemingly because of the personal ambitions of Arsinoë II, but this established the precedent that would remain to the end of the dynasty, with Ptolemy IV, VI, VIII, and XII all practicing it, although Ptolemy V, the obscure Ptolemy VII, and Berenike IV were the only direct products of brother-sister marriage who actually ruled. But Ptolemaic incest did not stop at brother-sister marriages. Ptolemy VIII married both his sister Cleopatra II and her daughter Cleopatra III, whose father was Ptolemy VIII's brother Ptolemy VI. This uncle-niece marriage produced both Ptolemy IX and X. Ptolemy X also married his niece Cleopatra Berenike III, who later married his son Ptolemy XI. Cleopatra VII briefly ruled jointly with her brothers Ptolemy XIII and XIV, and while it is not certain that any official marriage took place, the latter is called her husband in one source, although he would have been only 12 years of age.[37] What began as a pragmatic result of the intense political aspirations of Arsinoë II became state policy, with the historical objections to incest forgotten. In fact, royal incest became an extreme form of endogamy, marriage within the clan, which to some extent was a venerable Greek institution.[38] More tactful than his colleague Sotades, the poet Theokritos could remind all that the personal habits of Ptolemy II and Arsinoë II were exactly like those of the gods.[39]

With the accession of Ptolemy II around 282 B.C., the Ptolemaic Empire entered its most flourishing period. Over the next century scholars such as Archimedes, Aristarchos, Konon, and Eratosthenes, and writers such as Kallimachos and Apollonios, lived and worked in Alexandria. New disciplines and theoretical structures such as geometry, geography, and the heliocentric theory of the universe, as well as countless pieces of significant Greek literature, were the product of these years. Alexandria continued to develop, and in the early years of Ptolemy II a great lighthouse was built just east of Pharos, becoming one of the Seven Wonders of the Ancient World.[40] Ptolemy II sent explorers up the Nile, down the Red Sea, and into the western Mediterranean, expanding the economic reach of the empire: their reports were promptly filed in the Library for later scholars to use.[41] All this was part of the inheritance of Cleopatra VII.

Yet she is most remembered for her relationship with Rome, as her kingdom, the last survivor of those created after the death of Alexander, collapsed in the face of the overwhelming ascendancy of the Italian city-state. When her Ptolemaic dynasty began, in the late fourth century B.C., the Greek world barely knew about Rome, and it was not a factor in Greek politics. Rome had no territory outside Italy and had just begun to interact with the Greek states in southern Italy. Before long, however, the reach of Rome would extend into the eastern Mediterranean.

By the latter fourth century B.C. the Greek world had become aware of the rise of this new power in the west. The first mention of Rome in Greek literature seems to have been by Aristotle, who included the city in his discussion of the political organization of all the states of the Mediterranean world.[42] Rome was in direct contact with the Greek cities of southern Italy by 300 B.C. Shortly thereafter Pyrrhos of Epeiros, whose early career had been assisted by Ptolemy I and who had married his stepdaughter Antigone (an early daughter of Berenike I), was engaged in his lengthy futile war with the Romans. Ptolemy II supplied the troops to protect Pyrrhos' kingdom while he was in Italy.[43] Thus the Ptolemies were among the first in the eastern Mediterranean to become knowledgeable about Rome, and it is no surprise that in 273 B.C. Ptolemy II became the earliest major king to seek alliance with the city. This was only nine years before Rome's first war with Carthage, and Ptolemy may have seen what was coming.[44] He was still contending with his half-brother Magas in Cyrene, whose territory adjoined that of Carthage. Although Ptolemy had friendly relations with that city, it might have seemed wise to have as many alliances as possible in the western Mediterranean. As it was, he kept out of the First Punic War (264–241 B.C.), and while it was in progress Magas reconciled with his Egyptian relatives, sending his daughter Berenike II to marry the heir apparent Ptolemy III.[45] Both Ptolemy II and Magas died during the war, and after it ended the Romans sent an embassy to Alexandria to acquaint themselves with the new ruler, Ptolemy III. A generation later, under Ptolemy IV, relations between Rome and Egypt were close enough that a Roman was the Ptolemaic garrison commander at Itanos on Crete.[46]

What the early Ptolemies could not know, however, was that Rome would steadily grow in power and acquire territory closer and closer to Egypt. While Ptolemy IV was king, the Second Punic War (218–201 B.C.) began, which resulted in Roman occupation of a portion of main-land Greece. The Romans sought Ptolemaic support in the war, bringing lavish gifts to Alexandria and requesting grain, since the devastations of Hannibal in Italy caused serious difficulties.[47] But it seems that Ptolemy remained neutral, and when Rome invaded northwestern Greece in response to a treaty that the Macedonian king, Philip V, had made with Hannibal in 215 B.C., Ptolemy attempted to mediate, the first time that the Ptolemies involved themselves in the foreign policy of Rome.[48] This perhaps encouraged the Romans to become more interested in the affairs of Egypt. Rome came to the Ptolemies' defense diplomatically in 200 B.C. when Philip attempted to gain possession of their territories in the Aegean. At the same time the Seleukid king, Antiochos III, moved against Ptolemaic holdings in interior Syria and the Levant. This aggressiveness was possible because in 205 B.C. Ptolemy IV had been assassinated and his infant son Ptolemy V placed on the throne, and the kingdom entered into a lengthy period of internal strife.[49] Rome sent envoys to Philip to demand that he desist from taking Ptolemaic territory; the ambassadors continued on to Antioch and Alexandria in an attempt to negotiate peace between the Seleukids and Ptolemies.[50] Yet the lack of any diplomatic progress on this issue was one of the reasons that Rome initiated the Second Macedonian War in late 200 B.C.; when Philip was defeated three years later, he was required to give up all the Ptolemaic territory that he had acquired. The Ptolemaic government had also complained to Rome about the Seleukid activities in the Levant, and the Romans demanded that Antiochos III withdraw. But Antiochos made a brilliant and unexpected response: he announced that he and Ptolemy V were concluding an alliance which would be sealed by marriage. Since no one else seemed aware of these plans, it represents a remarkably innovative move by Antiochos, the most senior and experienced of the Greek kings, at the peak of his career. He was undoubtedly able to enforce his will on the Ptolemaic court and its adolescent king, and in the winter of 194/93 B.C. at Raphia on the Egyptian-Levantine border, Ptolemy V, by then 16, was married to the Seleukid princess Cleopatra I, who was 10 years of age.[51] Her dowry was the territory of interior Syria that her father had just seized from her future husband. The royal couple were the great-great-grandparents of Cleopatra VII, and this both joined together the two great dynasties of the late Hellenistic world and allowed the name Cleopatra to enter the Ptolemaic family.

Yet neither of the young monarchs lived long. Ptolemy V never learned how to be an effective ruler and was manipulated by court officials throughout his life; he was assassinated by his military staff in early 180 B.C., when he was about 30.[52] His youth and inexperience had not only seen the loss of Ptolemaic territory but constant internal instability.

Cleopatra I survived him by only four years, dying in 176 B.C. in her late twenties. She had been named regent for her adolescent son Ptolemy VI: had she lived longer, she might have been able to stabilize the kingdom. As it was, Ptolemy VI became as manipulated by court factions as his father had been.[53] These events mark the beginning of the decline of the Ptolemaic kingdom.

By the early second century B.C., Ptolemaic weakness and Roman ascendancy meant that the political destinies of both would never again be separated. A Roman embassy was received in Alexandria in 173 B.C., and a Ptolemaic one went to Rome a few years later.[54] Embassies would shuttle regularly between the two capitals as long as the Ptolemaic state lasted. In view of the continued hostilities among the Greek states it was in Rome's interest to keep its eye on the eastern Mediterranean and to have allies wherever possible. In addition to the diplomatic contacts, Roman officials began to play the role of tourists. In 112 B.C. L. Mummius, perhaps the son or nephew of the conqueror of Corinth, sailed up the Nile to see the antiquities. Officials along his route were told to receive him with magnificence, provide lodging and gifts, and to ensure that the sites be open for his visit.[55]

In 175 B.C., when further difficulties erupted between the Seleukids and Ptolemies, Rome quickly responded. The new Seleukid king, Antiochos IV, who came to the throne in that year, aggressively moved into coastal Egypt and even attempted to repudiate the dowry of his just-deceased sister Cleopatra I, demanding the return of interior Syria to Seleukid control.[56] Since Antiochos was the uncle of Ptolemy VI, he could claim that he was simply exercising his duties as the senior member of the combined Seleukid-Ptolemaic families. Ptolemy appealed to Rome, and the Senate compelled negotiations. In July 168 B.C. the Roman ambassador, C. Popilius Laenas, met Antiochos at Eleusis outside Alexandria and forced him to withdraw under humiliating conditions. Closely following these events was the historian Polybios, himself personally involved in the Roman relations with the Greek states, and who expressed the situation succinctly: "Thus the Romans saved the exhausted kingdom of Ptolemy."[57]

The Ptolemies were now totally beholden to Rome, and the two states became even closer, for better or worse, over the next century. Roman intervention at every level of dynastic operations was the rule. The Romans would advise and expect consent on military and territorial matters as well as the dynastic succession. The career of the brother of Ptolemy VI, Ptolemy VIII, demonstrates this. After the Romans forced Antiochos IV out of Egypt, the three children of Ptolemy V and Cleopatra I ruled jointly. These were Ptolemy VI and VIII and their sister Cleopatra II, whose cooperation with one another was less than harmonious. Only four years after Antiochos's withdrawal, the siblings were so much at odds that Ptolemy VI appealed to Rome and traveled there in person, the first Ptolemaic king to do so. He went in late 164 B.C. without a royal escort and lived under poor conditions with a certain Demetrios, an artist from Alexandria who was an acquaintance, until the Senate learned of his presence and placed him in suitable lodgings.[58] It is not known how the Senate reacted to this demonstration of extreme humility. Meanwhile Ptolemy VIII had seized sole control in Alexandria—the whereabouts of his sister Cleopatra II at this time are unknown—and the Romans stepped in and enforced a settlement.[59] Ptolemy VIII was sent to be petty king of Cyrene, and Ptolemy VI and Cleopatra II married and ruled the rest of the Ptolemaic realm as equals. Not unreasonably, Ptolemy VIII felt that he had been marginalized, and he went to Rome. The Senate refused to alter the arrangements that it had just made, although pressure by Ptolemy VIII over the next few years resulted in the Senate's gradually moving to support his position and to back away from that of his brother.

In the midst of these negotiations, around 155 B.C., an attempt was made on the life of Ptolemy VIII, probably by a dissident Cyrenaian, but perhaps by a member of his family. He promptly wrote his will,[60] stating that his kingdom (presumably Cyrene, but he may have been audacious enough to mean all the Ptolemaic territories) would be left to Rome if he did not have an heir. This is the first known example of what would become a common tool of eastern royalty, a will favoring Rome, not so much a wish for Roman acquisition of territory but a threat to those who might think of removing the king. Yet at the same time the very existence of such a stratagem demonstrates how much Roman and Ptolemaic fortunes had become entangled. In fact the will was never invoked. Ptolemy VIII lived 40 more years, and he became king of Egypt when his brother died in 145 B.C., marrying Cleopatra II, the sister of both, as well as marrying her daughter Cleopatra III, the most convoluted family relationship that the Ptolemies were to have. The succession of the dynasty was through Cleopatra III, as she and Ptolemy VIII were parents of both Ptolemy IX and X, the former Cleopatra VII's grandfather.[61]

The year after he wrote his will, Ptolemy VIII returned to Rome. Among his activities there was his unsuccessful courting of Cornelia, recently the widow of the distinguished Ti. Sempronius Gracchus, the consul of 177 and 163 B.C.[62] She was the mother of the famous Gracchi brothers, who would figure so much in the attempts to reform Rome during the following years. This is the first documented example of a Ptolemaic ruler attempting to enhance his position by a marriage connection to a member of the Roman elite. It was probable that on this trip he was also formally named a friend and ally of the Roman people, and he may even have been given Roman citizenship.[63]

Ptolemy VIII is not remembered favorably in the sources—he was called "Physkon" ("Pot Belly") because of the visible effects of his luxuriant lifestyle—and there were many internal problems during his reign, as well as the more entertaining family issues. Yet he was in power longer than any other Ptolemy, and his lengthy 24-book memoir, the *Hypomnemata*, although surviving only in a few fragments, provides a strikingly personal insight into his world.[64] Most important, he set further precedents for his great-granddaughter Cleopatra VII in his visits to Rome to strengthen his political position and his recognition of the viability of a personal liaison with a prominent Roman. By the time of his death in 116 B.C. it was inevitable that Rome, which half a century previously had prevented the Ptolemaic kingdom from dissolving, would continue to dictate its destiny.

CHAPTER THREE

Cleopatra's Youth
and Education

CHILDREN, ESPECIALLY FEMALE ONES, are not prominent in the historical record, and thus it is no surprise that Cleopatra VII does not appear until the end of her father's reign, in the late 50s B.C., when she was nearly 20. Nevertheless, some assumptions about her youth are possible. She was unusually well educated even for a royal woman of the period. To be sure, the intellectual environment in Alexandria was not what it had been in the third century B.C., when personalities such as Euclid, Kallimachos, Apollonios, and Eratosthenes frequented the royal court. Ptolemy VIII had severely weakened the academic atmosphere with the convulsions of his reign, creating an environment that offered little security to scholars. The king himself expelled a number of them, and the major intellectuals of the era, such as Polybios, Hipparchos, and Nikandros, kept away from the city. Significantly, Ptolemy filled the post of Librarian with a military officer named Kydas, who replaced the distinguished Homeric scholar Aristarchos of Samothrake, the king's own teacher.[1] Placing a crony in the position once held by Apollonios and Eratosthenes is clear evidence of the kingdom's decline; filling senior administrative posts with ideologues is typical of the syndrome of disintegration. This pattern seems to have continued into the next generation, when Ptolemy IX also appointed a confidant as Librarian, one Onesandros of Paphos, registrar of that city, who had become an intimate of the king during his exile in Cyprus.[2] His son Ptolemy XII, however, made some modest attempts to restore the intellectual prominence of the city, an effort continued by his daughter Cleopatra VII.[3] Despite an era of political interference, Alexandria still possessed the world's finest library and its adjacent research center, the Mouseion, and scholars sought out both for study. Medicine seems to have been especially favored, something that would affect Cleopatra's own scholarship. Apollonios of Kition wrote commentaries on Hippokrates' works, one of which survives, dedicated to a King Ptolemy—either Ptolemy XII or his brother, Ptolemy of Cyprus—and which records that Apollonios had been commissioned by the king to write the work.[4] Apollonios's teacher, Zopyros, a pharmacologist and surgeon, advised Ptolemy XII about antidotes to poison and was also connected to another court interested in medicine, that of Mithradates VI of Pontos; in fact Zopyros's Persian name suggests that he may have originally come from that region.[5] A certain Chrysermos, although little known, seems to have been an important physician of the era who survived into the period of Cleopatra.[6] His students, Herakleides of Erythrai, an historian of medicine, and Apollonios Mys, a pharmacologist who also wrote on perfumes, were still active in the 20s B.C.[7] Another member of the school was perhaps Cleopatra's own physician, Olympos, whose memoirs were used by Plutarch.[8]

Philosophy also enjoyed a renaissance, as the Mithradatic Wars and Sulla's sack of 86 B.C. caused an exodus of scholars from Athens, some of whom went to Alexandria. The Academic school—originated by Plato in the fourth century B.C. but having undergone many convulsions since—was represented by Antiochos of Askalon, whose lectures Cicero attended in Athens.[9] Coming to Alexandria, Antiochos established a philosophical circle that determined the nature of Academic philosophy in the city.[10] Those associated with him included his friend and, in time, violent opponent, Herakleitos of Tyre, and Antiochos's brother Aristos, who eventually returned to the Academy and was an intimate of Marcus Brutus. There were also Kratippos of Pergamon and Ariston of Alexandria, both Academics who became Peripatetics, adherents of the school of thought originated by Aristotle, but whose followers, like the Academics, were no longer attached to an institution in Athens. Ariston himself became involved in a plagiarism issue with Eudoros of Alexandria (perhaps a product of the same school) regarding suspiciously similar works about the Nile, but he also wrote an encyclopedia of philosophy that was generally respected, as well as on astronomy and mathematics.[11] Another member of the circle was the unfortunate Dion, leader of the embassy to Rome in the 50s B.C. to complain about Ptolemy XII and, as a result, to be murdered by his agents; little is known about him as a scholar.[12] The most famous student of Antiochos was Areios Didymos, who represented the third of the great philosophical schools of the Hellenistic world, the Stoics. He may also have studied with Eudoros, and he became one of the teachers of Octavian, advising him at the time of the fall of Alexandria.[13] Areios Didymos was offered the position of prefect of Egypt, but he went to Rome instead and continued to be close to the imperial family, especially Livia, surviving until at least 9 B.C. This variety of scholars—Academics, Stoics, and Peripatetics— demonstrates not only the eclectic nature of philosophy in Alexandria of the first century B.C., but that practically any point of view was available to those seeking it.

A scholar of great importance of the era of Ptolemy XII was Timagenes of Alexandria, the most significant historian of the period.[14] There is no specific evidence that he was at the royal court, although this is probable; he first enters the historical record when taken to Rome by Aulus Gabinius in 55 B.C., but he was probably not a young man at the time. Gabinius's aide Marcus Antonius may have been the insti-gator in encouraging Timagenes to come to Rome, because the two became intimates, and Timagenes facilitated Antonius's contacts with the Greek intellectual community. Among Timagenes' protégés were Strabo of Amaseia and Nikolaos of Damascus, both of whom returned to Alexandria, the latter, at least, becoming a member of Cleopatra's court. Timagenes was a prolific writer, whose major work was *On Kings*, seem-ingly a universal history structured on an examination of royal power, a particular interest of his. It included a discussion of the reign of Ptolemy XII. Eventually Timagenes became an advisor—perhaps on Egyptian matters—to Octavian. He is a significant personality in the flow of ideas between Alexandria and Rome, and although there is no evidence that he was a teacher of Cleopatra VII, he influenced some of those who were important in her life.

How Cleopatra profited from these scholars is not known, but one presumes that she could study at the Library and attend lectures at the Mouseion, both part of the royal palace complex. A medical writer herself, she may have studied with the physicians and pharmacologists at her father's court. A certain Philostratos was her tutor in philos-ophy, rhetoric, and oratory.[15] He was elderly in 30 B.C. and had prob-ably come to the court in the time of Ptolemy XII. Since Philostratos was the outstanding orator of his day, he would have been the one who gave Cleopatra her excellence in public speaking and her philological reputation. On the other hand, he misrepresented himself as a member of the Academy, which allegedly got him into difficulty when Alexandria fell to Octavian, although Areios Didymos intervened and was persuasive in having him pardoned. After time at the court of Herod the Great, he died in poverty some years later at Ostrakine on the eastern coast of Egypt.[16]

Cleopatra was a skilled orator. Plutarch wrote that the queen was gripping in her conversation and persuasive in her discussion, able to speak Ethiopian, Trogodyte, and the languages of the Hebraioi, Arabes, Syrians, Medes, and Parthians, and many others as well.[17] Egyptian is not specified but can be presumed because Plutarch referred to the ignorance of that language on the part of her royal predecessors. In addition to her native Greek, she also knew Latin, although the Romans with whom she came into contact would insist on speaking Greek. Greek had been used officially by the Romans since the early third century B.C., and in Cleopatra's day Cicero complained that there were still people who demanded interpreters, showing that this was neither normal nor expected.[18] Latin would have been useful to her not so much to speak to Romans but to read material in that language, such as the transcript of the trial of her father's banker Rabirius Postumus and senatorial actions relating to her kingdom. In addition, the Romans used Latin more than might be expected in the Levantine territories Cleopatra desired, because of a long-standing antipathy to Greek in this region,[19] and at least one of her decrees, directed to a Jewish community, probably in Leontopolis, uses some Latin.[20]

The seven languages recorded by Plutarch deserve some attention. The list is essentially geographical, from south to northeast. Ethiopia and Trogodytika had been associated with the Ptolemies since the time of Ptolemy II, who had sent numerous expeditions into both regions, especially to Meroë, the Ethiopian capital, where his agents had lived for extended periods and had explored far beyond.[21] This city, on the Nile above the Fifth Cataract, was the center of a powerful indigenous kingdom that was important to the Ptolemies because of its supply of resources, especially gold and elephants, the latter a valuable military tool. Ptolemy II also extended control over Trogodytika, the area between the upper Nile and the Red Sea, founding several cities along the coast, again for the supply of elephants as well as support of trade to India. These regions remained closely associated with the Ptolemaic Empire until its end—Cleopatra considered taking refuge somewhere in Trogodytika or Ethiopia after Actium[22]—and for her to know their languages was an important point in her favor.

Across the Red Sea was the Arabian peninsula. Although only small parts of it were ever under Ptolemaic control, this region was a vital part of the Ptolemaic kingdom's economy.[23] The great Nabataean trading center of Petra began to flourish in the late fourth century B.C., and a certain Anaxikrates explored the Red Sea for Alexander, reaching the wealthy aromatics-producing regions at its southern end. By the third century B.C. the trade route from Petra to these districts was well known, and frankincense and myrrh, the two most famous aromatics, were exported to processing factories in Alexandria. Knowing the Arabian language may have assisted Cleopatra in diplomatic and mercantile negotiations, and she may have acquired some Arabian territory in the 30s B.C.

Plutarch's next language, that of the Hebraioi, probably refers not to Hebrew but Aramaic. The Hebrew language was still spoken in isolated pockets in Cleopatra's day, but Aramaic was far more common, although the relative use of the two languages remains disputed.[24] Her constant involvement in the fortunes of the southern Levant again would have made knowledge of the local languages useful, although her lengthy relationship with Herod the Great would have been carried on in Greek. But it is possible that not all his agents spoke that language.

North of Judaea was Syria. The core of Syria had been a Roman province since the dissolution of the Seleukid kingdom in 64 B.C., but the Ptolemies long had had claim to various parts of the region, especially the interior district known as Koile ("Hollow") Syria, technically the deep upper Orontes valley but a term eventually applied to much of Syria except the district around Antioch. Koile Syria had been lost to the Ptolemies in the early second century B.C., and despite various attempts to regain it had remained Seleukid (and then Roman) until Antonius gave parts of it to Cleopatra in the 30s B.C. The geographical limits of Koile Syria were fluid and tended to expand, eventually even to include the Phoenician cities. Exactly what was the "language of the Syrians" to which Plutarch referred is uncertain, but it is clear that Cleopatra was deeply interested in this historically Ptolemaic region.

Plutarch's last two languages, those of the Medes and Parthians, were presumably of concern to Cleopatra because of Antonius's Parthian expeditions of 36–34 B.C. The two languages were closely related, and Plutarch's phrase may be the familiar tautology. Although the Ptolemies never controlled territory on the Iranian plateau, the region had been

Seleukid in the time of Cleopatra's Seleukid ancestors, and with that kingdom now defunct she could invoke a hereditary claim, believing, as the only reigning descendant of Seleukid royalty, that the Seleukid territories which the Parthians had conquered in the second century B.C. were actually hers. As a skilled linguist she would learn new languages when it was necessary to do so, in this case perhaps during the lengthy preparations for Antonius's Parthian campaign, thus being ready for the presumed amalgamation of the newly conquered territory of Parthia into her kingdom. In fact, her son Alexander Helios was named king of Parthia in the Donations of Alexandria (see p. 100).

Plutarch also stated that Cleopatra knew many other languages. One can only speculate what these might be, but other than Greek, Egyptian, and Latin, which can be taken for granted, the most obvious ones would be the languages of North Africa. The Ptolemies had had a long relationship with Carthage, remaining neutral in the Roman wars; their possession of Cyrene meant that they were territorially near to Carthage, with the inevitable trade contacts. Cyrene also had connections with the major indigenous kingdom of North Africa, Numidia, southwest of Carthage. Ptolemy VIII, while king of Cyrene, had visited the court of the legendary Numidian king Massinissa, and Massinissa's son Mastanabal had been honored at Cyrene.[25] The Numidian kingdom survived well into Cleopatra's reign until provincialized by Caesar in 46 B.C.,[26] and she may have had ideas of extending her influence in this direction, perhaps with Caesar's help. It would be expected that the queen would know something of the local languages of this region, yet she could not know that in 25 B.C. her daughter Cleopatra Selene would fulfill this promise by marrying Massinissa's descendant Juba II, becoming ruler of Mauretania, a vast region of North Africa extending from just west of Carthage to the Atlantic (see p. 154).

Although Plutarch's statement refers to speaking ability, it is probable that Cleopatra could also read some of these languages, a talent that would assist her in diplomacy. Again, her reading knowledge of Greek, Egyptian, and Latin are obvious. Scholars at the Library were constantly involved in the translation of texts, which implies that the originals were also on file. The most famous case is the Hebrew Bible, the circumstances of whose translation into the Septuagint are described in an extant letter allegedly by a certain Aristeas, which records how Ptolemy II commissioned Demetrios of Phaleron to supervise the task, effected by 72 scholars sequestered on the island of Pharos for 72 days.[27] The tale has problems: in addition to its obvious formulaic nature, Demetrios was not an intimate of Ptolemy II, as he had not supported him in the succession and was promptly forced into exile (see p. 35). Yet there is no doubt that a Greek version of the Bible came into existence in the third century B.C., and this may mean that an original was deposited in the Library.

Persian texts may also have been available, as Hermippos of Smyrna, best remembered for his biographical research that forms much of the extant material of Diogenes Laertios's familiar work on scholars, wrote on the writings of Zoroaster. As a student of Kallimachos, he was active in the third century B.C.[28] It seems obvious that Egyptian writings were in the Library: in the first half of the third century B.C. Manethon, an Egyptian, wrote a history in Greek of his native land.[29] One might also expect that emergent Latin literature would find its way to Alexandria in the first century B.C., and there is some evidence that Cleopatra was familiar with the poetry of Horace.[30] Although most researchers would find Hebrew, Egyptian, and Persian material more accessible in Greek translation, young Cleopatra may have used the originals to hone her linguistic skills.

Cleopatra's education would also be reflected in her own publications, although the tradition of her as an author is obscure and full of problems. Hellenistic royalty were expected to be scholars and writers. The literary achievements of her ancestors Ptolemy I and VIII have already been noted (see pp. 33, 42). Ptolemy III also seems to have written his memoirs.[31] Ptolemy IV wrote a tragedy called *Adonis*.[32] One might also add that Cleopatra's son-in-law Juba II of Mauretania would become one of the more prolific scholars of his era, ably assisted by his wife, Cleopatra's daughter.[33] Even Herod the Great wrote his memoirs.[34] Julius Caesar, certainly a major influence on young Cleopatra, was an extensive author: in addition to his familiar memoirs, he wrote poetry, including a tragedy on Oedipus, and technical works on language.[35] Yet a significant role model for Cleopatra, both politically and culturally, would have been Mithradates VI the Great of Pontos, who was a major player in the world of the eastern Mediterranean for more than half a century. He was famous for speaking more languages (22) than anyone known, and he was also a brilliant scholar, especially of medicine, with a notable library.[36] His vision of the future of the East was remarkably similar to that which Cleopatra and Antonius would develop, and, in fact, Cleopatra may have been seen as the successor to Mithradates as the great opponent of Roman expansionism.[37] Contacts at the scholarly level between the two courts have already been noted (see p. 44), and it is probable that with Mithradates' death in 63 B.C. some of his intellectual circle, such as the pharmacologist Zopyros, came to Alexandria.

Cleopatra, then, grew up and flourished in an environment in which literary output was expected of someone in her position, so the obscure notices of her writings must be taken seriously, although her short and turbulent life precluded the publication of memoirs, a great loss. There are several groups of literary fragments attributed to Cleopatra. All seem to be from a single work, the *Cosmetics*.[38] These are scattered through several sources, most notably Galen, and the late antique medical writers Aetios of Amida and Paulos of Aigina. Galen, at least, seems to have relied on the work of a certain Kriton (T. Statilius Crito), physician to the emperor Trajan. Fragment 1, from Galen, is a discussion of remedies for a type of hair disease. Fragments 2–3, also from Galen, examine cures for baldness and dandruff. Fragment 4, from Aetios, is a recipe for perfumed soap. Fragment 5, from Paulos, is about curling and dyeing the hair, and fragment 6, from Galen and the most ambitious, is a lengthy list of weights and measures. All six fragments are attributed to a Cleopatra. Only Aetios called her Queen Cleopatra, although there are Byzantine references that support this.[39]

Connecting these fragments to Cleopatra VII is, admittedly, difficult. Only one is assigned to a royal personage, and the attribution is from the sixth century A.D. By late antiquity Cleopatra VII was by far the most famous person of that name and there would be a tendency to assume that the fragments were hers. There is also the concern that fragment 6, on weights and measures, shows knowledge of the Neronian reforms of A.D. 64,[40] although this is in only one of the 31 entries in the passage, and it could be argued that it is a later addition, perhaps by Kriton.

Less credible is the modern argument that a work on cosmetics is somehow unworthy of Cleopatra VII. To be sure, such a treatise fits conveniently into the popular image of the queen as a seductress, but the *Cosmetics* is far deeper than a discussion of female adornment. It is rather a medical and pharmacological work, with eight prescriptions for curing *alopekia* ("fox-mange"), a disease in which the hair falls off,[41] and several additional remedies for hair loss and dandruff. Alexandria at the time of Cleopatra's youth was a major center of medical and pharmacological scholarship, and the *Cosmetics* is a natural product of this environment. The section on weights and measures, long and complex, a significant source on its topic, has obvious pharmacological relevance, but would also be useful in the trade and industrial aspects of the administration of the Ptolemaic kingdom. It may even belong to a separate work. Obviously the *Cosmetics* entered the mainstream of medical literature, cited by at least four later medical authors, and was a work typical of the direction of scholarship in the Alexandria of Cleopatra's day.[42] Attribution to her cannot be proved but is exceedingly probable.

Thus when Cleopatra VII came to the throne in late 51 B.C., she was a remarkably educated person. Intellectual royalty was common in Hellenistic times, but it was not inevitable—her brother Ptolemy XIII was said to have had little education[43]—and since women often did not have the opportunities that men did, even in the Hellenistic period, Cleopatra's achievement is all the more remarkable. Chronological details cannot be fixed, but it can be presumed that by her accession she could read and write several languages and was familiar with the history of her family, Ptolemaic Egypt, and Egypt and the Greek world in general. She was said to take an almost sensuous pleasure in learning and scholarship,[44] an intriguing variant on her best-known alleged attribute. She was probably more knowledgeable of Roman politics than were many of her generation, determined, if futilely, to avoid the traps into which her father had fallen. Her presumed scholarly writings, although their dates of composition are unknown, reflect her position in the intellectual mainstream of her kingdom. An early visit to Athens—and connections to that city throughout her life (see pp. 22, 135)—could only have enhanced her education, and one can speculate on what she learned in that prestigious city, still believed by many to be the intellectual capital of the world.

CHAPTER FOUR

Becoming Queen

(51—47 B.C.)

THE WISH OF PTOLEMY XII that his children live in harmony was not to be realized.[1] Perhaps his own execution of the eldest, Berenike, set a bad precedent. Problems arose almost immediately after his death, which had occurred by 22 March 51 B.C., perhaps in February.[2] The two older children, Cleopatra and Ptolemy XIII, who had been made joint rulers by their father, succeeded to the throne, but Cleopatra moved swiftly to assert herself. On 22 March she traveled to Hermonthis, just south of Thebes, to install a new Buchis bull, the first recorded event of her reign. The sacred Buchis bull was the terrestrial intermediary of the god Montu; its worship was one of the many animal cults that pervaded Egyptian society. Cleopatra was perhaps the first Ptolemy to attend this ceremony in person.[3] The journey of more than 400 miles up the Nile also served to make her visible to her new subjects. By late summer she had removed her brother from the joint rule, as documents beginning on 29 August list her alone. Within a few months of her father's death, the queen had managed to assume sole control, but this merely initiated a struggle that was to last even beyond the settlement by Julius Caesar three years later. In Rome, rumors of the death of Ptolemy XII began to circulate in late spring of 51 B.C., but they were confirmed only in July, and those in the city were anxious to learn who was in charge.[4]

Cleopatra had many problems in addition to her dynastic troubles. Her father's immense debt to various Romans was not totally paid. When Julius Caesar arrived in Alexandria in 48 B.C., he was still owed 17.5 million drachmas.[5] Scattered civil strife continued. In the first years of Cleopatra's reign, a provincial official had been attacked by a

FIGURE 2. Head of Cleopatra VII in Parian marble, in the Staatliche Museen zu Berlin (1976.10). Photography by Klaus-Dieter Braczyk; courtesy of Bildarchiv Preussicher Kulturbesitz and Art Resource, New York (ART177844).

certain Diokles, who seemed to have an extensive force at his disposal. Organized brigands were a continuing problem: reports use the term *anarchia* to describe conditions. This situation had existed since the late second century, as a decree of Ptolemy VIII from 118 B.C., the first significant hint of problems, offers amnesty to those involved in rebellious acts. Government officials were a major part of the problem, as they repeatedly misused their powers to extort funds, acquire the best land, and levy labor.[6]

In addition, drought and the resultant food shortages were becoming serious. A document from late 50 B.C. regulates the movement of grain, by royal order, and gave protection to those transporting it to Alexandria.[7] The governor of the Herakleopolite nome was told that any failure to account for the full harvest would be charged to him personally.[8] By 48 B.C. the Nile flood was extremely low, and food riots were imminent in Alexandria.[9] Moreover, there was the matter of the Roman troops that Aulus Gabinius had stationed there in 55 B.C., since with the death of Ptolemy XII they had become unemployed, and thus began to assimilate and gain a reputation for lawlessness, luxuriating in the delights of Alexandria and waiting for a new patron. In 50 B.C. they tortured and murdered two sons of M. Calpurnius Bibulus, proconsul of Syria. Bibulus had been politically active for years (he was consul with Julius Caesar in 59 B.C.) but was generally ineffective, one of the weaker

FIGURE 3. Basalt statue of Cleopatra VII in the Rosicrucian Egyptian Museum, San Jose, California (RC1586), used with permission of the Rosicrucian Egyptian Museum, San Jose, California, Rosicrucian Order, AMORC.

Roman figures of the era.[10] He took up his post in Syria in 51 B.C., accompanied by his two older sons. The sons were sent to Egypt probably to return the Gabinians to active duty, as Bibulus needed more troops because of problems in his province, since Crassus's disaster in 53 B.C. had not only seriously reduced Roman military strength but emboldened the Parthians. But the sons were killed, probably with the approval of the powers in Egypt, not the quarreling Ptolemaic siblings but the senior members of the administration, especially the regent Potheinos and the military commander Achillas. Cleopatra, in her first recorded diplomatic act regarding Rome, had the killers sent in chains to Bibulus in Syria, but he returned them to her, stating that punishment was the role of the Senate, a strange rebuke to the queen for having interfered in internal Roman affairs, something that must have been confusing to her given the history of entanglements between Rome and Egypt.

This seemingly minor incident had astonishing repercussions. It was Cleopatra's first official contact with the Roman government, and her swift action to smooth a potential diplomatic incident only a year into her reign, even if not appreciated, demonstrates how seriously she considered relations between the two powers. All her life she had seen difficulties with the Romans, issues that her father could never resolve, and she was determined to do better. Moreover, in opposing the government officials that she had inherited from her father, she set herself up for a collision with them that would almost cost her the reign. Bibulus himself seems never to have recovered and became increasingly erratic. In early 48 B.C., as a naval commander on the Pompeian side, he was charged with preventing Caesar from moving toward Greece, something that he failed to do. This hastened Caesar's ultimate victory (and his involvement in Egypt). Bibulus died on board his ship in the midst of these engagements.[11]

Cleopatra also devoted effort to establishing herself as a ruler concerned with the historic culture of Egypt, shown not only by her visit to Hermonthis but her deep involvement in the burial rites of the Apis bull in 50/49 B.C. This was the most famous bull cult, long known to the Greek world because of Herodotos's detailed description.[12] Cleopatra contributed a large sum of money and endowed the festival, especially providing food and oil. Yet despite her interest in ancient Egyptian traditions, or the economic and financial issues afflicting Egypt, her priority was the survival of her reign, which promptly was called into question, as she was soon feeling the effects of sibling rivalry. Her brother

Ptolemy XIII, who was only about 11 years old, had a powerful group of advisors committed to making him sole monarch, in part because they resented being ruled by a woman.[13] Most notable, or notorious, was Potheinos, legally his tutor and the administrator of his property and finances, whom the Romans saw as the true power in Egypt after the death of Ptolemy XII and was probably the one behind the killing of Bibulus's sons.[14] Others included another tutor, the rhetorician Theodotos of Chios (or Samos), and the military commander Achillas. This cabal—and there were probably others in addition to the three known—presumably all holdovers from the reign of Ptolemy XII, was devoted to the ascendancy of Ptolemy XIII at the expense of his siblings, and would play a dominant role in Egyptian events until after the arrival of Caesar, who saw Potheinos as the effective ruler.[15] Cleopatra's response to the empowerment of her elder brother may have been to seek alliance with the younger one, Ptolemy XIV, but this seems to have lasted only a few months in 50 B.C.[16] By autumn Ptolemy XIII was in a dominant position, and on a document of 27 October—the one regulating the transport of grain—his name appears before that of his sister. Soon he began his own regnal dating, equating his Year 1 with Year 3 of Cleopatra (49 B.C.).[17]

Cleopatra still held her own, however. She remained in Alexandria and was there in the spring or summer of 49 B.C. when Gnaeus Pompeius, the son of Pompeius the Great, arrived in the city with a request from his father for military support.[18] In the six years since Gabinius had restored Ptolemy XII, Rome had continued to drift toward civil war, and the senior Pompeius and Julius Caesar were headed toward collision. Cleopatra was well aware of this, because she knew, either personally or by reputation, all the major players. Gabinius himself, after his trials connected with his role in restoring her father, had gone into exile and was no longer involved in politics,[19] but Cleopatra certainly had clearer memories of Gabinius's cavalry commander, Marcus Antonius, who was now Julius Caesar's most important subordinate. Caesar himself she had never met, and he had never been in the Levant or Egypt, but Cleopatra would have known that in 59 B.C. he had obtained legal recognition of her father as an allied and friendly king (see p. 21). She also would hardly forget that her kingdom was heavily in financial debt to Caesar because of her father's largesse. But it was Pompeius the Great who was most involved in Egyptian affairs. Cleopatra would not have remembered his presumed visit to the court of her father—she was only three at the time—but she would have heard about it and the assistance that Ptolemy had provided Pompeius three years later for his efforts in the southern Levant, and she would have been aware that her father had lived with Pompeius during his exile in Rome. She would also know that Pompeius had the Roman copy of her father's will, which seemed— at least in the way Pompeius interpreted it—to put him in a state of guardianship of her and her siblings.[20] It seems highly probable that Cleopatra and Pompeius would have corresponded about the realities of this relationship.

The reason that Pompeius's son Gnaeus appeared in Alexandria in the spring or summer of 49 B.C. was the imminent war with Julius Caesar. After many years of virtual exile in Gaul, Caesar had returned to Italy in January, causing Pompeius and his supporters to abandon Italy and to seek a power base in Greece. Drawing upon his 20 years of contacts with the eastern Mediterranean world, Pompeius swiftly built up a large force with which to oppose Caesar. It was inevitable, given their mutual history, that the Ptolemies would be expected to play a role in Pompeius's plans, and thus young Gnaeus was promptly sent to Alexandria.

The younger Pompeius was the first Roman to visit Cleopatra when she was queen and an adult—she was 20—and he was the first to feel the effect of her charm.[21] His visit was successful, for Cleopatra and Ptolemy XIII, in perhaps their last joint action, sent the elder Pompeius 60 ships and 500 troops, the latter conveniently mobilized from the troublesome Gabinian contingent. This helped discharge the debt that the monarchs owed Pompeius for his efforts on behalf of their father. The younger Pompeius used the fleet in activities around Orikon (modern Orikuni in Albania) and Brundisium, but these raids did not, in the long run, assist the fortunes of his father.[22] The Gabinians were at the Battle of Pharsalos.

Shortly afterward, the breach between Cleopatra and Ptolemy XIII became permanent. It did not help the queen that Pompeius decided to violate the terms of the will of Ptolemy XII and name Ptolemy XIII sole ruler,[23] although it is not clear how this fact (mentioned only by Lucan) fits into the sequence of events of early 48 B.C. Clearly, however, Potheinos and the others around the boy king had gained the upper hand. Cleopatra either was formally exiled or finally felt it necessary to leave Alexandria. She retreated upriver to the region around Thebes, perhaps seeking the historic heartland of Egypt.[24] Since she was related to the priesthood of Ptah, the venerable religious center of the Thebaid may have seemed attractive, especially the ancient temple of Ptah at Karnak, or even Hermonthis, where she had recently been. Her mother may have had contacts in that region. Nothing is known about her, but since Cleopatra was only 21, it is quite possible that her mother was still alive and could provide some protection for her daughter. But the Thebaid did not work out as a place of refuge, and by spring 48 B.C. Cleopatra was in Syria collecting an army. Her sister Arsinoë allegedly accompanied her. She was younger than Cleopatra, probably in her early teens, and first appears in the historical record at this point.[25]

There is no explicit information as to why Cleopatra went to Syria, presumably Antioch, in early 48 B.C., or why she believed she could raise an army there. She did, however, have contacts in the city. It had been only 16 years since Pompeius had terminated the Seleukid kingdom, and Cleopatra was related to the Seleukids. Members of the family were still alive, and a few years previously her sister Berenike IV had twice attempted to marry Seleukids.[26] Cleopatra may have been seeking a husband herself: it was an obvious issue, given her age and status, and there were no reasonable candidates within the Ptolemaic family, but possibilities certainly existed among her Seleukid relatives. By establishing herself in Antioch, the queen could exploit these family connections to her advantage.[27] Moreover, Antioch was a center of increasing opposition to Pompeius,[28] and by now Cleopatra could feel nothing but betrayal from him. She may also have obtained some support from the southern Levantine city of Askalon, on the borders of Egypt, which commemorated her on its coinage and whose powerful local citizen Antipatros had assisted in the restoration of her father.[29] A few months later, perhaps even after Caesar's arrival, Cleopatra attempted to return to Egypt with an army—it is unknown how she obtained it—but found her way blocked by her brother and thus took up a position near the eastern Delta city of Pelousion.

During these months—the spring and summer of 48 B.C.—events in Greece were to have their own immense impact on the future of Egypt and its exiled queen. By late spring Pompeian and Caesarean forces were engaging in repeated skirmishes. Pompeius's eastern connections, which allowed him steadily to augment his troops, meant that Caesar needed a prompt and decisive action. Loyally assisted by Antonius, he moved into Thessaly, thereby largely isolating Pompeius from his fleet, which had been used unsuccessfully by Bibulus to keep Caesar in Italy. The two armies met at Pharsalos on 9 August 48 B.C. Defeat for the Pompeians could not have been more overwhelming: Caesar's report lists 15,000 dead and 24,000 captured against merely 200 killed on his side. When Pompeius's headquarters was about to be overrun, he escaped to Larisa and then Mytilene, and eventually to Tyre.[30] After some consideration of North Africa as a refuge, he decided that his best option was to go to Egypt, where he could invoke his historic relationship with the Ptolemies and replenish his forces.

In Egypt, Ptolemy XIII had spent the past several months consolidating his position. He used the leftover Gabinian troops as a personal bodyguard, and mobilized some of them under the command of Achillas when Cleopatra returned from Syria, sending them to Pelousion to bar her way to Alexandria. But the boy was hardly in control of events. His advisors, led by Potheinos, had no intention of letting Pompeius use Egypt as a base; as holdovers from the times of Ptolemy XII they well knew what would happen when Romans controlled Egypt and its resources. Perhaps naively, they wanted to keep Egypt out of the Roman civil war. Thus—it was said to be the idea of Theodotos—they laid a trap for Pompeius. When he arrived off Pelousion, he sent messages requesting safe-conduct. These were accepted, but as he attempted to land he was killed by a force led by Achillas. Caesar, who eventually determined where Pompeius had gone, arrived in Egypt shortly thereafter.[31]

Presumably, Ptolemy XIII's advisors believed that proving to Caesar that Pompeius was dead—Caesar was sent his head—would neutralize the situation. But all the parties were unaware of how complex things had become. Cleopatra, it was thought, had been successfully marginalized and was blocked at the eastern edge of Egypt or possibly in Syria.[32] At any rate, no one took her seriously. Ptolemy XIII, although the pawn of his advisors, felt that he was in control, demonstrating his authority by standing on the beach in the midst of his army, wearing a purple robe, as Pompeius was eliminated.[33] The two other children, Ptolemy XIV and Arsinoë, were too young to be considered politically. Caesar believed that affairs in Egypt were indeed Rome's concern, as they had been for some time. He established himself in a suite in the royal palace at Alexandria—not without some difficulty—and sent messages to Cleopatra and Ptolemy XIII strongly suggesting that they disband their armies and reconcile with one another. Nevertheless he also enjoyed the cultural delights of Alexandria and seemed to have the situation under control, but wisely ordered reinforcements from the remnants of Pompeius's army in Asia.[34]

Whether Caesar felt that he had inherited Pompeius's obligations to the Ptolemaic dynasty is not clear, but he himself had long been involved in Egyptian matters. He had been responsible for recognition of Ptolemy XII as an allied and friendly king, and therefore believed that his quarreling children needed some Roman persuasion. Provincialization of Egypt, as Pompeius had done with the Seleukid kingdom, was not an option with so many heirs available. Thus Caesar decreed that Cleopatra and Ptolemy XIII should settle their differences by negotiation before him. He also asked for partial payment of the 17.5 million drachmas that he was owed, as he needed funds to maintain his troops. Potheinos, the real power in Egypt, offered to pay at some future date if Caesar were to leave and was rebuked for the sly suggestion.[35]

Ptolemy XIII thus came to Alexandria but kept his army. Cleopatra sent representatives, who evidently reported that Caesar was not only susceptible to royal women but had a history of affairs with them. She then decided to appear before him in person. Of the two detailed accounts of this meeting, that of Dio[36] is more mundane: she asked for permission to see him without telling her brother and dressed herself to appear as beautiful and pitiable as possible, charming him with her demeanor and her skill at language. But the more famous account is that of Plutarch, who described how she had herself tied up in a bedsack and was smuggled into Caesar's presence.[37] There is a certain credibility to Plutarch's account, however romantic, because a name is provided, Apollodoros of Sicily, who helped Cleopatra implement her plan and who was perhaps the source of the story. On the other hand, it is almost a demeaning way for the queen of Egypt to appear before the consul of the Roman Republic, especially given that Cleopatra was always conscious of her regal status, to the point of arrogance.[38] Yet the bedsack device may have been common at the time: a certain Antius escaped the proscriptions of 44 B.C. by removal from his home in the same way.[39] In whatever manner the queen appeared before him, Caesar was immediately captivated. If he had had any thought of excluding her from the settlement,[40] it vanished, and he decided to effect a reconciliation between Cleopatra and her brother. As soon as Ptolemy arrived, he realized what had happened—as far as he knew, his sister was still east of Pelousion—and he now understood that Caesar was no longer neutral. In a dramatic scene, probably staged by Potheinos, he rushed from the palace and with an impassioned speech incited the waiting populace to riot, ending it with tearing the royal diadem from his head. Quick thinking by Caesar saved the situation: he arrested Ptolemy and used his own outstanding oratorical skills to talk down the crowd.

Cleopatra, who witnessed all of this, was taken with her brother to a meeting of the Alexandrian assembly, where Caesar produced Ptolemy XII's will—his quick acquisition of it shows exceptional foresight—and upheld it through his authority as consul, reasserting the Roman guardianship over the siblings and stating that Cleopatra and Ptolemy XIII would be joint rulers in the Egyptian tradition.[41] Unlike Ptolemy XII, Caesar made a specific provision for the two other children, realizing that they were no longer so young that they could be safely ignored. Arsinoë, perhaps in her early teens, and Ptolemy XIV, about eleven, were together given Cyprus, presumably under a traditional sibling marriage. The island had been occupied in 58 B.C. by the Romans in a revenue-producing action, deposing its king, Cleopatra's uncle Ptolemy of Cyprus (see p. 22). In returning this historically Ptolemaic territory, Caesar was politically astute, for it not only was an attempt to mollify the restive Egyptians (loss of Cyprus had driven Ptolemy XII into exile) but removed from the Egyptian settlement two potential royal rivals. Cleopatra was probably in no way unhappy at having two of her siblings sent far from Egypt, but the arrangement was never implemented because of subsequent events.

All seemed to be well. But Caesar had failed to take into account the realities of Eastern politics. Potheinos and his cabal were not to be bypassed so easily, for he understood that the allegedly unbiased settlement really favored Cleopatra, the only adult among the four siblings. Potheinos also realized that Caesar had little military support, as he had arrived in Egypt with only about 4,000 men and no obvious way to pay them. The Egyptian army, including the remaining Gabinians, had 20,000. Thus, allegedly while the reconciliation was still being celebrated, Potheinos put into effect a plan to remove Caesar and Cleopatra. Potheinos sent to Achillas, in command of the army at Pelousion, orders to attack Caesar, thus beginning the events known as the Alexandrian War.[42]

The Alexandrian War lasted the rest of 48 B.C. and into the early months of the following year. Despite a detailed report by one of Caesar's senior staff, the extant treatise known as *de bello alexandrino* (*On the Alexandrian War*), the tactical details are not relevant to the career of

Cleopatra, and only the outcome is of importance. Presumably she spent the entire war in the palace.

Its most infamous event was the burning of the Library.[43] Caesar, who had created a defensive perimeter in the area of the palace, used fire to repel an attack, which got out of control and, according to the primary sources, burned the Library. It was said that hundreds of thousands of books were destroyed, or indeed the entire collection. The account seems to have become more terrifying as time passed. Loss of the entire collections, or even much of them, is clearly impossible, as research by major scholars such as Didymos and Strabo continued into the Augustan period: any decline in Alexandrian scholarship was through other causes. Although remembered as an archetype of Roman insensitivity to Greek intellectualism, the accidental fire may have been limited to a portion of the collections or even a warehouse. Nevertheless it remains canonized as one of the great disasters of antiquity.

The major effect of the Alexandrian War on Cleopatra was that it eliminated most of her rivals for power. Although the exact sequence of events is not clear from late summer 48 B.C. into the spring of 47 B.C., Caesar soon realized that his major opponent was Potheinos, who had implemented most of the difficulties. This problem was solved by executing him. Then a faction in support of Arsinoë flared up, led by her tutor Ganymedes. Having returned from Syria, she left the palace and joined Achillas and his army, and was declared queen, but the new allies soon fell into dissension, and Arsinoë persuaded Ganymedes to kill Achillas and to take command of the army himself. Ganymedes in his brief career showed himself to be a brilliant military tactician and almost defeated Caesar. One of Ganymedes' ruses was to request the presence of Ptolemy XIII as a negotiator, who promptly joined the side of Arsinoë and her army.[44]

Yet just as things seemed impossible for Caesar, reinforcements began to arrive from Asia, the Nabataeans, and Antipatros of Askalon.[45] The assistance given by Antipatros would have lasting repercussions for Cleopatra and the region, as in reward Caesar would give him numerous honors and Roman citizenship, all inherited by his son Herod, slightly older than Cleopatra and certainly involved in the events. Cleopatra and Herod would have a tangled relationship for the rest of her life.

The last engagements of the war occurred early in 47 B.C. Ptolemy XIII and Arsinoë had established their headquarters along the Nile, which fell to a vigorous attack by Caesar. The king fled the battle by boat, which capsized: his body was later found buried in the mud. Ganymedes disappeared and was probably killed, but Arsinoë was captured, never to become queen of Cyprus. She appeared in Caesar's Roman triumph in 46 B.C. and went into exile at the Temple of Artemis in Ephesos, as her father had done a decade earlier.[46] Theodotos, the third member of the original group around Ptolemy XIII and the one who suggested the murder of Pompeius, was discovered some years later in Asia by Marcus Brutus and was tortured and executed.[47] Caesar entered Alexandria in triumph, to the acclamation of the citizenry.

Strangely absent from these events is Cleopatra. As the chaos swirled around her, she resided quietly in the palace, not involved in the circumstances that resulted in the removal of two of her siblings and the elimination of several members of the senior palace administration. The detailed account of *de bello alexandrino* mentions her only once, regarding the settlement at the end of the war.[48] It is probable that with Caesar as her protector, Cleopatra was content to play it safe and watch her rivals destroy one another. But another factor may have entered into her withdrawal from activity: she was pregnant. Her child would be born on 23 June 47 B.C., so conception was probably in September, slightly over a month after Caesar's arrival in Egypt. Although it seems improbable that the father was anyone but Caesar, the matter of parentage became a complex political issue that would last until after Cleopatra's death (see pp. 69–70).

With the war over and most of the protagonists dead, Caesar had to make new arrangements for the rule of Egypt. His consular term had expired at the end of 48 B.C., but in the autumn he had been named dictator for one year (through October 47 B.C.). Antonius, who had returned to Rome after Pharsalos, engineered the appointment and became his *magister equitum*, or chief lieutenant. It was under this authority—as well as the will of Ptolemy XII—that Caesar would continue to settle Egyptian affairs.[49] Provincialization was still not an option even with the reduced number of claimants to the throne, since the dictator was perceptive enough to realize that an aggressive provincial governor could use Egypt as a power base.[50] Caesar's closeness to Cleopatra also meant that he would inevitably seek a solution favoring her. Since Arsinoë had effectively led the war against him, she was removed from the succession. Cleopatra was the obvious choice even without her personal relationship with Caesar, but in accordance to Egyptian tradition, which still had distaste for a woman ruling alone (it had been only a decade since Cleopatra's elder sister, Berenike IV, had attempted this unsuccessfully) (see pp. 22–25), Caesar made Cleopatra's surviving brother, Ptolemy XIV, joint ruler, including—at least in theory—the expected sibling marriage. It is probable that few took the liaison between the 22- and 12-year-old seriously, even though Egyptian inscriptions tend to subordinate Cleopatra to her brother.[51] It was all seen as a pretence, and the queen lived with Caesar, not her husband.

Cyprus, it seems, was folded into these arrangements, although the evidence is far from certain, since Strabo recorded that Antonius gave it to Cleopatra and Arsinoë,[52] and somewhat later a certain Demetrios seems to have been Antonius's governor on the island.[53] Strabo's comment may be a conflation of Arsinoë's stillborn rule with Cleopatra's later control, as it was hardly likely that the politically astute Antonius would give the territory to two sisters who by that time had been hostile for years. By 41 B.C. Cleopatra would persuade Antonius to have Arsinoë killed.[54] The island was definitely under Cleopatra's control in 42 B.C. as the activities of her governor, Serapion, are known. It may also be that Cleopatra did hold Cyprus from 47 B.C., yet the uncertainties at the time of the Battle of Philippi five years later—when Serapion supported Brutus and Cassius—led Antonius to intervene as part of the arrangements made at Tarsos the following year (see p. 79), perhaps officially returning it to the queen at the Donations of Alexandria a few years later.[55]

His work finished, Caesar could leave Egypt. There was no political reason for him to stay. He had been away from Rome for a year, leaving it in charge of Antonius, and objections were increasing regarding the quality of the latter's administration.[56] It would have been prudent for Caesar to return to Rome promptly—Cicero began to express increasing frustration that the dictator remained in Alexandria[57]—but he lingered in Egypt for three more months.

During the time that Caesar remained in Egypt with Cleopatra, the couple seem to have taken a Nile cruise, although the existence of the journey has been disputed because it does not appear in the most contemporary sources.[58] The earliest known reference is a century later by Lucan, in passing;[59] the first detailed accounts are by Suetonius and then by Appian, the latter promising further details that are not extant.[60] The cruise is not mentioned by Strabo, Velleius, Plutarch, or Dio. This is perhaps evidence that the tale is a romantic elaboration of what it is thought that Caesar might have done during his weeks with Cleopatra, since a Nile cruise had long been a required activity for Romans of importance. But this latter point argues in favor of the trip, and it would have fit in with Caesar's geographical interests and Cleopatra's political needs. It is impossible to be certain, yet the first to report in detail on the tale, Suetonius, may have been led by reading Lucan to search the Roman archives for evidence and to find it.

As reported in the sources, the Nile cruise of Cleopatra and Caesar was a grandiose expedition employing more than 400 ships and using Cleopatra's *thalamegos*. This was the opulent state boat of the Ptolemies, first constructed by Ptolemy IV, half a *stadion* (perhaps 300 feet) long and 40 *peches* high (perhaps 80 feet), fitted with dining rooms, state-rooms, and promenades around the outside on two decks. In fact the entire boat resembled a grand villa, elaborately decorated with precious woods, ivory, and gold, and including architectural entablatures and sculpted reliefs. Shrines to Dionysos, Aphrodite, and the royal family were also on board.[61] Presumably Cleopatra's version, 200 years later, was no less lavish, although the *thalamegos* was a type of boat, not a specific vessel, and there are no details about hers. In fact Strabo wrote generically about them, noting that they were housed at Schedia, a dockyard just southeast of Alexandria on the Kanobic mouth of the Nile.[62] Cleopatra's *thalamegos* would figure again in another notable and mythic event of her career, her visit to Antonius at Tarsos (see p. 77). The journey up the Nile went some distance, almost to Ethiopia, when the accompanying troops insisted that it turn back. The voyage should not be seen merely as a pleasure cruise, for Caesar was unusually geographically astute and familiar with the latest scholarship of his day. He had used Eratosthenes' *Geographika* in his expeditions in north-western Europe, and he was aware of the seminal work of Pytheas and Poseidonios.[63] His surviving treatises all show a particular interest in geography. The Ptolemies had sent expeditions far up the Nile into the northern parts of central Africa, and the reports of these journeys were easily available to Caesar in Alexandria. It is possible that he wanted to find the source of the Nile, not an unreasonable goal, as it had long been an issue in Greco-Roman culture.[64]At the very least, he would want to visit Syene at the First Cataract, the point from which Eratosthenes had been able to measure the entire known world. Cleopatra herself would wish to see more of the kingdom that she finally controlled. The Nile cruise was as much geographical reconnaissance as vacation.

Caesar also used his remaining time in Alexandria to initiate a building program in the city, making him the first Roman to do so. He made plans for a Kaisareion, a cultic structure honoring himself and his family, and an early example of both the enclosed portico that would become so typical of Roman architecture, as well as the Roman Imperial type of personal cult. It is unlikely that he was able to do anything beyond suggesting its plan and location, and like so many of Caesar's architectural endeavors, it fell to his successors to complete, in this case Cleopatra and perhaps Antonius.[65]

In spring, probably in April, Caesar finally left Egypt.[66] The ostensible reason was the activities of Pharnakes, a son of Mithradates the Great, who was causing difficulties in Pontos. A more pressing reason, perhaps, was that Cleopatra was near the end of her pregnancy, and Caesar, respectably married to the eminent Roman matron Calpurnia, may have wanted to distance himself from the imminent birth. But he left a Roman garrison of three legions with Cleopatra, soon to be increased to four. These would not only provide support for the queen, as her position was still weak, but would be a restraint to any actions on her part that might be detrimental to Roman interests. In leaving a trusted freedman, a certain Rufio, in charge of the legions, and indeed the very stationing of troops outside Roman territory to assist and watch an allied ruler, Caesar was foreshadowing policies of the Imperial period.[67]

CHAPTER FIVE

Consolidating the Empire
(47–40 B.C.)

ON 23 JUNE 47 B.C., according to the best evidence, Cleopatra's child was born. The date is from a stele at the Serapeion in Memphis, supplemented by Plutarch's account in his biography of Caesar.[1] It has been suggested that he was not born until after Caesar's death, based primarily on interpretation of a passage in Plutarch's *Antonius* (that Cleopatra was "left pregnant"),[2] the absence of any mention of the child in Greco-Roman sources before the death of Caesar, and the rumors of Cleopatra's pregnancy that Cicero heard in May of 44 B.C.[3] Yet the statement in the *Antonius* probably refers to Cleopatra's being left behind in Alexandria, and indeed the same verb is used elsewhere by Plutarch where there is no connection to Caesar's death: "Cleopatra, left on the throne of Egypt, a little later had a child by him."[4] Moreover, a birth-date in the late spring of 44 B.C. would make the boy rather young to be enrolled among the Alexandrian ephebi 12 years later (see p. 142), and to assume that the father was some unknown person misses the point about Cleopatra's careful choice of partners. Yet given the extent of confusion about the parentage of the child, it is remotely possible that Cleopatra invented Caesar's role after his death, but the answer will never be known. It also seems probable that (at least in Rome) there would be uncertainty about his birthdate, and the explicit information at the Sarapeion (not subject to Roman tampering) seems the best evidence.[5] His official name, "Pharoah Caesar," was recorded on the stele. As was customary for male children in the dynasty, he was also Ptolemaios, and so is often called Ptolemy XV by modern reckoning. But his most familiar name was one given to him by the Alexandrians,

Caesarion, a patronymic, probably not a part of his official title at first but a testament both to popular gossip in the city and his mother's assiduous insistence that Caesar was the father, something repeatedly announced in public documents. Caesar himself, who was still in Asia confronting Pharnakes when the child was born, may hardly have appreciated this. When Caesar returned to Rome later in the year, he was faced with negative public reaction, but the issue of Cleopatra was only one of his problems, given his long absence from the city and the general instability there.[6] Although it was well known that he had had affairs with royal women, children may not have been involved, or at least children whose parentage had been so vigorously promoted by their mother. Moreover Caesar was married. This was not itself an issue, but his wife was the distinguished Calpurnia, daughter of the consul of 58 B.C. and a member of a prominent family of late Republican times that would continue to be important into the early Empire. They had married in 59 B.C. and now, more than a decade later, the marriage remained childless, an additional complication that made Calpurnia seem a victim. Thus Caesar returned to a public relations nightmare and had every reason to be diffident about whether he was Caesarion's father, although later it was said that the boy had his looks and mannerisms.[7] The matter of parentage became so tangled in the propaganda war between Antonius and Octavian in the late 30s B.C.—it was essential for one side to prove and the other to reject Caesar's role—that it is impossible today to determine Caesar's actual response. The extant information is almost contradictory: it was said that Caesar denied parentage in his will but acknowledged it privately and allowed use of the name Caesarion.[8] Caesar's associate C. Oppius even wrote a pamphlet proving that Caesarion was not Caesar's child, and C. Helvius Cinna—the poet who was killed by rioters after Antonius's funeral oration—was prepared in 44 B.C. to introduce legislation to allow Caesar to marry as many wives as he wished for the purpose of having children. Although much of this talk was generated after Caesar's death, it seems that he himself wished to be as quiet as possible about the child but had to contend with Cleopatra's repeated assertions. In fact, Cleopatra and her eldest child had an unusually close relationship, unique in Ptolemaic history (her father had killed his eldest child), with not only the vigorous promotion of Caesarion's parentage but numerous representations of him in art and citation of him on inscriptions, even suggesting a parallel with the divine single mother Isis and her child.[9]

FIGURE 4. South wall of the Temple of Hathor at Dendera, showing Cleopatra VII and Caesarion on the right making offerings to the gods. Photography by Erich Lessing; courtesy of Art Resource, New York (ART 80662).

For more than a year after the child's birth, nothing is known about Cleopatra's activities other than her publicity campaign. In the latter part of 46 B.C. she and Ptolemy XIV went to Rome, probably after Caesar's great triumphal display that summer, which included her sister Arsinoë.[10] Whether Caesarion accompanied them is not known. A trip to Rome by the reigning Ptolemy or any eastern monarch was perfectly expected and had been normal for generations. Cleopatra and Ptolemy XIV were not the only dynasts in Rome during these months: Ariarathes of Kappadokia was attempting to gain the throne held by his brother and came to the city in the spring.[11] Yet Cleopatra's relationship with Caesar meant that her visit had unusual implications. The royal couple were given space in Caesar's villa in the Horti Caesaris, across the Tiber.[12] In lodging her here, Caesar not only acknowledged her status (as queen, not lover), but to some extent protected her and the Senate from each other; it would not have been forgotten that Ptolemy VI had to live poorly with an artist until the Senate noticed him and defused a potential diplomatic incident.[13] How long Cleopatra and Ptolemy XIV stayed in the city is not certain. Although she was there when Caesar was assassinated a year and a half later, there is evidence of two visits, and it is difficult to imagine the young queen neglecting her kingdom for so long.[14] Her presence did not enhance Caesar's reputation, although he gave the couple legal status as friendly and allied monarchs and may have allowed Caesarion to bear his name.[15] Any visiting royalty in Rome was an object of interest, and Cleopatra received distinguished visitors during her stay. Certainly Antonius was one.[16] Cicero took an immediate dislike to her.[17] They had known each other by reputation— Cicero had long been involved in Rome's relations with Egypt—but it is uncertain how much, if any, previous contact they had had. Cicero, always on the lookout for books, had approached one of her advisors, Ammonios, who had been the Roman agent of Ptolemy XII, for copies from the Alexandria Library, but something went wrong, and Cicero never received them. A visit to Cleopatra across the Tiber left him with a sense of her arrogance, perhaps a typical Roman attitude toward Greek royalty.

While in Rome, Cleopatra saw some of the effects of her influence on Caesar. She would have been aware of the preparations for his calendar reform that went into effect 1 January 45 B.C., using the calculations of Sosigenes of Alexandria, a member of her court (see p. 126). Plans for the first public library in Rome and Caesar's appointment of the famous scholar M. Terentius Varro as Librarian were also certainly a result of the time spent in Alexandria,[18] as well as Caesar's particular interest in hydraulics.[19] Caesar's Forum Julium, with its Temple of Venus Genetrix, had been dedicated on 25 September 46 B.C. as part of the triumphal festivities, probably before Cleopatra's arrival, but she may have been there when a golden statue of her was placed in the precinct, seemingly still visible in the third century A.D.[20] Cleopatra was now alongside Venus, physically and culturally: the ultimate mother of the Roman people was associated with the mother of Caesar's child, perhaps undercutting Caesar's aloofness. The statue not only suggested that Cleopatra, like Venus, was a divine mother goddess but subtly connected Isis, historically associated with the Ptolemies, with Roman religion. Caesar may also have planned a temple to Isis, since construction of one was voted the year after his death, probably another of his leftover projects.[21] Even the disastrous incident at the Lupercalia, the month before Caesar's death, may reflect the queen's influence. As is well known, Antonius attempted to place a royal diadem on Caesar's head, and a tussle resulted in which Antonius repeatedly tried to crown Caesar and the latter just as repeatedly rebuffed him.[22] This event, certainly staged, seems designed to test the interest of the Roman populace in Hellenistic monarchy. Cleopatra

FIGURE 5. View of Forum Julium in Rome. Courtesy of Duane W. Roller.

was probably in the city at the time, perhaps even a witness to the events. Cicero, also there, pointedly asked, "Just where did that diadem come from?"[23] The answer seems obvious, but the public disapproved, and Caesar's death six weeks later meant that the plans, whatever they were, were never fulfilled. It is no surprise that Cicero abhorred her.

The diplomatic needs that brought Cleopatra to Rome in 46 B.C. would not have taken long, and there was every reason for the queen to return to her kingdom promptly.[24] Suetonius reported that she left Rome while Caesar was still alive,[25] presumably before Caesar departed for Spain late in the year on an expedition to eliminate lingering Pompeian support there. On this campaign, as was his custom, he would have a personal relationship with royalty, in this case Eunoë Maura, the queen of Mauretania.

Thus Cleopatra was back in Alexandria by the end of 46 B.C. The year 45 B.C. is a total blank in her biography, as she devoted herself to consolidating her kingdom with the tools that Caesar had given her. In early 44 B.C., however, she made another journey to Rome. Caesar himself had returned from Spain the previous year, eliminating all his opposition. There is no explicit evidence as to why the queen made a second trip to the city, but it probably was to assert her needs within the new Roman order that had been established, as Caesar was actively engaged in his reform program. She may even have been afraid that the annexation of Egypt—a topic festering in Rome for 20 years—was on the agenda. The fact that her journey by necessity would have been in midwinter demonstrates how important the trip was to her. She came without her brother Ptolemy XIV, who was rapidly fading as a person of importance.

Whatever was the reason that Cleopatra was in Rome in early 44 B.C., her relationship with Caesar was a contributing factor in the conspiracy of M. Brutus and L. Cassius Longinus that led to his assassination on the Ides of March. Cicero's comments in the weeks following indicate how distasteful her presence had become.[26] But the queen did not immediately leave the city after Caesar's death—another indication that it was the Roman government, not merely the dictator, that brought her to Rome—perhaps because she saw an opportunity to put forward Caesarion as his heir, though these hopes failed when it became apparent that Caesar's will offered no recognition and may even have denied parentage. She departed Rome in mid-April, at the same time that her future nemesis, Caesar's grandnephew Octavian, arrived in Italy on his way to the city, having been named his primary heir. Within a few weeks rumors developed that

Cleopatra was pregnant but suffered a miscarriage and that Caesarion was dead, but just as quickly the gossip faded away. A few months later the queen took the matter of succession into her own hands by killing Ptolemy XIV, allegedly with poison, and elevating her son.[27] Of her four siblings, only Arsinoë remained alive, living in exile in Ephesos.

In 43 B.C., Antonius (who had been surviving consul at the time of Caesar's death), Octavian, and M. Aemilius Lepidus (the consul of 46 B.C.) constituted themselves for a five-year term as triumvirs for the restoration of the Republic and moved to dispose of Caesar' assassins. Early the same year, P. Cornelius Dolabella, proconsul of Syria and a Caesarian loyalist, requested from Cleopatra the four legions that Caesar had left in Egypt. He was not the only one aware that these troops might be useful in the renewed civil war, since Cassius, Caesar's assassin, also sent a message to Cleopatra and may even have considered invading Egypt.[28] The queen temporized with Cassius, saying that she could not provide assistance because of internal problems in her kingdom, and sent the legions to Dolabella. Her sentiments would be with the Caesarian side, but she kept her options open with the assassins. She also prepared to send a fleet to Dolabella, yet it never set sail because of adverse weather. But as the legions were being moved from Egypt to Syria by Dolabella's legate A. Allienus, they were captured in Palestine by Cassius. Cleopatra's governor of Cyprus, Serapion, also joined Cassius, sending him ships. Meanwhile, she provisioned her own fleet and set sail under her own command for the west coast of Greece to assist Antonius and Octavian. As a naval commander (a role that she would repeat in the Battle of Actium) she was a rarity among Greek queens, recalling the great Artemisia of Halikarnassos in the early fifth century B.C. It also connected with her identification with Isis, since two of the festivals of the goddess were nautically oriented.[29] Cassius sent L. Staius Murcus with 60 ships to lie in wait off Tainaron, the southernmost point of the Peloponnesos, but the fleets never engaged as the queen's ships were heavily damaged in a storm and she was prostrated by seasickness. By the time she recovered, her forces were no longer needed. Yet in return for her services she requested from Dolabella official recognition of Caesarion, something he had no authority to grant but which was approved by the triumvirs. There is no further evidence of her involvement in this phase of the civil war, and the Battle of Philippi, fought in the autumn of 42 B.C., resulted in the defeat and suicide of Brutus and Cassius by Antonius. Once again the civil war seemed over.

After Philippi, Antonius emerged as the strongest member of the triumvirate. Powers and territory were divided between him and Octavian—Lepidus was essentially ignored—and within a year Octavian was established in the west and Antonius in the East.[30] By late 42 B.C. he was in Athens, and then moved through the eastern territories repairing the damage left by Brutus and Cassius. In settling the affairs of Asia Minor, he developed a personal relationship with Glaphyra, companion of the priest-king Archelaos of Komana, making Glaphyra's son, also named Archelaos, king of Kappadokia.[31] By summer 41 B.C. Antonius was at the ancient city of Tarsos.

At 42 years of age, Antonius was at the peak of his career, having gained a military reputation that began with his service with Gabinius in the Levant and Egypt 14 years previously. He had become Caesar's colleague in the consulship for 44 B.C. and since late 43 B.C. had been triumvir, which gave him broad magisterial powers. He was currently married to the dynamic Fulvia, who was actively involved in the political and military maneuvering after Philippi. Fulvia was said to have had no interest in traditional women's pursuits such as spinning wool or housekeeping; rather, she wished not merely to rule a man but to rule rulers and commanders. It was also said that life with Fulvia prepared Antonius for Cleopatra, since he was acquainted with an environment controlled by a woman.[32] This marriage produced two sons, M. Antonius Antyllus and Iullus Antonius, and there was also a daughter from a previous marriage. Antonius already had a reputation for being erratic, a heavy drinker, and a womanizer, but he was an outstanding orator—immortalized by his speech at Caesar's funeral—and a brilliant military tactician.[33] Yet his character flaws would be stressed in the propaganda wars of the 30s B.C. The later literary tradition emphasized that these deficiencies were exactly what Cleopatra was able to exploit: she could flatter his ego, act swiftly in time of crisis, and be his companion in fun and games but use his ability at humor and playfulness to her own advantage.[34] Although some of this was certainly later revisionism, it was also largely true.

In the summer of 41 B.C., Cleopatra—whose activities since just before Philippi are unknown—received a summons from Antonius at Tarsos. She was reluctant to go and ignored repeated letters.[35] Her procrastination may have been a matter of status and the impropriety of a Roman magistrate to demand that a queen leave her kingdom at his bidding. It was only when Antonius sent his trusted aide Q. Dellius to appeal in person that the queen actually went. Dellius would spend the next decade moving as liaison between Antonius, Cleopatra, and Herod the Great. He survived into the Augustan era and wrote a history of the period, which is probably one of the major sources for the last decade of Cleopatra's life. He became notorious for his ability to change sides, moving from the Caesareans to Cassius to Antonius to Octavian.[36] When he arrived at Cleopatra's court, he immediately sensed that she would be able to influence Antonius through her charm and well-spokenness, and he urged her to go to Tarsos as Hera had gone for her assignation with Zeus.[37] Cleopatra herself, now 28, felt that she was far more mature and sophisticated than when she had known Pompeius the Younger and even Julius Caesar and, in the proper style of eastern monarchs calling upon Roman magistrates, equipped herself with presents and money, but put her greatest faith in her own abilities.

The ostensible reason that Antonius summoned Cleopatra to Tarsos was to allow her to explain her alleged recent support of Cassius, more misinformation than reality. But it is inevitable that there was a personal motive as well: they had had occasional contact for 14 years, and although Antonius's claim that he had fallen in love when he first met her in 55 B.C. sounds like pillow talk,[38] it certainly was true that he now had the chance, not available previously, to pursue a personal relationship if he were so inclined. Cleopatra seemingly felt the same way, although neither gave up their current political needs.

Cleopatra also believed that it was necessary to establish herself with the new regime in Rome. At this point it was thought that the civil war was over. Octavian, in the west, was still an unknown factor, and Antonius was obviously the person in power. Moreover there were certain repercussions from the civil war that might destabilize Cleopatra's position. Her sister Arsinoë, still in refuge at Ephesos, was believed by some to be the legitimate queen of Egypt. One of Cleopatra's strongest allies, Antipatros of Askalon, had been poisoned at a banquet in 43 B.C.[39] His son Herod had been promised the kingship of Judaea by Cassius, but this offer was obviously defunct. Nevertheless the whole question of the future of the southern Levant was of vital interest to Cleopatra. She herself was suspected of giving aid to Cassius, something that she had to explain to Antonius.

Cleopatra thus eventually answered the summons and sailed up the Kydnos River to Tarsos in her *thalamegos*,[40] an approach that has become one of the most famous events of Greco-Roman history. Tarsos today lies 10 miles inland but was somewhat closer to the coast in antiquity.

FIGURE 6. View of modern Tarsos. Courtesy of Duane W. Roller.

The Kydnos was a major stream (in the fourth century B.C. it was two *plethra*, or about 200 feet, in width).[41] Today Tarsos is a hot dusty town, and the Kydnos almost invisible, but the city still invokes its dynamic past. In the first century B.C., however, the approach up the broad river would have been an event of grandeur. Plutarch's description is based on an eyewitness account of someone standing on the riverbank, seeing, hearing, and smelling it all, as Cleopatra's procession passed by. The source is probably someone close to Antonius, given the perspective and the personal comments about the triumvir that follow, perhaps his chronicler Dellius or the historian Sokrates of Rhodes, another member of Antonius's entourage.[42] It was a carefully constructed scene demonstrating a strong theatrical sense on Cleopatra's part. She made the intended impression on Antonius, who, along with his officers and entourage, was invited on board her boat to dine and was presented with a meal lavish beyond description, especially remarkable for the lighting within the cabin, whose walls were covered with tapestries woven with gold and purple. There were 12 dining tables, and the service was finely made of gold inlaid with precious stones. The following evening there was a more lavish banquet, and the guests were allowed to take away many of the furnishings, escorted home in litters or on horseback.[43] On the third day Antonius reciprocated, but his banquet was embarrassing in its simplicity. Yet Cleopatra was not finished. On the fourth day her dining room was strewn with spiral decorations of roses to the depth of a *peches* (about two feet). The Romans were always impressed with the lavishness of the Eastern courts, but clearly Cleopatra was making the most of the opportunity: whatever Antonius might have heard about her from Caesar and others, she was determined to outdo it. She probably was also well aware of his taste for extravagance and luxury.

Cleopatra acquitted herself of the charge of having aided Cassius by recounting that she had actually helped Dolabella and had sent her own fleet to Greece with herself in command while telling Cassius that she was unable to assist him. It was an easy charge to deflect, but Antonius may not have had accurate information, since Dolabella had committed suicide a year previously when, despite Cleopatra's assistance, he had failed to withstand an attack from Cassius at Laodikeia in Syria.[44]

Cleopatra also had her own agenda to pursue. She had Antonius eliminate her sister Arsinoë, her sole surviving sibling and the one person who could be a rival for her throne.[45] Arsinoë was dragged to her death from the Temple of Artemis at Ephesos. The priest of Artemis was also called to account, having acknowledged her as queen, but the Ephesians successfully petitioned Cleopatra for his release. The renegade governor of Cyprus, Serapion, was found at Tyre and delivered to Cleopatra, and Antonius may have taken direct control of Cyprus until matters quieted down (see p. 65). And finally, there was another suppliant, living in the Phoenician city of Arados, claiming to be Ptolemy XIII, Cleopatra's brother, who allegedly had died at the end of the Alexandrian War. He too was eliminated. The fact that such a rival could exist, living, like Arsinoë, in obscure refuge waiting for his chance, showed that Cleopatra's position was still insecure. All these actions were within Antonius' broad powers as triumvir and were necessary for settling the East after the defeat of Brutus and Cassius. But they cleared the way for Cleopatra to become the most powerful allied ruler of the region. How personal Antonius's motives were can never be known since Cleopatra was not the only prominent woman of the East whom he favored.

The queen probably did not stay at Tarsos long, having accomplished her twin objectives of ingratiating herself to Antonius and absolving herself of her conduct in the civil war. She soon returned to Egypt, but she had invited Antonius for a visit, and when it was time for him to move his forces into winter quarters, perhaps in November of 41 B.C., he himself went to Alexandria.[46] He was instantly popular with the

Alexandrian populace, in part because there were many who remembered his visit of 14 years previously and his almost heroic actions in restoring Ptolemy XII. Unlike Caesar, he brought no legions with him, thereby avoiding the appearance of leading an army of occupation, an unfortunate by-product of Caesar's visit. Although Antonius was still triumvir, he was no longer in Roman territory and was thus a private citizen, Cleopatra's personal guest.

In creating a connection with Antonius, Cleopatra was following the same pattern that she had with Caesar, personally allying herself with the most prominent Roman of the era, something that the Ptolemies had been doing for a century. She understood that her kingdom would survive only if Rome allowed it; the career of her father was enough proof. Her relationship with Caesar had not turned out as she had expected. Although it did solidify her position, it also involved her in the Roman civil war. Caesarion had received official recognition from Rome, yet he was her sole heir, a definite weakness insofar as the question of succession was concerned. Potential heirs were always a problem. They were necessary for the continuation of the kingdom but could turn against either their ruling parent or each other—there were many examples of both in Ptolemaic history. But to depend on a single heir was also dangerous. More were necessary, and traditional Ptolemaic sibling marriage was no longer an option for Cleopatra. It is possible that early in her career she had sought a Seleukid husband, as had her elder sister Berenike IV, but none was forthcoming. Yet as a ruling woman, Cleopatra had issues that ruling men did not have. Although there had been many powerful women in the Hellenistic dynasties, few had actually ever been sole queen. Among the Ptolemies it was limited to the brief reigns of Cleopatra's aunt and sister, Cleopatra Berenike III in 81 B.C. and Berenike IV after 58 B.C. Both reigns had been turbulent and obsessed with finding male consorts for the queens, and both had ended in their violent deaths. Attempts to make Cleopatra VII's other sister, Arsinoë IV, sole queen had been ineffective and also had ended in violence. Elsewhere independent queens had been rare, although there are occasional moments of power for ruling women between husbands. No queen ever ruled alone in either the Seleukid or Macedonian dynasties. In fact, queens ruling alone in the Greco-Roman world were few. At Halikarnassos—which produced more woman rulers than anywhere else outside Egypt—there was the elder Artemisia, the heroine of the Persian Wars in the early fifth century B.C., and her younger namesake, the sister-wife of Maussolos, in the mid-fourth century B.C., as well as their sister Ada, who ruled alone briefly after the death of her brother-husband Idrieus in the 340s B.C.[47] These four siblings were a brilliant moment in the history of the region, responsible for one of the great monuments of antiquity, the Mausoleion. Their theory of rule, with its patronage of the arts, sibling marriage, and prominence of women rulers, greatly influenced the Ptolemies. The only other independent queens of the Hellenistic period were later than Cleopatra: Dynamis of Bosporos (17 B.C.–A.D. 7/9) and Pythodoris of Pontos (3/2 B.C.–A.D. 33), who was a granddaughter of Antonius.[48] The one remaining famous queen in classical antiquity was Zenobia at Palmyra (A.D. 267–7?), who saw Cleopatra as her role model. All these were married during most of their careers. There was no one like Cleopatra VII, ruling for 22 years and married only in name and perhaps briefly at the end of her life. Actually, given her ancestry, she may have been more influenced by the handful of indigenous Egyptian queens, most notably Hatshepsut (1479/3–1458/7 B.C.).

Moreover, as a queen ruling alone, Cleopatra had to take into account the realities of creating an heir. A king could have minimal personal involvement, with the possibility of producing many in a brief period of time. For a queen, however, having an heir meant devoting the better part of a year to the process, a time during which she might not be in the best of health and would be vulnerable to usurpation. Unlike a king, with his several wives and consorts, Cleopatra could not discard herself if a problem developed in the production of an heir. Moreover, she would take a great personal health risk, entering into a process that was often fatal. After the birth of the child, the queen as mother had a responsibility that a father did not. It is clear that Cleopatra scheduled her pregnancies carefully (48, 44 [possibly], 41, and 37 B.C.), spreading them out as much as possible to limit any medical repercussions and political weakness. Three or four pregnancies in 18 years would be substantially less than what might be expected, even given the intervals with no known partner. Abortion was always a possibility, and many contraceptive methods were available.[49] And a pregnancy was possible only with a suitable partner, something that she also chose carefully. In selecting Antonius, Cleopatra followed all these criteria. Her rule was relatively stable, the world was at peace, and it had been several years since her last pregnancy. Antonius was the most powerful Roman, an obvious choice for producing further heirs, and this would also provide the useful political connections resulting from intimacy with a Roman of his stature.

Many anecdotes survive of the few months that the couple spent together in Egypt. Although the later negative tradition may have tilted the accounts against the pair, it is clear that Antonius, at least, regarded the period essentially as a vacation, time to be spent in games, hunting, fishing, and even wandering the city in disguise. Their life together was extremely lavish, and they called themselves the Amimetobioi, or "Inimitable Livers," an association with Dionysiac overtones.[50] The physician Philotas of Amphissa, a member of the royal court and later an acquaintance of Plutarch's grandfather Lamprias, provided some eyewitness details of the royal kitchens in operation: eight boars for a dinner party of 12, and meals always ready so that they could be served at a moment's notice.

Cleopatra's agenda with Caesar had been assuring her position on the throne and neutralizing rivals, as well as producing an heir. With Antonius it was somewhat different, although the matter of an heir remained a factor. At this moment in her life she had few political rivals, as all her siblings were dead and her sole child was only seven years of age. There was no one among the dynasts of the East who could compare with her stature or even be worthy of notice. But the Ptolemaic Empire was only a portion of what it had been in the third and second centuries B.C., and Cleopatra was committed to restoring its territory.[51] A first step had been taken when Caesar returned Cyprus after several years of Roman control, although Antonius seems to have temporarily repossessed it (see p. 65). Just to the north was Kilikia, the mountainous region of coastal southern Asia Minor, which historically had been associated with Cyprus and moreover had Ptolemaic connections. Ptolemy I had attempted unsuccessfully to conquer it during the wars of Alexander's Successors. Ptolemy II had actually acquired the region, only to have it lost to the Seleukids shortly thereafter.[52] Since the end of the second century B.C. Kilikia had primarily been under Roman control, although an indigenous king, Tarkondimotos, ruled parts of it. The record is silent as to whether any of his territory was given to Cleopatra, which probably means that it was not, and he died at Actium fighting on her side. Cleopatra's meeting with Antonius at the ancient Kilikian city of Tarsos may have inspired her to suggest that the region be returned to the Ptolemies—especially since it had been an area of political instability for the previous half century—an obvious way to start the rebuilding of the empire. Kilikia would also provide her with timber for shipbuilding. Just as Caesar had restored Cyprus to Ptolemaic control in 47 B.C., Antonius would now do the same for Kilikia, although the Ptolemaic claim to it was ephemeral. The transfer had occurred by 19 November 38 B.C., when a certain Diogenes was Ptolemaic military governor of both Kilikia and Cyprus, and the probable time for such an action was during the winter of 41–40 B.C. when Cleopatra and Antonius were together.[53] It would be perfectly legal under Antonius's wide-ranging triumviral powers.

Just as the Romans had supported favorable monarchs at the borders of their territory, Cleopatra seems to have done the same. Tarkonditimos of Kilikia may have been one. The ancient temple state of Olbe (modern Ura), known for its sanctuary of Zeus, lying just to the west of Cleopatra's Kilikian regions, was placed under the rule of a certain Aba, who had impressed both Cleopatra and Antonius and who was related to the indigenous royal family.[54] She would serve as a buffer between Cleopatra's empire and the free states and cities of western Anatolia. Although she was soon overthrown, the mysterious Aba, otherwise unknown, remains an intriguing example of both a ruling queen and an attempted network of Cleopatran allied monarchs.

By the spring of 40 B.C. Antonius found it necessary to bring his vacation to an end. A certain Q. Labienus, who had been sent to Parthia by Cassius before Philippi, had remained in the service of the Parthian government and now invaded Syria, killing the governor, L. Decidius Saxa, whom Antonius had appointed the previous autumn. Labienus also took possession of Saxa's army, decidedly tilting the balance of power toward the Parthians. Antonius had probably known about this for some time (as well as increasing instability in Italy, another concern), but had postponed dealing with it as long as possible.[55] Yet finally he had to leave Alexandria and to return to a more active role as triumvir. Cleopatra sent him on his way with a fleet of 200 ships, payment for support of her territorial ambitions. The queen and triumvir were not to meet again for three and a half years, although they kept in contact; it was said that Cleopatra had a spy in Antonius's entourage.[56]

With one exception, there is a gap in the written record of Cleopatra's life from spring 40 to late 37 B.C. This parallels closely the situation after Caesar's departure seven years previously, from early 47 to late 46 B.C. In both cases the reason for the gap may be because she was pregnant. Her administration would attend to running the kingdom while her pregnancy advanced to childbirth and she nurtured her newborn children.

Although the exact birth date cannot be determined, it seems that in the latter case, at least, Cleopatra continued to be withdrawn from public life for nearly two years, a year longer than in the case of Caesarion. Part of the silence of the sources must be ascribable to the deficiency of the record to detail the activities of a woman without a man in her life, but her pregnancies and the early stages of motherhood would play a role. At these times, being a mother was more important than being a queen.

Thus sometime between Antonius's departure in the spring of 40 B.C. and the end of the year, Cleopatra gave birth to twins. They would be named Alexander Helios and Cleopatra Selene, although their surnames may not have been applied until their parents met again in 37 B.C.[57] For Cleopatra to give her own name to her first (and only) daughter was nothing extraordinary, for this had been the practice since the name had entered the Ptolemaic family in the early second century B.C., when Ptolemy V had married the Seleukid princess Cleopatra I. The boy's name had less dynastic usage despite its distinguished heritage. Alexander was not a common Ptolemaic name, used only as surnames for Ptolemy X and XI, Cleopatra's great-uncle and cousin, not particularly strong precedents. There is little reason to dispute that the child's name came from the obvious source, Alexander the Great, not forgetting that the original Cleopatra was his sister. The surnames, Helios and Selene, the Sun and Moon, reflected the inauguration of a new era that parents and children would begin, inspired in part by Cleopatra's role as the new Isis. Such talk of rejuvenation of society was common: the children were born at the same time as the publication of Vergil's *Eclogue* 4, with its environment of renewal through the birth of a child. How much of this prophetic nomenclature was applied at the time of the birth of the twins is uncertain, as it may reflect the situation in 37 B.C. when Antonius and Cleopatra came together again and Antonius, who had not previously seen the children, acknowledged his paternity.[58]

In the summer of 40 B.C., Antonius's plans regarding Labienus and the Parthians were disrupted because of news from Italy, where the situation had begun to deteriorate once again, with Antonius's wife, Fulvia, a major player. As with the Parthian situation, it is probable that Antonius had long known about this. Fulvia had been managing his affairs in Italy, and increasing tension between her and Octavian had resulted in the episode called the Perusine War, largely orchestrated by her.[59] It was said that this was her attempt to create a disturbance in Italy that would encourage Antonius to leave Cleopatra and return home, although this seems chronologically impossible, as the problems in Italy were well under way even before the meeting at Tarsos.[60] It is possible that Fulvia had heard of the earlier relationship with Glaphyra;[61] even before Antonius and Cleopatra had become personally involved, Octavian had written a scatological poem complaining about Antonius and Glaphyra,[62] an early example of the literary propaganda that would erupt with greater violence a decade later. Regardless of Fulvia's motives, the Perusine War was a disaster for her. She and Antonius's brother Lucius Antonius were besieged by Octavian in Perusia (modern Perugia) and eventually driven out of Italy. Fulvia hurried to her husband but died en route at Sikyon on the Gulf of Corinth. Since she had been the perpetrator of the recent difficulties, her fortuitous death created a chance for reconciliation between the two senior triumvirs, and thus in September they met at Brundisium.[63]

Two things resulted from this meeting that would have a direct effect on Cleopatra, at the time either still pregnant or a new mother of twins. First, Antonius and Octavian divided the world between themselves, with Antonius in the East and Octavian in the west, the boundary at the Ionian Sea. This was good news to Cleopatra, for she already knew that Antonius would be of assistance in fulfilling her needs, and, by creating a personal alliance with him through their children, she was assured of his support.

The second result of the Brundisium agreement was less favorable. In typical Roman fashion a marriage was concluded between the new allies. Antonius would marry Octavian's sister Octavia, herself just widowed from the distinguished C. Claudius Marcellus, consul of 51 B.C. Octavia—a "marvel of a woman," in Plutarch's words—was known for her charm and skills as a mediator. She was the same age as Cleopatra and had the legitimacy of being a Roman matron rather than a foreign queen. Moreover, it was perfectly clear that Octavia would not be content to stay in Italy while Antonius moved through the world having liaisons with royalty. Unlike Calpurnia and Fulvia, she would accompany her husband on his return East. Although sources tend to contrast the virtuous Octavia with the foreign seductress Cleopatra, perhaps to the point of exaggeration, Octavia was unusual—her actions after Antonius's death demonstrate this (see p. 152)—and thus for the first time in her relations with prominent Romans, Cleopatra had a genuine rival. Plutarch's account of Octavia is the fullest in ancient literature, but she still remains elusive and often formulaic. Yet whatever Cleopatra's plans were for Antonius in late 40 B.C. as her twins were born, she would find Octavia a problem.

As noted, there is little information about Cleopatra during the months of her pregnancy and early motherhood. Nevertheless, during this time, probably in December 40 B.C., she received an unexpected guest.[64] This was none other than the tetrarch of Judaea, Herod, son of Cleopatra's former ally Antipatros of Askalon. Herod had not yet earned the title "the Great," and this was long before he became entangled in the Christian nativity, but he was a promising petty dynast in great difficulty. His father had been assassinated three years previously, in the unstable period after the death of Caesar, and when Herod appealed to Antonius in late 41 B.C., the latter had made him tetrarch of Judaea. This had happened at Daphne near Antioch just after Antonius had met Cleopatra at Tarsos.[65] Antonius had confidence in the young man's promise and had consistently defended him against various delegations of Jewish leaders that had accused him of treason. As a Roman citizen, Herod was worthy of Roman support, a potential ally in the ever-volatile southern Levant. Yet the year after he was made tetrarch, his situation deteriorated. Rivalry between Herod's family and that of the Hasmoneans, who had ruled the region for more than a century, reached a deadly level. Herod's brother Phasael, whom Antonius had also made tetrarch, had been imprisoned by the Hasmonean king Antigonos II, and it was clear that Herod would be next. In December of 40 B.C. he decided to flee Judaea, first going to his cousin, the Nabataean king Malchos, where he was rebuffed because the Parthians had warned the king not to receive Herod. Herod then decided to call upon Cleopatra, a recognition of her position as the dominant ruler of the region. While on the road he learned that his brother had been killed.

Although Cleopatra received him in her usual magnificent way, it is difficult to determine exactly what her thoughts were regarding this uninvited visitor. Their paths had crossed before because of the contacts between Cleopatra and Herod's father, and certainly Antonius, who had met Herod and shown his support, would have discussed the young tetrarch with Cleopatra. In later years, when Herod was king, she would actively covet his territory, but how far such ideas had developed in 40 B.C. is not known. It is equally uncertain what Herod hoped to gain from the queen, yet he probably felt that she had an obligation to him because his father had helped put her (and her father) on the throne.

Cleopatra, like Antonius, saw potential in Herod and offered him an unspecified military command, probably part of a developing campaign against the Parthians. Herod, however, rejected the offer and, despite the queen's attempts to encourage him to stay in Alexandria, decided to appeal directly to Antonius and soon set off for Rome. He arrived in the city after a difficult voyage—winter was not the time to travel on the Mediterranean—and the newly reconciled triumvirs named him king of Judaea, probably the last thing Cleopatra wanted to hear. The visit by Herod to Cleopatra inaugurated a contentious relationship between the two dynasts that lasted the remainder of Cleopatra's life. Before long she found herself embroiled in the complex politics of Herod's family.[66]

CHAPTER SIX

The Peak Years

(40–34 B.C.)

IT IS PROBABLE THAT WHEN CLEOPATRA learned of the marriage of
Antonius and Octavia, she believed that the triumvir would no longer
be a part of her life. Antonius had assisted her in many of her goals,
expanding her kingdom and increasing her number of heirs to three. Yet
he seemed firmly committed to his new life. By summer 39 B.C. Octavia
had the first of their children, Antonia, who would be the grandmother
of the emperor Nero, and the family moved to Athens, Antonius's headquarters for the next two years.[1] Soon Octavia was pregnant again, and
in 36 B.C. she bore a second and more famous Antonia, who would
become the mother of the emperor Claudius. There seemed to be no
room in Antonius's personal life for Cleopatra, and whether he would
continue to fulfill her political needs remained to be seen. Cleopatra's
own world was stable, as her largest potential problem, Herod, was
having difficulties claiming the kingdom that the Romans had given
him. A civil war was raging in Judaea, which lasted until 37 B.C. and
was only ended through extensive Roman military assistance ordered
by Antonius and provided by C. Sosius, governor of Syria.[2] Significantly,
Cleopatra offered Herod no help.

Whether or not it can be believed that Antonius had spent the years
since he had seen Cleopatra languishing for her—a detail not necessarily at odds with the picture of him as a happy family man[3]—an
opportunity presented itself in 37 B.C. for a renewal of their relationship.
That summer Octavia and Antonius returned to Italy, largely because
the triumvirate had expired the previous 1 January, and the relationship between him and Octavian needed to be redefined. At a meeting

in Tarentum managed by Octavia the triumvirate was renewed to the end of 33 B.C.[4] Arrangements for war against the Parthians—which had been in the planning stage for more than a decade—were intensified, and Antonius returned east determined to prosecute it, with two legions from Octavian and 1,000 additional soldiers from Octavia. Because Octavia could not accompany Antonius to war, she remained in Italy as he went to Antioch. Before long he sent his legate C. Fonteius Capito to Egypt to request the presence of Cleopatra.

Although the sources present a love-struck Antonius surrendering his better instincts to the wiles of the queen, this was hardly the case. To be sure, the absence of Octavia was a convenience, but queen and triumvir had needs for each other that were not merely personal. Herod had resolved his civil war, and this meant that he was now a significant threat to Cleopatra's ambitions. Antonius's resources were inadequate for his forthcoming Parthian expedition, and the queen could assist in this.

She arrived in Antioch in late 37 B.C. with her three-year-old twins, whom their father had never seen. It was probably at this time that they received their surnames Helios and Selene, a suggestion of grandiose plans by the parents, perhaps as yet not still fully formed.[5] In Antonius's ongoing reorganization of the East, which involved the redistribution of

FIGURE 7. View of Antioch from Daphne. Courtesy of Duane W. Roller.

many territories and the establishment of several new kingdoms with rulers friendly to Rome, Cleopatra was the clear winner. The arrangements made perfectly good sense regardless of any personal relationship between queen and triumvir: Cleopatra was the only tested ruler of the eastern Mediterranean. Herod had just secured his throne, and all the others were petty dynasts with limited territories. Moreover, the ease with which Brutus and Cassius had been able to disrupt the Roman governments of the region may have suggested to Antonius that a more compact Roman presence was the better choice, with large areas under the control of indigenous royalty beholden to Rome. Thus Antonius established a network of friendly states ruled by new dynasties that he essentially created, often bypassing the existing claimants. In Galatia, the central part of Asia Minor, Rome's long ally Deiotaros had supported Brutus and Cassius but had not yet been punished when he died naturally in 40 B.C. Antonius gave his kingdom and surrounding territories to his secretary Amyntas, who survived until 25 B.C.[6] To the north was the kingdom of Pontos, where a certain Polemon was placed on the throne after the convenient death of King Dareios. Polemon seems to have had no connection with any indigenous royalty, and his father, Zenon, was a rhetorician. Eventually Polemon would marry into royalty, first by wedding Dynamis and then Pythodoris, the latter a granddaughter of none other than Antonius. Polemon survived until the last decade of the first century B.C.; his widow, Pythodoris, would rule alone until she married the third of Antonius's friendly kings, Archelaos of Kappadokia.[7] Archelaos also came from outside established royalty, although it is possible that he was related to Mithradates the Great. One of his credentials, perhaps a minor one, was the personal relationship Antonius had had with his mother Glaphyra, but the triumvir was too astute to base kingship on this alone, and Archelaos's abilities and lineage were what resulted in his placement on the throne of Kappadokia when he expelled the king, Ariarathes X.[8] The fourth friendly king enthroned by Antonius was Herod the Great, also not a part of the existing royal line, that of the Hasmoneans, although he promptly married into it. Thus these four kings, none of whom was the expected heir to his throne, created a dynastic network that established a new order in the East.[9] Eventually there were marriage connections among all of them except Amyntas, who died too soon.

Yet there was a fifth friendly monarch in Antonius's plan. This of course was Cleopatra. At first glance she might not seem to fit the pattern, since her ancestors had ruled Egypt for nearly 300 years. But she too was an anomaly, unlike traditional Hellenistic dynasts. She was personally connected to Antonius—although, as in the case of the Kappadokian royalty, this alone was not sufficient to confirm her rule—and she was a woman. As the only queen to have a lengthy independent reign in the Hellenistic system of dynastic rule, she was as distinct from tradition as were Antonius's four kings. Moreover, with Glaphyra, Dynamis, and Pythodoris, it can be seen that Antonius's system brought women into positions of prominence. In addition he had no easy way of reaching outside the Ptolemaic dynasty for a new ruler of Egypt, if he had been so inclined (the only possibility might have been one of the dispossessed Seleukid princes). But in supporting Cleopatra and substantially enlarging her kingdom he was following exactly the same philosophy of rule as with Amyntas, Polemon, Archelaos, and Herod: creating a new order beholden to him that was to make the East a stable part of the Roman world. Although Cleopatra would die within a decade, it is significant that all the other monarchs outlived Antonius, Archelaos by half a century.

Nevertheless Cleopatra profited far more than her male colleagues in the territorial adjustments, which came close to achieving her goal of returning the Ptolemaic Empire to its maximum territorial limits. Over the next several years—the exact chronology is uncertain—Antonius steadily enlarged her kingdom. The list of acquisitions is long.[10] Probably the most important was the coast of Phoenicia and Palestine, although the implication is that Cleopatra obtained only the cities, and the ancient Phoenician centers of Tyre and Sidon were excepted. Her northern boundary was the Eleutheros River (the modern Nahr el-Kebir on the Syrian-Lebanese border). She received a number of important Levantine coastal cities, including Gaza, Ptolemais, and Byblos. Her possible acquisition of Askalon, Herod's ancestral home, would create more contention with that dynast, and in fact Herod may have immediately leased the territory back from the queen, thus retaining nominal possession of his family's lands. Cleopatra does not seem to have minted coins at Askalon after 38 B.C., suggesting her control of the city was minimal after that date.[11] Most of this coastal territory had been Ptolemaic until lost in 200 B.C. as a result of the aggressive policies of Antiochos III against Ptolemy IV. The queen's claim was strengthened by being a descendant of both these kings. The city of Ptolemais had been a foundation of Ptolemy II, on the site of ancient Akko, so return of it must have been especially gratifying to Cleopatra.

Because there was no longer a Seleukid Empire, Antonius was able to give Cleopatra some other regions historically Ptolemaic but which had been under Seleukid control since the second century B.C. As a reigning descendant of the Seleukids, she could assert such a claim, even believing that she was the legitimate Seleukid monarch, and she used her coinage from the region to emphasize this.[12] All these donations were in the interior of Syria. Koile ("Hollow") Syria—the upper Orontes valley—included the important city of Apameia, founded by Seleukos I and noted as a trade and cultural center, the home of the famous polymath Poseidonios. Nearby was the independent kingdom of Chalkis, whose king, a certain Lysimachos, had recently died.[13] There was also Ituraia, where the king, Lysanias, was eliminated by Antonius on the claim that he was pro-Parthian.[14] His son Zenodoros leased the land from Cleopatra and retained the territory after her death.[15] Regardless of the exact limits of these three districts, they were probably contiguous and gave the queen a rich and fertile area of interior Syria. Coinage indicates that her territory extended as far south as Damascus.[16] Koile Syria had been one of the major economic resources of the early Ptolemaic Empire. It provided timber for shipbuilding and was rich in agriculture, including extensive wine-growing regions. In the third century B.C. it had been the seat of large estates owned by important officials in the Ptolemaic government, and Cleopatra may have had visions of re-creating this traditional Ptolemaic royal economy.[17]

FIGURE 8. The date orchards of Jericho. Courtesy of Duane W. Roller.

To the south, she received the territory around Jericho—part of Herod's dominions—because of its production of date palms and the medicinal herb balsam, the latter allegedly growing nowhere else.[18] Some of the bitumen-producing regions of the Dead Sea area may also have been included.[19] Eventually Cleopatra leased Jericho back to its original owner, Herod.[20]

Still farther south, Cleopatra received "the part of Nabataean Arabia that slopes toward the External Sea."[21] Plutarch's precise terminology demonstrates that the sea cannot be the Mediterranean or the Dead Sea portions of Arabia, but must be the territory adjoining the Ailanatic Gulf, including the port city of Ailana (modern Aqaba), important as an outlet for eastern trade but also serving a protective role for Cleopatra since the Nabataeans had historically used this area to attack Egypt.[22] Yet the Nabataean king Malchos (probably a cousin of Herod), who had been on the throne since the early 50s B.C., was not to forget his loss of territory, something that Cleopatra would learn to her detriment near the end of her life (see p. 142).

Certain districts on the island of Crete were also given to the queen. Although there are no details, this probably meant two former Ptolemaic naval bases on the east end of the island, Itanos and Olous, which had been established by Patroklos, the naval commander of Ptolemy II.[23] Crete had been a Roman province since the early first century B.C., but the two cities would have been detached and returned to Ptolemaic control. Also included as part of the donation was Cyrene, which usually had been Ptolemaic throughout the history of the dynasty.

Thus Cleopatra could see her empire restored almost to its greatest territorial extent. What she did not receive were the former Ptolemaic possessions in the Aegean and southwest Asia Minor, most of which had been lost in the early second century B.C. with the rise of Pergamon and Rhodes, and which were probably too close to the Greco-Roman heartland to be considered. As it was, Antonius's arrangements met with intense disfavor in Rome and marked the beginning of the turning of public sentiment against him, soon to be skillfully exploited by Octavian. Antonius failed to realize the role of public sentiment in Rome and Octavian's ability to use it for his own needs. Moreover, Antonius was not sensitive to his moral position as Octavian's brother-in-law and the way that disagreements about the future of the Roman state were becoming entangled with the family dispute resulting from Octavian's perception of the mistreatment of his sister and his willingness to adopt this to his own political agenda.[24] In fact, late in 35 B.C., Octavian granted his sister as well as his wife, Livia, extraordinary privileges, including sacrosanctity and the right to administer their affairs without a guardian, a virtually unprecedented step.[25] Moreover, statues were erected in their honor, only the second time that there were public monuments to living Roman women. The previous recipient was Cornelia, daughter of P. Cornelius Scipio Africanus, the conqueror of Hannibal, who was also the mother of the reformist Gracchi brothers and object of the affections of Ptolemy VIII, Cleopatra's great-grandfather.[26] The fact that about 80 years later Octavia and Livia received the same unusual honor (as well as others) demonstrated not only their significance and the emergent status of the women of the nascent imperial family, but was an obvious response to the stature of Cleopatra, whose own image could be seen in the Forum Julium, and where, in fact, the two new ones might also have been located.[27] The other privileges that Octavian gave his sister and wife at this time particularly benefited Octavia, whose financial and legal dependency on Antonius was significantly reduced. At any rate, Cleopatra's actual rule of much of her new territory was nominal, even nonexistent, whether she leased it to its former owners or, as in the case of Cyrene, merely restructured the chain of command, with local Roman officials (often appointed by Antonius) reporting to her rather than to Rome.[28] Her greatest benefit was financial, including the revenues from the balsam and bitumen of Judaea, the agricultural districts of interior Syria and Cyrene, the trade centers of Ailana, Gaza, and Phoenicia, or the copper mines of Cyprus. Restoration of the Cretan naval bases was perhaps a hint of plans for the future. By the time the arrangements were completed—and it is not clear whether they all happened in the winter of 37–36 B.C. or over the next couple of years—Cleopatra was the strongest ruler in the eastern Mediterranean, but there were already ominous rumblings, not only from Rome but from those who had suffered, especially Herod and his cousins the Nabataeans. Nevertheless the queen saw it as the beginning of a new era for the Ptolemaic kingdom, and sometime in late 37 or early 36 B.C. began to double-date her coinage, with a new Year 1 equivalent to her traditional Year 16.[29]

Finally, in the spring of 36 B.C., the much-postponed Parthian expedition set forth. The Romans had had half a century of contentious relations with the Parthians, culminating in the disaster Crassus had suffered at Carrhae in 53 B.C.[30] In the 17 years since, plans to move against the Parthians had always been a central part of Roman policy, but implementation was repeatedly postponed because of the civil war, in which the Parthians actually became involved. A potential Parthian expedition was given further status since it was one of Caesar's many unfulfilled plans. Antonius's campaign is well documented, as Dellius, one of the field commanders, wrote a report that is probably the source of the detailed existing accounts,[31] but its tactics are not relevant to the career of Cleopatra beyond the effects of the result of the expedition. She did provide funds for it and accompanied Antonius as far as the Euphrates, probably to Zeugma (modern Balkis in Syria), the traditional crossing point for travel into interior Asia. She could not have expected to see Antonius again for some time, and rule of her kingdom would take precedence over any personal relationship with the triumvir. To be successful any Parthian expedition would be long and complex: Julius Caesar had planned on three years in the field.[32] Plutarch's suggestion that Antonius expected the war to be over in one season so that he could promptly return to Cleopatra[33] is totally unreasonable strategically (the march to Armenia alone was 8,000 *stadia*, several hundred miles, and would itself take weeks) and is at odds with Antonius's attempt to establish winter quarters in Armenia. The assertion is either a revisionist view based on what actually happened, or a slander on his military skills.

Leaving Antonius at Zeugma, Cleopatra then embarked on a tour of some of her new territories, such as Apameia in Syria. Continuing south through Damascus, she called on Herod in Judaea, who attempted a reconciliation, agreeing to lease back Jericho and escorting her in royal fashion to the Egyptian frontier at Pelousion. He was astute enough to recognize that offending the queen was not in his best interests, although he could hardly have been pleased with the situation.[34]

Despite her tour, Cleopatra had reason to return home because she was pregnant again. Her third son was born probably in the summer of 36 B.C., while Antonius was on campaign. As a boy he would be named Ptolemy, but he was also given the surname Philadelphos, a deliberate reference to the most notable of Ptolemaic kings, Ptolemy II Philadelphos, and the magnificent empire under his rule.[35] The name was especially appropriate at this time because the recent territorial adjustments had brought Cleopatra close to restoring her ancestor's geographical boundaries. All three children of Antonius and Cleopatra now had prophetic surnames, which implied that the Ptolemaic Empire was in the process of being restored to its greatest days, a true rival to Rome.

Meanwhile the Parthian expedition had turned into a total disaster. It was suggested in the later tradition that Cleopatra was to blame because Antonius was so preoccupied—even under the influence of magic and drugs—that he was uninterested in what was before him and wanted only to return to her. This is highly unlikely, but it is one of the earliest examples of the anti-Cleopatra tradition that begins to pervade the reports of the last few years of her life. Antonius was a brilliant military tactician, yet Roman expeditions into Parthian territory were doomed to fail. Although the massive Roman force outnumbered that of the Parthians,[36] Antonius was caught by the weather and lost 24,000 men, more than half by disease. The treachery of the Armenian king, Artavasdes II, was also a problem.[37] By late autumn Antonius realized that the expedition was futile, and he sent a message to Cleopatra to meet him on the coast. He hastily retreated, covering 300 miles in three weeks and losing 8,000 more men. In December[38] he arrived at Leukokome, between Berytos and Sidon, and spent the days until the queen arrived in heavy drinking and staring out to sea. Eventually she appeared with money and clothing for the troops.

This disaster, although in many ways inevitable, was a turning point for both Antonius's career and the relationship between triumvir and queen. Although Octavia offered to finance a new expedition, Antonius probably felt that he could not return to Rome, at least for the time being. The optimistic reports that he had been sending to Octavian had fooled no one.[39] The master tactician had been responsible for one of Rome's greatest military disasters. One of the purposes of the campaign was to avenge the death of Crassus and thousands of his men in 53 B.C., but Antonius had lost even more. He had nowhere else to turn, and by late 36 B.C. he was back in the palace at Alexandria to meet his new son and to make plans for the following year.

In the spring of 35 B.C., the Parthian expedition was renewed.[40] Among the major problems of the previous year had been the inability to establish winter quarters in Armenia, where Antonius would be better positioned to attack Parthia, and the desertion of Artavasdes II, the Armenian king, at a crucial moment, so the new campaign would be directed against his territory, including revenge against the wayward monarch. Before he left Alexandria, Antonius received a message from Octavia announcing that she was on her way to Athens with supplies and 2,000 troops, a project encouraged by her brother and seen by some as an attempt to embarrass Antonius. Cleopatra certainly saw the approach of Octavia as a major threat. She pressured Antonius by what-ever means possible to convince him that his relationship with Octavia was purely a matter of political convenience but that the one with her was actual love and affection. Plutarch described the queen's convenient tears, mood changes, and her embarkation on a weight-loss program, this perhaps because she had just completed another pregnancy. There were even hints of suicide. How true all of this is cannot be determined, for it fits too conveniently into Cleopatra's formulaic role as a seductress, and the account may be designed to explain Antonius's rather enigmatic actions thereafter. Yet whether or not this portrait of the queen is accu-rate, the situation prompted Antonius effectively to abandon his life in Italy, thereby not only providing Octavian the opportunity to control the dialogue (and public opinion) there, but eventually giving him no alternative but Cleopatra, not only emotionally but financially and mili-tarily. Had the triumvir spent some time during these years in Italy, the outcome of his and the queen's careers might have been quite differ-ent.[41] Antonius thus told Octavia not to come east of Athens—although accepting her supplies and men—actually a quite reasonable suggestion, as previously, to keep his wife from entering a war zone. He then moved from Alexandria to Antioch, perhaps accompanied by Cleopatra. But for some reason he then abandoned campaigning for the year and returned to Alexandria: it may be that although he had to make a gesture in response to Octavia's support, he had no real interest at this time in another long and difficult military operation.

When Octavia returned to Rome, she was immediately cast by her brother into the role of wronged victim and was told to leave Antonius's home and return to her own, something that she refused to do. Octavian and Antonius were moving toward polarization: the last two years had seen the elimination of all Octavian's rivals in the west, including Sextus Pompeius, the surviving son of Pompeius the Great, and the unfortunate third member of the triumvirate, Lepidus. The former had fled to the East and was playing a double game between Antonius and the Parthians, even perhaps involving Cleopatra, an old family acquaintance. He was killed that summer at Miletos.[42] Lepidus, after an ill-advised revolt in Sicily, had been removed from the triumvirate—although its two surviving members continued to call themselves triumvirs—and would live quietly under guard for the remaining quarter-century of his life. By 35 B.C., the Roman world was divided solely between Antonius and Octavian, with the latter astutely using the treatment of his sister as a potent weapon.

But there never was to be a Parthian expedition. After the disaster of 36 B.C. and the noncampaign in 35 B.C., efforts in 34 B.C. were limited to dealing with Artavasdes II of Armenia. Dellius was sent to negotiate with the king, authorized to offer the older son of Cleopatra and Antonius, Alexander Helios, in marriage to the king's daughter. Artavasdes saw this for the trick that it was and declined, whereupon Antonius himself marched into Armenia and arrested the king, sending him and his family to Alexandria. As royalty, they were entitled to travel bound in gold chains.[43]

Upon his own return to Alexandria, Antonius celebrated a triumph.[44] A triumph was a venerable Roman institution, as old as the state itself. Having its origin in the Greek *thriambos*, part of the Dionysiac festival, and passing to Rome through the Etruscans, it was a procession of a victorious Roman general to the Temple of Jupiter on the Capitol in Rome, and included captives, all the Roman magistrates, and elaborate musical and visual details.[45] Its Dionysiac connections and the elevation of the human to the divine would have been especially pleasing to Antonius. He drove into Alexandria in a chariot and presented Artavasdes and his family, along with the spoils of war, to Cleopatra, who was seated in a gold chair on a silver dais. Yet the event was more farce than religious solemnity: Antonius was dressed as Dionysos, the captives refused to play their proper role of deference and obeisance despite threats, and of course the event neither celebrated a victory nor took place in Rome. It gave Octavian another point of contention, and the sources are unanimous in their distaste, calling it "a sort of triumph" and noting that the beautiful and sacred ancestral rites of Rome had been perverted by being given to the Egyptians for the sake of Cleopatra, something that the Roman citizenry took particular offense at. The queen, sensitive to the power of religion and tradition and quite knowledgeable about what a Roman triumph meant, may have begun to wonder how much of an asset Antonius actually was.

Nevertheless Cleopatra's worries would have been assuaged, for the moment, by the ceremony that took place in the Gymnasium of Alexandria shortly thereafter, perhaps even part of the pseudo-triumph. Although the two major sources, Plutarch and Dio, are not in full agreement about the details—or even whether some of the territorial dispositions were part of one ceremony in 34 B.C. or scattered over the previous two years—what happened in the Gymnasium in 34 B.C., popularly called the Donations of Alexandria, was a lavish and theatrical demonstration of the vision of the future that Cleopatra and Antonius had conceived, yet based on Ptolemaic precedents, most notably an elaborate ceremony that Ptolemy II had produced early in his reign.[46] Conflating the sources, one can determine that a large crowd gathered in the Gymnasium for a banquet, where they saw the queen and Antonius on golden thrones, with lower thrones for her four children. Cleopatra, dressed as Isis, was declared to be queen of kings, queen of Egypt, Cyprus, Libya, and Koile Syria. Caesarion, whose activities are little known for the previous decade, was now 13 years of age and was declared king of kings and joint ruler along with Cleopatra.[47] Alexander Helios, now six, was dressed as a Median and also received the title king of kings; he was declared ruler of Armenia, Media, and, bizarrely, Parthia. Iotape, the daughter of the king of Media Atropatene (modern Azerbaijan), came to Alexandria and was engaged to Alexander. Two-year-old Ptolemy Philadelphos, dressed in the style of the Successors, was also king of kings; he received Syria and Kilikia and, in one report, all Asia Minor. Alexander was given a Median bodyguard, and Ptolemy a Macedonian one. Cleopatra Selene, also six, received Crete and Cyrene. In return, Cleopatra may have given Antonius estates in Egypt, although he had little time to enjoy their revenue. Upon his death they passed to his daughter the younger Antonia. Papyrus documents show that her holdings in Egypt were extensive, mostly in the Fayum, where the estates were so considerable that a district was named after her. Although there are other ways that Antonia could have obtained the lands, inheritance from her father seems the most probable.[48]

Cleopatra and Antonius may even have married at the time of the Donations of Alexandria, although the sources are so scattered and often polemical that this is difficult to determine,[49] and one must question what purpose a marriage might have served, since it would severely diminish Antonius's status in Rome. It is significant that such a marriage is not mentioned by Josephus or Dio, is cited only in passing by Plutarch,[50] and is not documented in Egyptian sources.[51] The ambiguity of the situation is stressed by the fact that at the Donations, Antonius emphasized that Cleopatra was Caesar's wife.[52] Thus any marriage between Antonius and Cleopatra may have been more one of semantic convenience that eventually came to be exploited by Octavian's propaganda. Nevertheless coin portraits from this period show the couple in the standard posture of married Hellenistic royalty.[53] At about the same time, the queen took the title Philopatris ("She Who Loves Her

Country").[54] This is both an allusion to her Hellenized origins, as it is a term from Greek political history,[55] and also stresses her role as an *Egyptian* monarch, not one limited to Alexandria, as her linguistically challenged ancestors had been. Her connection with all of Egypt had been demonstrated by her vigorous actions to improve the economy early in her reign.

Although such honors and territorial distributions were fully within Antonius's powers as triumvir, if taken literally they stripped Rome of all its territory east of central Asia Minor. Needless to say, such arrangements were not popular in Rome. Antonius sent a report to the city requesting ratification of his actions, the proper legal process, but even though Octavian, recognizing a propaganda coup, wanted it made public, the two consuls, both Antonian loyalists, wisely suppressed it.[56]

CHAPTER SEVEN

The Operation of
the Kingdom

Royal Administration

WHEN CLEOPATRA BECAME QUEEN she inherited an ancient royal administration that was far older than the Ptolemies. She also became ruler of a kingdom in serious financial difficulty. The large debts incurred by her father were still not paid off. Caesar personally was owed millions, and although in 48 B.C. Potheinos attempted to bribe him into leaving Alexandria by a promise of payment, there is no indication that the debts were ever paid in full, one of the reasons that Octavian, as Caesar's heir, eventually attempted to conquer Egypt. The lifeblood of the country, the Nile, was at historic lows. As early as 48 B.C. it rose only five cubits—a century later this was still the lowest recorded rise—and in the two seasons of 42 and 41 B.C. it did not flood at all.[1] This resulted in famine during much of the 40s B.C., used by Cleopatra as her excuse for not joining Brutus and Cassius at Philippi. For the same reason, the tyrannicides themselves could not obtain supplies from Egyptian merchants.[2] The lack of flooding and subsequent famines caused an outbreak of plague, which was discussed in a treatise by the physician Dioskourides Phakas, a member of the queen's court.[3] A village named Tinteris—west of the Nile above Memphis—had to be abandoned in 50/49 B.C. because of a lack of water, thus resulting in a loss of tax revenue.[4] There are other examples of depopulation, such as at Hiera Nesos, where the priests complained that this isolated them and interfered with the performance of their religious duties.[5] Cleopatra moved to alleviate the problem: she could do nothing about the low level of the Nile, but contemporary documents testify that she attempted to restrain rapacious royal officials who were harassing farmers, and she distributed grain from the royal storehouses. She was later accused of omitting the Jewish community of Alexandria in her program of famine relief,[6] yet this is hardly believable since her broad religious policy allowed her to renew the inviolability of a synagogue, probably at Leontopolis.[7]

How effective her attempts were to stabilize the economy of her kingdom cannot be determined, although it is significant that the reports of civil chaos seem to diminish after her first few years.[8] Her expenditures were high, but probably no more so than those of her predecessors. Roman efforts to emphasize her lavish personal life say more about the relative wealth of Rome and Egypt. Both Caesar and Octavian realized that the Ptolemaic kingdom was dangerously rich by Roman standards—a corrupting influence—and while they were quite willing to use its resources for their own needs, they also sought to put restrictions on Roman access to the territory. A greater expense than lifestyle for Cleopatra would have been her elaborate military preparations, from her support of the Parthian expedition to the 200 ships used in the Battle of Actium. But the continual expansion of her kingdom brought new revenues, many of which had not been available to the Ptolemies for some time. The return of Cyprus, which her father had lost to the Romans, meant a renewal of the traditional income from its copper mines, eventually to pass to Herod the Great.[9] Cyprus as well as Kilikia provided timber for her great shipbuilding program, although possession of Kilikia carried with it the obligation of making an effort to control the perennial piracy that emanated from the region.[10] The Romans had not been effective in eliminating it, something of particular concern to Antonius since both his father and grandfather had been futilely involved in the matter.[11] The triumvir decided that suppression of piracy was better handled by the allied rulers, and he set Cleopatra and her colleague Archelaos of Kappadokia to the task, although there is no evidence that they were any more effective than the Romans.

Other new sources of revenue for Cleopatra included the land leases—and presumably some of the commodities produced on these lands—in Koile Syria, Judaea, and the Nabataean territory. But she also had available traditional Ptolemaic income. Egypt was most noted for its abundance of grain, although it is difficult to say how the low levels of the Nile affected this. Theokritos had written that no place was as agriculturally productive, but he also emphasized that this was ascribable to the Nile. In the first century A.D., Egyptian grain could supply Rome for four months of the year.[12] Other agricultural commodities were less significant, and the quality of Egyptian wine was openly criticized.[13] Yet the Ptolemaic government had many royal monopolies, including vegetable oil (olive oil was not a major product), papyrus, textiles, and aromatics, the last an Arabian import.[14] It also owned a vast amount of land that could either be directly productive or leased. Cleopatra's royal textile mill was in the hands of a Roman senator, Q. Ovinius, who after the fall of Alexandria was put to death by Octavian, ostensibly because running a business was conduct unbecoming to a senator.[15] One suspects that there is more to the tale.

The government also had trade relations with areas outside their own territories, especially to the south and east. As early as the third century B.C., Ptolemaic explorers had gone far up the Nile and established contacts with the city of Meroë, creating a permanent presence there from which Ptolemaic agents could learn about interior Africa. Others established a number of trading and elephant-hunting stations along the Red Sea.[16] Aromatics were imported from the frankincense-growing region of southwestern Arabia. Cleopatra's knowledge of the relevant languages—Ethiopian, Trogodytic, and Arabian—would have assisted in further developing these contacts. Relations with India were also an important priority of the queen's: the repeated mention of India as a refuge after Actium demonstrates that she had some knowledge of the region. Direct trade between the Ptolemies and India began in the late second century B.C. with the activities of the adventurer Eudoxos of Knidos; in the early years of the following century 20 ships a year went between the Red Sea and India, a number that Strabo found minimal, as the traffic had drastically increased in his day—the years immediately after Cleopatra's death—presumably because of the Roman peace.[17] To implement the Indian trade Ptolemy XII obtained landing rights on the island of Dioskourides (modern Socotra) off the eastern tip of Africa,[18] an important point on the sailing route, although the island seems to have been controlled by local rulers from Arabia and was neither a permanent Ptolemaic possession nor acquired by the Romans.[19] The detailed account of trade to and from India known as the *Periplous of the Erythraian Sea*, dating from about a century after the time of Cleopatra, provides insights as to processes and commodities, probably little changed from Ptolemaic days. Items such as oil, olives, grain, wine, textiles, and metals headed east while sugar, ghee, rice, raw cotton and silk, precious stones, aromatics, and spices came west. If the queen actually wore Chinese silk, this is one of the earliest documentations of it in the Mediterranean.[20] In fact, late Ptolemaic trade with India was extensive enough that there was a member of the royal administration specifically devoted to the management of the operation, the "Overseer of the Erythraian and Indian Seas." From early in the reign of Ptolemy XII well into that of Cleopatra this post was held by a certain Kallimachos, documented from 74–73 to 39 B.C. As an indication of the hereditary nature of Ptolemaic offices, his son Kronios succeeded to at least some of his positions around 51 B.C. (perhaps with the regime change), and another son, also named Kallimachos, was in the government as late as 39 B.C.[21]

Yet despite this flourishing trade and agrarian economy, Cleopatra was plagued with financial problems. The net income of Ptolemy XII varied between 6,000 and 12,500 talents, although it is not known what these figures mean. Strabo, who quoted the larger amount, wryly noted that this was an astounding sum for a kingdom totally mismanaged financially.[22] As is well known, governments are adept at hiding financial excess, and how the massive loans from Roman bankers fit into this cannot be determined, but it is significant that both Ptolemy XII and his daughter had to debase the coinage.[23] The stories of confiscations and outright robbery at the end of Cleopatra's reign are so tangled into the negative view of her prevalent at this time that it is difficult to determine whether this represented genuine financial straits, though this seems a contradiction with Octavian's persistence in conquering Egypt because of its great wealth.

The wide geographical range of Cleopatra's coinage indicates both her attempts at economic solvency and her extensive territorial ambitions.[24] It reflected her self-image and often included representations of Isis. Her Egyptian series runs throughout her reign, from her Year 1 (51 B.C.) to Year 22 (30 B.C.); only a few years are missing. The issues reflect the economic problems of the era, for no gold coinage is known, and her silver was debased to 40 percent or less.[25] She also reestablished the minting of bronze at Alexandria, dormant since the days of Ptolemy IX.[26] The lack of gold was not a major issue, as there had been no Ptolemaic gold since probably the time of Ptolemy V,[27] and in fact gold coinage by the allied kings was becoming less common, eventually to be prohibited by the Romans.[28] Yet Cleopatra's relationship with Rome was loose enough that she was not bound by these strictures, unlike her grandson Ptolemy of Mauretania, whose minting of gold coins led directly to his death,[29] and her lack of gold was probably more because it was no longer a Ptolemaic habit. Bronze coinage is known for most of the queen's regnal years and silver from two, her sixth and eleventh (47–46 and 42–41 B.C.). The emphasis on baser coinage demonstrated her financial problems, and it is perhaps no surprise that the queen seems to have written a treatise on weights and measures.[30] In addition to the Egyptian coins, ones are known from Antioch, Askalon, Berytos (fig. 11c), Chalkis in Syria, Cyprus, Damascus, Orthosia, Patrai, and Ptolemais and Tripolis in Phoenicia. Caesarion appears on a coin probably from Cyprus showing him as Eros, along with his mother (fig. 11a). Other coins imitate the types of her ancestor Arsinoë II, the greatest of the early Ptolemaic queens.[31] A denarius from an unknown mint has Antonius with "Armenia devicta" on one side and the queen with "Cleopatrae reginae regum filiorum regum" on the other, demonstrating the titulature of the Donations of Alexandria (fig. 11e). Although the coinage is ambiguously Roman, this seems the first time that a foreign woman had appeared on assumed Roman coinage with a Latin inscription, something that could easily be used against Antonius.[32] Also associated with the queen are a series of crocodile coins from the Cyrenaica, minted under the authority of P. Canidius Crassus, probably the royal governor after the Donations affirmed Cleopatra Selene's control of the district.[33] Cleopatra VII's coins are not only known from the regions in which they were minted, but have been found on the Adriatic at Split, and at Este in the Veneto of northern Italy, perhaps an indication of trade efforts by the queen up the Adriatic and into the Po valley.[34]

Cleopatra's royal administrators were in many cases inherited from her father, as demonstrated by the long career of Kallimachos. Although some, like Potheinos, who was chief financial officer, ended up on the wrong side of the Alexandrian War, bringing their careers fatally to an end, many continued on, producing a prosopography of about 100 names from the queen's administration. Practically all these are found on papyri or inscriptions rather than in literature.[35] Most are merely names. A certain Diomedes was her secretary in 30 B.C.;[36] in 38 B.C. her majordomo was Noumenias. Someone named Chelidon was one of the court eunuchs, but his role is uncertain, although important, since he became famous for the great wealth that he amassed.[37] Apollodoros of Sicily is only known from when he helped her sneak into Caesar's presence, but he must have been a close associate to be trusted with such a delicate task (see pp. 169–70). Dexiphanes of Knidos was her royal architect; since an earlier Dexiphanes was the father of Sostratos, the architect of the Lighthouse, the position may have been hereditary.[38] In the period 46–41 B.C., at least, a certain Theon was the official in charge of current business—essentially her chief of staff—who implemented royal orders.[39] More than 20 of her regional governors are known, some with solid Hellenistic Greek names such as Alexandros, Leonnatos, Ptolemaios, or Seleukos, and others with Egyptian ones such as Pachom and Pamenches. It was still normal for the higher officials to be Greeks while the lower ones were Egyptian: Kallimachos, among his many posts, was royal governor (*epistrategos*) of the Thebaid, but his subordinates (*strategoi*) were the Egyptians Haremephis in the Panopolite nome, Pachomios at Dendera and Edfu (his statue can be seen today in Detroit),[40] and Monkores in the Peritheban nome.[41] Other administrators known by name include regional financial officers, granary managers, tax officials, and scribes. One should also add her devoted ladies-in-waiting Eiras and Charmion, who are documented regularly during the queen's career and were dramatically involved in her death.[42] The list is interesting, although not particularly informative. When Octavian turned Egypt into a Roman province in 30 B.C., he not only legally became its ruler but kept much of the royal administration, placing only a handful of Roman officials in direct charge.

The Royal Building Program

A royal building program was a standard part of the policy of a Hellenistic dynast. Cleopatra's ancestors, especially Ptolemy I and II, had built and enhanced the city of Alexandria and had also bestowed their architectural patronage elsewhere, such as the gymnasium constructed in Athens by Ptolemy VI or, more probably, Ptolemy III.[43] Cleopatra's nemesis Herod the Great began the largest royal building program ever in 40 B.C., which lasted for 30 years and extended throughout the eastern Mediterranean. Yet despite these precedents, the queen was not a major builder. In part this was because Alexandria, which had seen steady royal patronage for more than 250 years when Cleopatra came to the throne, had little need of major new constructions. By her father's time, it had grown immensely and was the largest city in the world.[44]

Nevertheless, early in Cleopatra's reign Alexandria suffered serious damage as a result of the Alexandrian War. Areas were demolished for military purposes. Caesar removed all the structures on the island of Pharos, building fortifications and modifying the approach causeway. The famous Lighthouse that sat on the small Proteus islet at the east end of the island was partially destroyed. The Alexandrian defenders turned the roof beams of major public buildings, including the gymnasia, into oars for ships.[45] During the actual hostilities, fire broke out in the ship-yard district and spread through warehouses, primarily those containing grain, and damaged the Library, although the details and extent of this are still disputed.[46]

Thus when Cleopatra was securely on her throne after Caesar's departure in the spring of 47 B.C., a serious repair program was essential under the supervision of the royal architect, Dexiphanes of Knidos. The main gymnasium was restored and became the location of major public events throughout and after her reign, although nothing is known about its earlier history. About the time of the queen's death Strabo described it as a particularly beautiful building with colonnades a *stadion* long, situated on the main east-west street.[47]

Cleopatra also had to attend to the island of Pharos and the adjacent Lighthouse.[48] The island itself was primarily an Egyptian residential district and probably not a target for royal patronage, and it remained desolate even into the Roman period. But the Lighthouse had to be recon-structed, for it was in poor shape, perhaps virtually demolished. It had been built by Sostratos of Knidos in the 280s B.C. for Ptolemy II because access to the harbors was difficult and dangerous.[49] As Alexandria's most famous and visible monument, the first thing seen by those approaching the city, prompt repairs were essential. They were so extensive that in later years Cleopatra received credit for building the entire structure.[50] Connecting Pharos to the mainland was a causeway, the Heptastadion, its name reflecting its seven-*stadion* length, first mentioned during the reign of Ptolemy II. It had been reworked by Caesar for his defensive needs, and Cleopatra reconstructed it in seven days and then ceremoni-ously rode along it in her carriage.[51]

What repairs were necessary to the Library are not recorded. The story that Antonius absconded with the Pergamene collections for the benefit of Alexandria,[52] while implausible and from an unreliable source, may reflect some attempt to replace lost volumes, but nothing is known about the buildings themselves. Yet the Library continued to flourish into the Roman period, as scholarship by Strabo, Juba II, and others demonstrates.

The most significant architectural construction of Cleopatra's Alexandria was a Kaisareion, a precinct in honor of Julius Caesar. Caesar himself, a major architectural innovator, suggested the project during his stay in Alexandria.[53] He had already begun his building program in Rome, including the Forum Julium, and shortly after leaving Alexandria he was to pass through Antioch and commission a Kaisareion there.[54] All these structures seem to have been enclosed porticoes of the Pergamene type, important in the cross-fertilization between Hellenistic and Roman architecture. Because Caesar never returned to Alexandria, it fell to Cleopatra to supervise the progress of the Kaisareion, presumably using the Forum Julium in Rome as the prototype, something that she would be familiar with, at least after 46 B.C. How far construction had progressed by 30 B.C. remains uncertain, but it was enough along to hold a statue of Caesar, because notoriously Antyllus, the son of Antonius and Fulvia, vainly sought refuge at it but was dragged to his death.[55] A head of Caesar in green diabase now in Berlin may have been part of this statue.[56] There are some hints that the complex also honored Antonius, but this seems a misreading of Dio's account, perpetuated by the tenth-century encyclopedia known as the *Suda*.[57] The precinct seems to have been placed in the center of the city facing the harbor, east of the Heptastadion. There is also evidence that Cleopatra either expanded the project into a Forum Julium or built a separate structure of that name nearby. The primary source is the original inscription on the obelisk now in front of St. Peter's in Rome (brought to the city in A.D. 37 by the emperor Gaius), which refers to a Forum Julium built by C. Cornelius Gallus, who was with Octavian at the fall of Alexandria and shortly thereafter was named prefect of Egypt.[58] Since the inscription does not give Gallus that title, it was probably written before Octavian left in late 30 B.C., and thus, since it is unlikely that Gallus was able to build a forum in the few months since Cleopatra's death, he probably completed a structure under construction. Although the evidence remains vague, it seems probable that Cleopatra began the project but that it was finished under the new regime, since honoring Caesar served Octavian as much as it had the queen. Yet it is important to realize that her efforts to memorialize Caesar were not because he was a former lover but were a necessary part of her positioning of herself in the contemporary Roman world. After Cleopatra's death, the complex—whether one structure or two—was turned into the temple of the Imperial cult: a description by Philon from the late 30s A.D. provides an account of it in its complete stage, with stoas, libraries, and a rich collection of art, although how much of this was the work of Cleopatra remains uncertain.[59] In 13/12 B.C., when Augustus became Pontifex Maximus, the two famous obelisks from the New Kingdom, known today as "Cleopatra's Needles," were erected in front of the complex, at the waterfront.[60] In the late nineteenth century one was still standing, and the other lay buried next to it: the latter was sent to London in 1877, and the standing one was removed to New York in 1880.

The only other structure in Alexandria associated with Cleopatra was her tomb, where she buried Antonius and where, a few days later, Octavian buried her.[61] It was distinct from the tombs of her Ptolemaic ancestors, the Ptolemaion, which itself was separate from that of Alexander the Great, although all these were in the palace precinct.[62] Cleopatra's tomb is not mentioned until the last weeks of her life, and it is unknown whether it was a long-standing project or something generated in the summer of 30 B.C. when she realized that her death was imminent.[63] In fact it was unfinished at her death and allegedly completed by Octavian. If it was a hurried effort it cannot have been very substantial, which may explain why it does not seem to have lasted long. The tomb was near the Temple of Isis—an affirmation of her status as the New Isis—a structure that Alexander had marked out as part of his original plan for the city,[64] but the location is not known today, and by Cleopatra's time Alexandria had many temples of Isis. It may have had a window that overlooked the sea. It also had an ingenious contrivance that made it impossible to open the doors once they had been sealed, reminiscent of traditional Egyptian tombs: for this reason the dying Antonius had to be hoisted into the tomb through a window or the roof. It is by no means certain whether the queen actually died there or in the palace, but she does seem to have a room fitted out for habitation. Astonishingly it remains one of the least-known monuments of ancient Alexandria, seemingly not surviving past the first century A.D. The last reference to it is at the end of that century, a poetic allusion that may not even have a temporal context.[65] Explanations regarding its early demise have included willful destruction by the Alexandrians or Roman officials (somewhat at odds with the care that Octavian took to ensure its use as well as the reputation Antonius retained long after his death), or that it was a temporary tomb and the queen was buried with her ancestors (a speculation that is unsupported by the literature). Even if it were better to forget Cleopatra, the tomb was also that of Antonius, and this, one might think, would ensure its survival, as his descendants included three emperors and others who were prominent in Rome for nearly a century after his death. Though his grandson Germanicus visited Egypt in A.D. 19, a remarkably detailed account of his trip includes no mention that he saw his grandfather's tomb, despite recent visits to Actium and the camp of Antonius, indicating that he was interested in his grandfather's memorabilia.[66] The tomb of Cleopatra and Antonius must have disappeared quickly, but the matter is curious and unresolved, and it is possible that Antonius's body was soon removed to Rome and the tomb of Cleopatra quickly forgotten or even demolished, perhaps with her remains joining those of her ancestors.[67]

Nevertheless the tomb came to have important symbolic significance. Upon returning to Rome, Octavian—soon to be Augustus—almost immediately began construction of his own dynastic tomb at the northern edge of the Campus Martius. Like Cleopatra, he forsook the ancestral burial site of his family and built a new structure. Strabo would see it under construction and apply the name *mausoleion* to it, the first use of this term in any context other than the famous tomb of Maussolos of Karia. Within a few years Herod the Great would begin work on his tomb at Herodeion and Juba II his at Tipasa east of Mauretanian Caesarea.[68] All three of these remain conspicuously visible today. The little-known and long-vanished tomb of Cleopatra and Antonius is the prototype for the dynastic tombs of both the Roman imperial family and the allied kings.

There is no solid evidence about the palace of Cleopatra, which she inherited from her father and may not have significantly altered. It stood on and southwest of the promontory of Lochias, east of the harbors,[69] and was commissioned by Alexander the Great.[70] The best description of the palace is by Strabo, writing a few years after the death of Cleopatra. He related that it took up nearly one-third of the city and that each of the Ptolemies had added to it—presumably this would include Cleopatra—so that there were many complexes connected with one another. The Mouseion, with its lecture halls and dining rooms, was one of these, as well as the royal burial precinct, including the tomb of Alexander himself and the Ptolemies, with the tomb of Cleopatra and Antonius a separate structure. The palace contained numerous gardens and pavilions, and had its own private harbor. Offshore there was another palatial complex on a small island. It all was as grandiose a structure as Hellenistic architecture allowed, with decoration of the highest quality. Archaeological finds in the region of the Lochias promontory include fine mosaics, colonnades, Greek roof tiles, and evidence of gardens; as expected, the earliest material recovered is from the late fourth century B.C.[71] The palace continued in use in Roman times, with the Mouseion functioning under Imperial patronage and the administrative areas presumably being used by the Roman government.[72]

Although there are few details specific to the palace as remodeled or used by Cleopatra, a description of it exists in Lucan's epic of the Roman civil war, written approximately a century after the queen's death, a poetic account of her entertaining Caesar.[73] Obviously the material must be treated with extreme caution, and much of it is formulaic and based on the Roman view of the opulence of Hellenistic dynasts, as well as the palaces of Nero that Lucan would have known. Lucan recorded marble walls, a dining room the size of a temple, ivory and emerald decorations, scented herbs, and an abundance of flowers. There are also specific decorative details, such as ebony from Ethiopia, citron-wood tables from Mauretania, and tortoiseshell from India. Despite its problems, the account provides the best sense of the luxury of Cleopatra's palace, and like her tomb it became an important prototype for future generations, of great influence on the many palaces of Herod and the Roman residential complex on the Palatine.

There are some hints of construction by Cleopatra elsewhere in Egypt, structures that follow the long-established rules of Egyptian architecture. A relief of the queen with Caesarion, both of whom are in traditional Egyptian royal dress, appears twice on the rear wall of the Temple of Hathor at Dendera in the Thebaid (fig. 4). The temple was begun by Ptolemy XII and completed by the queen. The relief emphasizes her role as mother, appearing with the attributes of Isis, with Caesarion in front of her.[74] The symbolism on this relief deserves some attention. Cleopatra and Caesarion are making offerings to Hathor, who is the goddess of the temple, and her son Ihy. Hathor's consort Horus is not present because he lived at Edfu, more than 60 miles upriver, although he would visit Dendera on occasion. The scene therefore becomes a metaphor for Cleopatra's personal situation: mother and child but an absent father (Julius Caesar). The queen could thus use her own life to emphasize her parallelism with a major Egyptian goddess, strengthening her position among the religious elite and the population as a whole.[75] Interestingly, after Cleopatra's death Augustus enlarged the temple and added his name, a subtle indication that whatever the official view in

Rome, in Egypt the queen was still a source of power. At Koptos is a boat shrine that may commemorate her Nile voyage with Caesar.[76] Further upstream at Hermonthis is the unfinished Kiosk, another effort by the queen.[77] Also at Hermonthis was a shrine, popularly considered a birthing temple (demolished in 1861), where Cleopatra was depicted at the birth of Isis's son Horus, a clear allegory to the birth of Caesarion.[78] She also built a temple to Isis near Ptolemais Hermiou in Upper Egypt; the project was implemented in 46 B.C. by Kallimachos, the long-standing governor of the region.[79]

A further prerogative of Hellenistic royalty was the foundation of cities, and there are at least three places named Kleopatra/Kleopatris in Egypt.[80] The best known is at the head of the Gulf of Suez, where the city of Suez is now, at the mouth of the ancient canal that connected the Mediterranean with the Red Sea.[81] This was probably the Ptolemaic naval base for operations on the Red Sea and to India, and although not well located (aside from being the point on the Red Sea closest to Alexandria) it continued in use until the nineteenth century. It was here that Aelius Gallus, prefect of Egypt, embarked on his ill-fated Arabian expedition in 26 or 25 B.C., with Strabo on his staff. The city was formerly called Arsinoë, and Cleopatra may have wished to remove her hated sister from the topographic map of Egypt, especially such an important place, although the name probably belongs to Arsinoë II. Another Kleopatris or Kleopatra (whether this is one site or two is not clear) was west of the Nile near Hermopolis but is virtually unknown archaeologically, although the toponym was still known in the eighth century.[82] There is no certain association of Cleopatra VII with any of these towns, but she was more likely than her homonymous predecessors to be involved in city foundation.

Isis and Dionysos

From the beginning of Ptolemaic rule Isis and Dionysos had been associated with the dynasty, culminating in the adoption of their divine attributes by Cleopatra and Antonius. Isis was a popular divinity who was not only an agricultural and harvest goddess but also one of marriage and maternity issues, equated with Greek Demeter. As a single mother, she would have resonated with Cleopatra. The father of Isis's child Horus (or Harpokrates in more Hellenized versions) was her brother Osiris, whom Greeks saw as a version of Dionysos, the most popular of Greek gods, given his association with the grapevine. His ecstatic retinue had long been a part of Greek culture. As soon as Greeks learned about Egypt, they came to see Isis/Demeter and Osiris/Dionysos as a divine couple worthy of interest and respect.[83] The divinities could be connected with Alexander the Great, since Isis figured in his plans for the city of Alexandria, and Dionysos was not only said to be one of his ancestors but a constant role model.[84] Thus it was natural that the Ptolemaic monarchs would have a close relationship with both divinities. On his coinage Ptolemy I first placed Alexander, and then himself as Dionysos.[85] The Ptolemaic promulgation of Isis caused worship of that goddess to be established in their overseas possessions.[86] Even as early as the fifth century B.C. she had been identified with Demeter[87] and was probably worshiped in Athens before Ptolemaic times,[88] perhaps brought by Egyptian merchants. Arsinoë II, the wife of Ptolemy II, was designated a goddess after her death in 270 B.C., with Isis as one of her attributes. The spread of the queen's cult throughout the Ptolemaic world also included Isis, especially in the cities named Arsinoë, but also in places as diverse as Halikarnassos and Thera.[89] Isis was known in Italy since at least the second century B.C., especially in seaport towns. The Romans were always ambivalent about the cult—as they were about foreign cults generally—and in the 50s and 40s B.C. there were repeated reactions against it and expulsions, perhaps not by coincidence during the very years Ptolemy XII and Cleopatra were visiting the city.[90]

With the association of Arsinoë II, the greatest of early Ptolemaic queens, with Isis, the precedent was established that the goddess would be an attribute of her successors, most notably Cleopatra III in the latter second century B.C.[91] Cleopatra VII is attested as Isis from as early as 47/46 B.C.—the year she became, like the goddess, a single mother[92]—eventually always appearing at state functions dressed as her.[93] Exactly what this meant is uncertain, but it probably included a crown with a circlet of cobras, cows' horns, and a sun disc, an Egyptian wig, and a large knot between her breasts that secured her *himation*, or outer garment. She may have carried the *sistrum*, a ritual bronze rattle, and the *situla*, a bronze bucket. Furthering her connection with Isis, the queen was presumably also responsible for encouraging Caesar to commission a Temple of Isis in Rome,[94] probably in the central part of the Campus Martius near the Saepta Julia,[95] to replace and enhance a shrine of Isis that had been on the Capitol but had been demolished in 48 B.C. after being taken over by swarms of bees.[96]

The Ptolemaic cult of Dionysos is documented as early as the time of Ptolemy II, when, at a great festival early in his reign, the Ptolemaia, the god played a prominent role, with his gigantic statue drawn in a cart adorned with rich offerings, accompanied by a multitude of celebrants and adherents carrying a vast number of containers of wine.[97] Since Dionysos was a traditional Greek god there was no need to spread his cult through the eastern Mediterranean, but clearly the Ptolemies gave him special recognition, perhaps because of his connection with Alexander. Ptolemy XII took the title "New Dionysos"[98] and was known as "Auletes," the Flute Player, a sobriquet that had Dionysiac overtones. He depicted himself as the god,[99] although holding divine titles by Hellenistic royalty did not mean actual divinity in a theological sense but was a recognition that the rulers had special qualities and achievements that made them divine in character.[100] But the Romans also had their own interest in Dionysos, again emanating from Alexander, who was a role model for many of the prominent leaders of the first century B.C. Pompeius's African triumph of 79 B.C. was a distinct imitation of Dionysos's alleged Indian triumph, and Caesar may have created a shrine of Dionysos on his property.[101] It was reported to be in the "royal gardens," which in the context of the anecdote—29 B.C., connected with Octavian's return to Rome—can hardly mean a nonexistent Imperial palace but probably the Horti Caesaris, Caesar's gardens across the Tiber.

Thus Dionysos and Isis came together in the Rome of Julius Caesar. The dictator assumed divine characteristics even before his death, as Antonius eloquently pointed out in his funeral oration, passing over the fact that this presumption contributed to his death.[102] Cleopatra came to Rome and lived in the Horti Caesaris with its shrine to Dionysos, and soon her statue was in the Forum Julium alongside the Roman divine matriarch Venus (fig. 10). Her identity as Venus (Aphrodite) had already appeared on coinage at the time of the birth of Caesarion,[103] where queen and son appeared as the goddess and Eros (fig. 11a). This connection was further suggested in her carefully staged approach to Antonius at Tarsos, when the popular rumor was that Aphrodite had come to play with Dionysos: his Dionysiac revels in Ephesos, just previously, had set the stage.[104] Antonius himself, Caesar's successor, assumed the role of Dionysos no later than 41 B.C. and the Tarsos encounter: the connection of the god with wine and his general festive nature was of great appeal to the darker side of the triumvir. Shortly thereafter he was calling himself the New Dionysos and allegedly gave instructions that others should address him in the same way,[105] undergoing a symbolic marriage to Athene at the urging of the Athenians, a highly profitable endeavor, as the dowry was immense. Antonius also took on the persona of Osiris, perhaps more through expediency than belief, but the god had long been equated by Greeks with Dionysos.[106] In deference to her father, Cleopatra called herself the "daughter of Dionysos,"[107] and she and Antonius had their portraits and sculpture commissioned as divinities:[108] when their statues on the Akropolis of Athens were struck by lightning before the Battle of Actium, it was seen as an ominous portent.[109] Antonius's supposed triumph after the Parthian disaster was another Dionysian extravaganza, and Cleopatra minted coins showing herself as Isis.[110] By the time the couple met their end, their divine roles were firmly established, and even Roman officers respected the queen's identity as Isis, as C. Julius Papius made a dedication to the temple of that goddess at Philai in 32 B.C.[111] Yet early in the morning of 1 August 30 B.C., the day that Octavian entered Alexandria, sounds of Dionysiac revelry were heard passing through the city toward and through the eastern gate, beyond which he was camped.[112] There were numerous precedents for encouraging the enemy gods to change sides,[113] and Greeks had long believed that a defeated city was abandoned by its gods.[114] Thus this staged event was interpreted as the worst portent of all, that Dionysos had deserted Antonius. Cleopatra's death by asp, if it truly happened, furthered the connection with Isis and may have been the official Egyptian version of her end.[115] Octavian could ridicule divinity of the pair, as he did just before Actium[116] and refuse divine honors himself while bestowing them on Julius Caesar, but Cleopatra as Isis was totally serious to the Egyptians.[117] Nevertheless Octavian would be deified after his death, and the Hellenistic idea of ruler cult was a forerunner of the Imperial cult, which promptly took hold in Alexandria not long after the couple's demise.[118]

Foreign Policy and the Matter of Herod the Great

Cleopatra's foreign policy was so tangled with her relationship with Rome—as had been the case with the Ptolemies for several generations previously—that it is difficult to detect any activities that were not affected by Rome. Her primary goals were to return her kingdom to its greatest territorial extent, that of the third century B.C., and to ensure its survival by a stable transition to her heir. The latter eluded her, despite her efforts, but this was hardly surprising since a succession without violence had not been a feature of the Ptolemaic dynasty for nearly 200 years. Yet throughout her reign she was obsessively concerned with who would succeed her, something that her Roman antagonists and even Antonius may not have fully understood.

She was more successful in her territorial ambitions. She persuaded first Caesar and then Antonius to enlarge her kingdom, beginning with the return of Cyprus in 47 B.C. and followed by the extensive bestowals of the following decade. These arrangements were not the whims of her smitten Roman lovers but a valid part of Roman policy of the era, an attempt to restrain the rapid and almost uncontrolled Roman expansionism into the eastern Mediterranean that had begun with the acquisition of the Pergamene kingdom in 130 B.C. and included both the Seleukid Empire 60 years later and numerous minor territories, such as Cyprus in 58 B.C. Both Caesar and Antonius, although perhaps without the deeper clarity of modern hindsight, saw that internal problems for the Roman state resulted from these acquisitions, and they sought to create a network of friendly kings and queens who could rule as proxies for Roman interests while retaining a local connection. Cleopatra was the most famous of these allied rulers; others included Archelaos of Kappadokia, Malchos of Nabataea, and Herod the Great.[119]

Yet the Romans may have failed to realize the extent of the allied rulers' own agenda and the ways in which their interests might collide outside the Roman sphere of influence. Herod the Great and Cleopatra were the most contentious, and he proved the greatest obstacle to the queen's territorial needs. Second only to Cleopatra in power and prestige—as well as later reputation—Herod came to the throne in 40 B.C., halfway through Cleopatra's reign, and survived her by 26 years. In his later years he would become infamous in Christian literature for his activities at the time of the birth of Jesus of Nazareth, but his relationship with Cleopatra was during the first decade of his reign. During these years, 40–30 B.C., king and queen were constantly at odds, and Herod's kingdom was where Cleopatra's ambition to restore her dynasty's territorial greatness came to a dead end.

The queen's relationship with Herod was the most frustrating of all her associations. The sole source is Josephus, much of whose material came from someone that both dynasts knew well, Nikolaos of Damascus, tutor to Cleopatra's children and then a longtime advisor to Herod. The families of Cleopatra and Herod had been in contact with one another since Herod's father Antipatros of Askalon had assisted in the restoration of Ptolemy XII in 55 B.C. (see p. 24), when both future dynasts were in their teens. Eight years later Antipatros aided Caesar in the Alexandrian War and received Roman citizenship for his efforts (see p. 63). Power passed to the younger generation, with Cleopatra and Herod as rulers of their respective territories and eyeing each other suspiciously. Although Herod owed his kingship directly to Antonius and Octavian, the various territorial arrangements from 37 to 34 B.C. favored his rival Cleopatra, who allegedly would have preferred all of his kingdom.

Nikolaos's account, which made extensive use of Herod's own memoirs,[120] is highly positive, even eulogistic, toward Herod, and exceedingly negative about Cleopatra, but it presents a vivid picture of two dynasts who were highly competitive about their conflicting territories.[121] It was perfectly reasonable for Herod to believe that the queen was plotting his ruin, for he saw her, especially in her treatment of her siblings, as a bloodthirsty, aggressive ruler.[122] Given his own later history, these were unusual charges for Herod to make, but they were an acceptable interpretation of events of the early 30s B.C. as he saw them, when Cleopatra acquired vast areas of his territory almost as soon as he obtained them himself. Herod's own tortuous relationship with his cousin, the Nabataean king Malchos,[123] was also entangled into the matter of Cleopatra, since Herod felt, again not unreasonably, that the queen was playing the two kings against each other, something that would eventually lead to open warfare between them. In fact Herod became so afraid of Cleopatra's ambitions, believing that the queen wanted Antonius to kill him and take his throne, that he fortified Masada as a possible refuge.[124]

Yet despite the animosity between the two dynasts, Cleopatra found herself involved in Herod's turbulent family relations. While Herod was besieging Jerusalem in 37 B.C., as a final act toward gaining his kingdom, he married the Hasmonean princess Mariamme.[125] Her uncle Antigonos II was the reigning king of Judaea, Herod's opponent, and was soon defeated and handed over to Antonius for execution. Since Antigonos was also high priest, this vacancy had to be filled. Rather than appoint Antigonos's nephew (and Mariamme's brother) Aristoboulos III, the obvious candidate as the senior eligible male in the Hasmonean family,

Herod claimed that he was too young and gave the office to an obscure priest from Babylon, one Ananel, his attempt to weaken both the priesthood and the Hasmonean family.[126]

At this point the matriarch of the family, Alexandra, moved into action. She was the sister-in-law of the late king Antigonos and the mother of Mariamme and Aristoboulos. She appealed to Cleopatra to help her family against Herod, since she knew that the two rulers were at odds.[127] Herod could not have been happy at having his formidable mother-in-law and his greatest rival in alliance. Alexandra had to use a trusted member of her entourage to sneak a letter to Cleopatra asking her to appeal to Antonius to give the priesthood to her son. Antonius, not surprisingly, was reluctant to become involved, but to investigate the situation he surreptitiously sent Dellius, who seemed more interested in the Hasmonean women than his task. Herod, who probably had spies in Cleopatra's court,[128] of course knew all that was happening, and although he accused Alexandra and Cleopatra of plotting together for his throne, he also agreed to appoint Aristoboulos to the priesthood. But he put his mother-in-law under house arrest, and she again wrote to Cleopatra, who suggested that Alexandra and Aristoboulos come to Egypt. Herod, however, learned of the plan and caught them in the process of departing. He took no action against Alexandra, but shortly thereafter Aristoboulos mysteriously drowned in the swimming pool at Herod's palace in Jericho. Ananel was reappointed high priest. Alexandra again wrote to Cleopatra, who pressed Antonius to become more active in the dispute. The triumvir summoned Herod to Laodikeia in Syria, where the plans for the stillborn Parthian expedition of 35 B.C. were under way. According to Herod, Antonius rebuked Cleopatra for her involvement and exonerated Herod: this outcome may have been eased by Herod's offer to help fund the Parthian expedition.

The tale must be considered cautiously because of its perspective of being highly favorable to Herod, who himself was probably the source of much of the account, but Cleopatra's attempt to adjudicate the dysfunctional lives of the Hasmoneans and Herodians was of little profit to her. The families needed no outside help to be destructive toward one another, but they could also destroy outsiders whom they drew into their quarrels. Antonius's diffidence demonstrated this, and his "rebuke" to Cleopatra was probably to point this out. She was attempting to exercise her role as the dominant ruler of the region—with an eye on additional Herodian territory—but it is significant that there is no evidence of any further involvement in Herodian domestic life. In later years the family would repeatedly drive the emperor Augustus to despair during much of his long reign.

Despite such an implication by Josephus, it seems unlikely that Cleopatra attempted to further her needs by trying to seduce Herod:[129] again the source is Herod himself, who allegedly evaded her solicitations and even considered killing her but could not decide whether this would earn the gratitude or wrath of Antonius. The extant account by Josephus is presented as a mixture of Herod's attractiveness to women and astuteness in the face of danger, contrasted with Cleopatra's promiscuity, and it ignores the political unlikelihood of such a move by the queen. Exactly when this supposed attempt at a liaison took place is also uncertain. The context of the tale assumes a visit by Cleopatra to Herod in Judaea, and Josephus, whose chronology is far from clear, seems to have placed the failed seduction in 36 B.C., the only time that she is known to have been at his court, when, incidentally, she was pregnant.

Another point of contention between Cleopatra and Herod was Idumaea, the region southwest of the Dead Sea, potentially volatile because it was bordered by Nabataean possessions on the south and Cleopatra's coastal cities on the west. As Hasmonean territory it had passed to Herod in 37 B.C., and he placed a certain Kostobaros, a native, as governor, who married Herod's sister Salome.[130] For a short time he was also in charge of Gaza, but this quickly became part of Cleopatra's realm. His Idumaean nationalism soon overrode his loyalty to Herod, and he reached out to Cleopatra as the one who would be most effective in supporting Idumaean interests. The queen asked Antonius for Idumaea, a request that was denied, as the triumvir realized that its value to her was minimal but its loss to Herod would offend and weaken an important ally. He may also have seen that Kostobaros intended for Idumaea to become independent of both dynasts. It is clear that Antonius was trying to balance the conflicting needs of Cleopatra and Herod, and after the territorial settlement of 37 B.C. regularly decided in favor of the latter. Cleopatra's empire was extensive and secure, but further dismemberment of Herod's kingdom would cause serious problems in the region between Roman Syria and Egypt. Even if Cleopatra were as territorially aggressive as the pro-Herodian account implies, to gratify her would be disastrous. Nevertheless the queen probably continued to hope that she could profit from the continued animosity between Herod and Malchos: Herod, at least, believed that this was her plan, and when open warfare broke out between the two kings in 32 B.C., she was blamed.[131] The immediate cause of the war was Malchos's failure to pay his tribute to Cleopatra—probably actually land rentals—which Herod had guaranteed. By then, however, Cleopatra and Antonius had other issues on their minds.

CHAPTER EIGHT

Scholarship and Culture at the Court of Cleopatra

THE INTELLECTUAL CULTURE OF THE COURT of Cleopatra VII was the most distinguished that Ptolemaic Alexandria had seen since the expulsion of many scholars from the city by Ptolemy VIII a century earlier. An astonishing number of personalities are known, although many are quite obscure today. Cleopatra presided over the last of the genuine Hellenistic courts, providing inspiration not only for the intellectual world of Augustan Rome but the Romanized kingdoms of that era, such as those of Herod the Great, Archelaos of Kappadokia, and Juba II of Mauretania. When Cleopatra died, many of her court's scholars and artists went to Rome or the allied kingdoms. Yet analysis of the intellectual side of court life in Alexandria is difficult because not all the scholars who were studying in the city were attached to royalty, whereas in other places the circle around the monarch might be the only intellectual presence in a kingdom. But in Alexandria, especially in the latter days of Ptolemaic rule, one could work at the Mouseion and Library and have little if any contact with the royal family. Intellectual life continued in Alexandria after 30 B.C. without royal support: the facilities, not the court, drew scholars. Nevertheless what follows is an attempt to outline the scholarly life of Alexandria in the middle of the first century B.C., with the understanding that not all those mentioned may have benefited directly from royal patronage.

Cleopatra inherited the scholarly environment of her father. Among those associated with Ptolemy XII who survived into her era are the physician Chrysermos and his student Apollonios Mys; the philosophers Eudoros, Ariston, and Areios Didymos; and the royal tutors, the rhetorician Philostratos (for Cleopatra) and Theodotos of Chios (for Ptolemy XIII). All these except Theodotos and perhaps Chrysermos continued to be active into the Augustan period. As was the case under Ptolemy XII, medicine seems to have been the outstanding discipline of the era, with the queen herself part of its written output. The prominence of medicine in Alexandria at this time seems largely ascribable to the work of Herakleides of Taras, who was a strong proponent of medical empiricism (opposition to speculation and theory) and wrote a treatise on that topic and a significant work on pharmacology. His works survive in nearly a hundred fragments, quoted largely by Galen and Athenaios.[1] One of his students was a certain Antiochis, probably from Tlos in Asia Minor, one of the most prominent female physicians known from antiquity.[2]

The younger generation included Philotas of Amphissa, the physician of Antonius's son Antyllus in the 30s B.C., who often ate at his house. He survived the convulsions of the collapse of the reign, which included the death of his patient, eventually moving to Delphi and living until at least A.D. 15. In Delphi he became a friend of Plutarch's grandfather Lamprias, supplying him with details, especially culinary, about the world of Cleopatra that Plutarch would eventually use in his biography of Antonius.[3] Most of the other physicians at the court are obscure.[4] The name Sostratos occurs in several contexts as a gynecologist, surgeon, pharmacologist, and zoologist, although all these may not be the same person.[5] He may have written on the pharmacological aspects of the queen's death. Another physician and medical writer was a certain Dioskourides Phakas ("Warted," presumably referring to his physical appearance), a native of Alexandria, who wrote more than 20 works, mostly on medicine,[6] probably the same Dioskourides who had been an ambassador to Rome for Ptolemy XII and was in the service of Ptolemy XIII when Caesar arrived in Alexandria in late 48 B.C., another example of a house intellectual being used as a diplomat. Although he was almost killed in the engagements of that time, he survived and was still active in the 30s B.C. There were also Olympos, Cleopatra's personal physician, some of whose remedies survive, and a physician named Glaukos, only known because he was a friend of Dellius's.[7]

Philosophy was represented not only by Eudoros, Ariston, and Areios Didymos, but also by Ainesidemos of Knossos, a member of the Academy who rebelled against its views and founded a new Sceptic school in Alexandria in the 40s B.C., reestablishing one that had died out in the third century B.C. His major treatise—*Pyrrhoneian Arguments*, outlining the ideas of the founder of Scepticism, Pyrrhon—was dedicated to L. Aelius Tubero, probably the friend and relative of Cicero, demonstrative of the influence of Alexandrian philosophy in late Republican Rome.[8]

There was also an emphasis on philology and its associated subjects such as grammar and lexicography. The most important scholar in this field was Didymos of Alexandria, known as "Chalkenteros" ("Brazen Innards") because of the fortitude and industriousness that allowed him to be such a prolific scholar.[9] He was said to have written nearly 4,000 books on many disciplines, including Homeric scholarship, lexicography, medical language, oratory, and grammar. He compiled commentaries on Archaic and Classical authors. In many ways he was more a collector of past scholarship than an original thinker, and his work was widely used in later times, with many fragments surviving. The extant biographical summary of his career records that he lived "from the era of Antonius and Cicero to that of Augustus," not mentioning Cleopatra specifically, but curiously his scholarship was compared to that of her son-in-law Juba II.

Other philologists of the era were Tryphon, a follower or student of Didymos, also a prolific grammarian and lexicographer,[10] and Theon, whose noteworthy contribution was to write the first commentaries on Hellenistic poets, such as Kallimachos and Theokritos, the basis of the extant later scholia on these authors.[11] Theon's father, Artemidoros, was from Tarsos and a student of Aristophanes of Byzantion, himself a student of the great polymath Eratosthenes, who was Librarian in the third century B.C., thus providing an intriguing unbroken chain of scholarship over 200 years from the greatest days of Alexandria to the end of the Ptolemaic dynasty and (through Theon's students) well into the Roman period. Antonius, when he had his headquarters in Tarsos in 41 B.C., may have given support to the family. Students of both Tryphon and Theon were active in Julio-Claudian Rome: Theon was the teacher of Apion, the nemesis of Josephus, immortalized in the latter's polemic *Against Apion*.[12]

Research in the sciences seems to have been minimal. There are only hints of contemporary activities in these areas, since after the expulsions by Ptolemy VIII, the scientific disciplines never recovered in Alexandria, and Rhodes, which supported both Hipparchos and Poseidonios, became the new center. Eudoros and Ariston, polymathic products of the school of Antiochos of Askalon, are remembered as geographers only because of their plagiarism dispute, which Strabo investigated but could not resolve.[13] Whether Strabo himself was part of the environment of Cleopatra is uncertain: he was in Alexandria in the 20s B.C. on the staff of the prefect Aelius Gallus, but it seems unlikely that Gallus's brief tenure of office can support Strabo's explicit statement, "I lived in Alexandria a long time."[14] Knowledge of Strabo's career is spotty, yet his lengthy *Geography*, with its awareness of numerous obscure sources, is clearly a product of many hours in the Alexandria Library. Nevertheless one cannot say if this was before or after his time with Gallus, and in 29 B.C., at least, he was in Greece. His scholarly career began in the early 30s B.C., but whether he came to Alexandria while Cleopatra was still in power remains unknown, although his *Geography* has personal details about the queen undocumented elsewhere.[15] Nevertheless, like the writings of his contemporary Didymos Chalkenteros, Strabo's work is typical of the exhaustive summarization of previous scholarship that marked the era of Cleopatra.

There is some evidence for astronomy and mathematics at the court of Cleopatra. Eudoros—perhaps the same as the geographer—excerpted the work of a certain Diodoros, which itself was a commentary on the astronomical poem of Aratos of Soloi of the third century B.C.,[16] another example of the highly derivative scholarship of the period. Also active in mathematics and astronomy, and at the court at least in 48–47 B.C., was Sosigenes, Caesar's advisor on his calendar reform.[17] The Roman calendar was two months out of phase, so that the winter solstice came in February, and Caesar not only inserted enough days into 46 B.C. to bring it into line but made other adjustments to keep future years more accurate. The necessary technical work was the effort of Sosigenes, with the calendar reform taking place just after Caesar's stay in Alexandria. He probably had Sosigenes in his entourage when he returned to Italy, and he implemented the reforms immediately thereafter. Although the notices of Sosigenes are predictably sparse, he was an astronomer of note, writing three treatises, one on the planet Mercury and perhaps one on his calendar theories. The lengthy passage in Lucan's epic, in which Caesar and the Egyptian priest Acoreus discuss the natural phenomena of Egypt, including astronomical matters, although fictitious and based on later sources, is an intriguing dramatization of the interchange that repeatedly took place between Roman officers and Eastern intellectuals.[18]

Literature is essentially totally unknown, except for the scant and dubious evidence of a four-line epigram attributed to Antipatros of

Thessalonike that mentions an amethyst cameo belonging to a Queen Cleopatra.[19] If the authorship is correct, and if it is about Cleopatra VII—both disputed facts, although there is no other possible queen—the epigram may be the only piece of poetry known from her court, yet none of the dozens of other poems by Antipatros indicates any connection with Egypt. Nevertheless his date as a contemporary of the queen is certain.[20]

Historiography is better documented. Since Nikolaos of Damascus, the tutor to the queen's children, was one of the major historians of the Augustan period, one suspects that he indulged in this talent while at the court. Sokrates of Rhodes wrote a history of the Roman civil wars that seems to have used sources from within the court and is more favorable toward Antonius than are Augustan accounts. His work seems to have been lost or suppressed during the Augustan period, not emerging until the late second century A.D.[21]

Little is known about the visual and performing arts, with only two names recorded. Artists tend to be invisible throughout antiquity, although there are occasional frustrating glimpses, such as the intimacy that Ptolemy VI had with the painter Demetrios (see p. 41). The visual arts are represented solely by the gem cutter Gnaios, whose signed portrait of Antonius is now in London. Eventually he ended up in the service of the daughter of Cleopatra and Antonius, Cleopatra Selene, at the Mauretanian court.[22]

At the court of Cleopatra VII there was also a certain M. Tigellius Hermogenes, a musician associated with the queen, Caesar, and Augustus.[23] The information is contradictory and obscure, but he may be the Sardinian musician whose death was reported by Horace,[24] although this person does not seem to have survived into the Augustan period. He may also be the one who had issues with Cicero in the summer of 45 B.C.[25] Horace's Tigellius seems to have been temperamental and showy as a musician and ostentatious in his personal life.

A final aspect of the cultural life of the court was the royal tutor. The position had been an important part of the Ptolemaic world since the earliest days, and the tutor was often the Librarian. The list of tutors comprises some of the most notable scholars who had been in Alexandria. The distinguished scientist Straton of Lampsakos, who succeeded Theophrastos as head of the Peripatetic school and was famous for his theories about the formation of the earth, was tutor to Ptolemy II. The polymath Eratosthenes of Cyrene—who invented the discipline of geography—was probably tutor to Ptolemy IV, and the

Homeric scholar Aristarchos of Samothrake held the same position for Ptolemy VIII, and probably his siblings.

Cleopatra VII's first child was born three and a half years into her reign; at its end her four children ranged in age from 7 to 17. Royal tutors would be a necessity, especially during the last decade of her rule. It is perhaps indicative of the era than three of the four known tutors have no apparent scholarly profile. Euphronios evidently had some diplomatic skills, because he was one of the negotiators with Octavian after Actium. Rhodon is remembered only for his involvement in the death of his pupil, Caesarion. There was also Theodoros, tutor of Antonius's son Antyllus, who betrayed his pupil.[26] Their total obscurity and quickness to join Octavian even if fatal to their charges indicates that they probably had little if any scholarly distinction, and it is unlikely that any of these tutors held the post of Librarian. But Cleopatra was fortunate to have at her court someone who would become one of the most significant scholars of the following era, Nikolaos of Damascus. He was probably near the beginning of his career, a student of the historian Timagenes of Alexandria, who had gone to Rome with Gabinius in 55 B.C. and became associated with Antonius. Nikolaos may have come to the court through Timagenes' recommendation. In later years, when service to Cleopatra and Antonius was not something that he would want on his résumé, he attempted to suppress this youthful indiscretion and almost succeeded.[27] After the collapse of Cleopatra's court, Nikolaos ended up at Herod's, serving as his ambassador to Rome and court chronicler. He also became an intimate of Augustus and shuttled back and forth between Judaea and Rome for more than a quarter of a century. He was involved in the succession struggles after Herod's death in 4 B.C. but then retired from politics. During his career he wrote an autobiography, an extant biography of Augustus, and a lengthy universal history, which survives in many fragments and was the primary source that Josephus used for the reign of Herod. Without Nikolaos, little would be known about that turbulent environment or about Cleopatra's involvement in it. Moreover, he almost certainly influenced his pupil Cleopatra Selene in her creation of a Ptolemaic government in exile at Mauretanian Caesarea: one would expect that the two continued in contact in Rome after 30 B.C. Although Nikolaos's interests were narrowly focused, and he came to be an apologist for Herod, he is the most extensive contemporary literary source for Cleopatra VII and the most probable candidate to have been her Librarian.

CHAPTER NINE

Downfall

(34—30 B.C.)

THE DONATIONS OF ALEXANDRIA were not well received in Rome, especially given the role of Cleopatra and her children in them, although oddly it eventually became so significant an event of the era that 20 years later, long after Cleopatra's death, Octavian—by now Augustus—felt compelled to envision his own counter-ceremony, the "Donations of Rome," known today through the scenes famously depicted on the Ara Pacis. It is even ironically possible that a grandson of Cleopatra participated in these events; descendants of Antonius certainly did.[1] For the time being, however, immediately after the Donations of Alexandria, messages went back and forth between the two capitals with charges and refutations, and the partisans of Octavian and Antonius argued in the Senate.[2] The animosity between the two triumvirs, going back to 44 B.C.—as long as they had known each other—centering largely on the issue of who was the true heir of Caesar, reached its peak. Antonius claimed that Octavian had acted illegally in deposing Lepidus and then had taken his troops and had not allowed Antonius to levy forces in Italy. He even offered to resign his offices, perhaps more a public relations gesture than an actual plan.[3] Octavian, whose case was somewhat weaker, charged that Antonius had no legal right to concern himself with Egyptian affairs, that his arrest of Artavasdes II of Armenia was unlawful, that he had illegally married Cleopatra (thus committing a personal insult against Octavian's family), and that it was wrong to claim that Caesarion—who, after all, was Octavian's cousin—was the legal heir of Caesar. This last item, that Cleopatra was the mother of the only known child of Julius Caesar, was in many ways the greatest danger to

Octavian.[4] Octavia continued to attempt to mediate between husband and brother, generally tilting toward the side of the former. But it was of course Cleopatra who was the unspoken target of the accusations. Whether or not she had married Antonius, this soon became assumed as fact and was a central cause for the animosity, for it directly affected Octavia and her brother. When Antonius began to place Cleopatra on his coinage (fig. 11e), this could easily be seen as proof of his intentions to turn Rome into a Hellenistic monarchy. At some point it became clear that it would all end in war.

For the time being it was merely a propaganda war,[5] which began in earnest in late 34 B.C. after the Donations. Although many of the charges are not to be believed or are exaggerations, they provide much of the familiar anecdotal information about the lives of Cleopatra and Antonius. Most of it is scurrilous and slanderous, and it was particularly directed toward the queen, although the other principals were hardly immune. These attacks and carefully laid rumors were the basis for the negative tradition about Cleopatra that found literary expression in the writers of the Augustan era and which has pervaded the popular view of the queen ever since. She was categorized along with Medea as a dangerous sorceress, seen as a drunken fornicator and a disgrace to the Ptolemaic dynasty whose only goal was to conquer Rome. She would be as destructive to civilization as Helen or indeed as the agents of vengeance, the Furies themselves, had been.[6] Horace's phrase, written shortly after her death, that Cleopatra was a "fatale monstrum," sums up popular prejudice against the queen—or what Octavian hoped would be such—invoking the creatures of mythology in suggesting that she was hardly human. She was said regularly to use monsters, magic, and witchcraft to achieve her ends, and was an infamous poisoner who almost tricked Antonius into drinking one of her concoctions.[7] Notoriously, it was also said that Cleopatra included in her official oaths a phrase stating that someday she would dispense justice on the Roman Capitol.[8] The extravagant lifestyle of the couple—Cleopatra allegedly sent love letters to Antonius on onyx or crystal tablets—was a constant cause for criticism, since Egyptian wealth, although avidly desired by Rome, was looked upon with suspicion.[9] The opulence and luxury of Cleopatra's court was thought to be unusual even within the standards of Hellenistic royalty, something that the austere Romans easily could seize upon. Her son-in-law Juba II later reported that she began calling her silver and gold table service simply "ceramics," demonstrating both her great wealth and her disdain for it, and that as the Romans became richer and more Hellenized, the Ptolemies remained far beyond their reach.[10] A "Cleopatran feast" remained a proverbial phrase even centuries later.[11] Lucan, in a detailed description, recounted the banquet that Cleopatra gave for Caesar in 48 B.C.[12] It is a world of gold table service, jeweled glassware, crystal water pitchers, exotic foods, flowers everywhere, and even the best Italian wine (Falernian) instead of the inferior Egyptian product. Although written a century after Cleopatra's death and based on the banquet Dido gave Aeneas, the account may reflect news coming to Rome in the late 30s B.C., suitably exaggerated for poetry. Vergil himself may have had these reports in mind.[13] Perhaps the most complete and concise polemic is that provided by Josephus in his *Against Apion*:[14] Cleopatra committed every kind of crime, killed her siblings, plundered tombs, corrupted Antonius but eventually deserted him, and even refused to provide famine relief to the Jewish community.

Generally Antonius was spared the worst, as he still had powerful friends in Rome, and his descendants would be prominent for a century after his death. If he was mentioned at all, it was to say that he had lost his judgment because of Cleopatra and had been a victim of witchcraft and magic or that he had become subordinated to a woman and her foreign ways, although it was also said he was even more extravagant than the queen, and it was considered ironic that in his younger days he had introduced a sumptuary law. Some thought that he had marshaled all the East—including places that he had had no contact with, such as Baktria and India—against Rome.[15] Yet Antonius's supporters could also create their own polemics, especially with explicit suggestions about Octavian's love life; in fact, sexual promiscuity was one of the most frequent charges on all sides.[16] Octavian was well prepared for such polemics: some years previously, at the time of the Perusine War, he had written an obscene poem about Antonius's relationship with Glaphyra and Fulvia's reaction.[17] Many of the slanders, especially the sexual ones, were made through the medium of graffiti that appeared in Rome. Even Antonius's legate Dellius, who was in trouble at the court because he criticized Cleopatra's taste in wine, was accused of writing obscene letters to her, which in fact may have been an epistolary piece of literature.[18]

Natural phenomena were also brought into play: the consistently low level of the Nile during these years was seen as a harbinger of disaster. Yet some of the propaganda took a higher road. As was common in times of difficulty, a Sibylline oracle conveniently appeared, stating that Cleopatra would repay Rome for its sins against her but that eventually peace would emanate from Asia and the queen would bring about reconciliation and a golden age,[19] based on the ideals that Alexander the Great had established long ago and that had pervaded Hellenistic thought.[20] The prophecy represents Eastern ideas about Cleopatra—outside the Roman worldview—and actually says less about her than the era, the same environment that produced other prophecies, Messianic thought in Judaea, Vergil's fourth *Eclogue*, and even the prophetic names that the queen used for her children. Since the days of Alexander the Great there had been a consistent idea that international unity should be the goal of humanity. This belief was credited to Alexander himself, and was a common political theory during much of the Hellenistic world.[21] Yet Cleopatra was perfectly willing to make use of such ideas.

Although most of the anecdotes from the propaganda war can be dismissed as slander, there are occasional insights into the activities of Cleopatra during this period, of note because there is little direct evidence of her between late 34 and early 32 B.C. Many of the familiar tales about palace life probably come from these years, largely from the account of L. Munatius Plancus, who had been governor of Syria, probably into 34 B.C., and then spent time in Alexandria as Antonius's secretary, probably the one who packaged the communiqués sent off to Rome. It was Plancus who reported on one of the best-known events of Cleopatra's career, her dissolving of a pearl in vinegar.[22] The queen, already known for the extravagance of her banquets, announced that she could spend two and a half million drachmas on a single dinner. She had prepared an ordinary banquet, probably expensive enough in its own right, and then took off one of her earrings and melted it in vinegar—perhaps a sleight-of-hand rather than the slow chemical process[23]—but Plancus prevented her from doing the same with the other earring, as the pair were the most expensive pearls known and an ancient family inheritance. The surviving pearl was reset into earrings that came to adorn the statue of Venus in the Pantheon in Rome. Although this has remained one of the more familiar episodes of the queen's life, it may be a created example of her excessive foreign extravagance, probably based on the similar tale of a certain Clodius[24] and his friend Metella that was in circulation in Rome at the time.[25] This story first appeared in Horace's *Satires*, perhaps evidence that, as one would expect, Cleopatra read contemporary Latin literature. Plancus also appeared at another party costumed as the water divinity Glaukos.[26] Eventually he felt that Antonius was not effective enough in refuting the charges originating in Rome and went over to Octavian's side. By summer 32 he was back the city, no doubt bringing with him numerous useful anecdotes about Cleopatra's court.

These tales of banquets reflect not only the Roman distaste for the extravagant lives of eastern royalty but also an increasing dislike of the involvement of a Roman magistrate in such happenings. Although entertaining, they are perhaps trivial. Some of the stories seem unimportant to the modern mind but reflect a contemporary perception (or at least Octavian's hope for such) of how much Antonius had debased himself, such as the report that he had massaged Cleopatra's feet in public, something only a slave should do. Perhaps more serious, and even true, were the constant charges of theft and sacrilege that surrounded the couple.[27] In most cases Antonius was the implementer but it was always said to be for the sake of Cleopatra. The most notorious was that he removed the library of Pergamon—all 200,000 of its volumes—to Alexandria and gave it to the queen.[28] The tale cannot be literally true, because the Pergamon library continued to flourish, and indeed Plutarch's language suggests that only copies were involved. If the story has any basis in fact, it may have reflected some attempt to restock the Alexandria Library after the fire of 47 B.C. But the perpetrator of the story eventually admitted that he had made it up. This was C. Calvisius Sabinus, consul of 39 B.C., a former Caesarian who in later years would be governor of Spain. He seems the source for many of the slanders against the couple, and he may have published a collection of them available to Plutarch.

A common and rather serious accusation against Antonius was art theft, with the Classical sculptor Myron seemingly a particular favorite. His Apollo was removed from Ephesos, as well as a Zeus, Athene, and Herakles from the Heraion on Samos. There was also a statue of Aias—the sculptor is not specified—from his temple-tomb at Rhoiteion (modern Baba Kale, just north of Troy). There were other unspecified cases of such acquisitions.[29] It was hardly unusual for Roman magistrates in the provinces to obtain art for their own purposes, but Antonius's crime was doing it for the sake of Cleopatra, and the stolen art was regularly returned after his death, although the Zeus from Samos was brought by Augustus to Rome.

Despite all these anecdotal incidents Cleopatra continued to devote her primary efforts to administering her kingdom. One of her official acts has achieved particular fame in recent years. In February 33 B.C. she approved an order granting certain tax exemptions to P. Canidius Crassus, who had been with Antonius for a decade and would be senior commander of the land forces at Actium. The relevant document is a papyrus recovered from mummy wrappings and first published in the year 2000.[30] Canidius was allowed to import 10,000 artabas of wheat and 5,000 amphoras of wine tax free, and the lands that he owned in Egypt were also exempt. What has excited interest is the subscript in a different hand: γινέσθωι ("make it happen"). There is little doubt that this is the writing of the queen herself, as there was a tradition in Ptolemaic Egypt of countersigning by the monarch, in part to avoid forgery of official documents.[31] This autograph of Cleopatra VII certainly is one of the more exciting discoveries of recent years: the only other known royal autographs from antiquity are of Ptolemy X and Theodosios II, both somewhat less interesting than the queen. The document also indicates the dichotomy that still existed at the very end of the Ptolemaic era between the rulers (and their Roman allies) and the ruled, where the former continued to obtain special privileges.

At the end of 33 B.C. the triumvirate expired. Needless to say it was not renewed. On 1 January 32 B.C., two Antonian loyalists entered into the consulship: C. Sosius, who had served Antonius in many positions and as governor of Syria had installed Herod as king in 37 B.C., and Cn. Domitius Ahenobarbus, who had been involved in the murder of Caesar but had exonerated himself and had been on the Parthian expedition. On his first day in office (1 February),[32] Sosius spoke out vehemently against Octavian and attempted to introduce legislation against him. Some days later Octavian entered the Senate with a guard and made counter-accusations against the two consuls. Properly intimidated by the armed presence, the next day they and Antonius's supporters in the Senate left the city secretly and joined him in the East, where he constituted a Senate of his own.[33] This was the final break between Antonius and Octavian, and the former's complete renunciation of any role in Italian affairs. For the time being, at least, the end of the triumvirate made little difference in Antonius's legal situation—he still had his military command and his status as a former consul and in fact refused to resign the triumviral post—but he now was in a position of greater dependence than ever on Cleopatra. The couple went to Ephesos early in 32 B.C. to collect a large naval force, with Cleopatra providing 200 (probably 140 transports and 60 warships) of the 800 ships and all the supplies.[34] The various allied kings were also summoned. Antonius seemed oblivious to the hints of a number of his senior officers that the queen was becoming a liability. Domitius Ahenobarbus, now with Antonius, was publicly insulting to Cleopatra and argued that she should play no role in the forthcoming military operations: having just left Rome, he knew that the propaganda war was effective.[35] Yet she was not totally without support on Antonius's staff. Canidius Crassus pointed out that not only was the queen essentially funding the war, but that she was in no way inferior in ability to the male allied kings and had ruled a major kingdom alone for a long time.[36] Antonius did attempt to persuade Cleopatra to return to Egypt, but she insisted on remaining. Although her primary interest was the defense of her kingdom, she was better positioned in Greece with her fleet to oppose any movement by Octavian toward Egypt. Yet her resoluteness resulted in the first defections from Antonius's side, not only Domitius Ahenobarbus but Munatius Plancus.

In the spring the couple moved on to Samos, where a great festival was held, and then went to Athens. This most venerable of Greek cities had long been favorable to the Ptolemies, especially Cleopatra, who may have lived there as a child. At least one member of her household was Athenian, whose mother had gone to Alexandria to nurse her in her final illness and then brought her remains back home.[37] When Cleopatra arrived in Athens in 32 B.C., she was honored by the city, although it was said this was extorted on her part because of her jealousy of similar attention paid to Octavia. Cleopatra may have been responsible for establishing a sanctuary of Isis at Teithras, modern Pikermi, east of Athens near the coast.[38] She also persuaded Antonius to send a formal notice of divorce to Octavia. This played directly into Octavian's hands, and Munatius Plancus, now back in Rome, suggested that he investigate Antonius's will. In violation of Roman religious and legal customs, Octavian seized it from the Vestal Virgins and found that it was a remarkably useful document, so much so that it has long thought to have been a forgery. Yet a forgery could easily have been exposed, especially by the scandalized Vestals, and Antonius himself acknowledged the seizure,[39] although Dio's report of this—in the speech Antonius was said to have given before Actium—may be a construct designed to elaborate on Octavian's acquisition of the document. In fact this would not be the only time that Octavian discovered convenient material in a temple, since some years later he alone was able to read a decayed ancient inscription in the Temple of Jupiter Feretius that happened to support his needs.[40] Forgery or not, Octavian held a highly selective public reading, pointing out that the will asserted that Caesarion was the heir of Caesar, that the Donations of Alexandria were perfectly legal, and especially that Antonius should be buried with Cleopatra in Egypt even if he were to die in Rome. It also suggested that Antonius was planning to transfer the capital of the Roman Republic to Alexandria: the same charge had been made against Caesar, perhaps representing a Roman's worst fear.[41] The reading had the desired effect, and war was promptly declared against Cleopatra.[42] Later in life Octavian, with some exaggeration, would claim that he had the support of "tota Italia" in this endeavor.[43]

Yet the vast amount of prejudice that had developed against Cleopatra was hardly legal grounds for war, although it did create a convenient body of public opinion that provided support for such an action.[44] As Octavian himself made clear,[45] it was Cleopatra's actions that were the cause for war; in other words, she had conducted herself in a manner improper for an allied monarch. The fact that Antonius had been a private citizen since the end of 33 B.C. (although still with a certain authority due, in the Roman fashion, to the cumulative weight of his career) weakened Cleopatra's position since he could no longer legally confirm her actions as an allied monarch. Presumably her foreign policy now needed approval of either the Senate or Octavian himself, something that she did not request. She was in the bind common to all allied monarchs of attempting to balance her (and her state's) needs with the legal requirements that Rome placed on her in return for its assistance of nearly 20 years.[46] In fact, everything Antonius had done for Cleopatra was perfectly legal (if impolitic) through his authority as triumvir— however much Octavian might disagree—and, as noted, Antonius did not always favor Cleopatra, especially in regard to Herod. Yet after the end of 33 B.C. Cleopatra was on her own, or, at least, had to reestablish her relationship with the Roman government (as Herod was famously to do after Actium). Even though Antonius had created certain arrangements through the Donations of Alexandria, legally Cleopatra should have these reconfirmed after he was out of power if she wanted them to remain in effect. Cyrene, for example, had been a Roman province until transferred into a kingdom ruled by her daughter. Armenia was, in theory, in possession of one of her sons, even though it had briefly been a Roman province. Because of this, and other arrangements under the Donations, Octavian could say that Cleopatra had given Roman territory to her children and desired further Roman possessions, a weak but technically legal argument.[47] More seriously, there was Cleopatra's continued military support of Antonius after he was a private citizen, something that he was no longer entitled to have. This was a true cause for a declaration of war. But Octavian was cautious enough not only to build patriotic support against Cleopatra but to go carefully through the most sacred and ancient formulas for war such as the throwing of a spear into (in this case, probably toward) enemy territory. He knew that he was on shaky ground, and it was really Antonius he was after, not Cleopatra. Yet despite the fact that she was the stated enemy, it was understood that the war was also against Antonius, who was deprived of his remaining authority, including a consulship scheduled for 31 B.C., although that year he issued coins with this title (see p. 183). This stripped him of any official position and had the effect of bringing into question the legality of any future action on the part of Antonius not only generally but in regard to Cleopatra.

With war inevitable, both sides put together extensive military forces. Octavian had 200 ships and 80,000 troops; Cleopatra and Antonius had 800 ships and more than 100,000 troops, as well as the support and resources of no fewer than 11 allied kings, including Herod, Malchos, Archelaos, Amyntas, and Polemon. Labor was levied in Central Greece for supply purposes: one of those drafted was Plutarch's great-grandfather Nikarchos.[48] Cleopatra probably used the officers and crews from the Red Sea—India fleet to man her ships,[49] but the couple's superior numbers were weakened by the fact that many of their ships did not have full crews, and the manpower that did exist—probably merchant rather than military—was not well trained, whereas the fleet of Octavian was in perfect shape with full complements. Antonius wanted to attack Octavian while his ships were in port at Tarentum and Brundisium, probably strategically wise, but Cleopatra dissuaded him because she did not believe that an attack on Italy was viable for the defense of Egypt, her primary and indeed sole concern. She persuaded Antonius to withdraw and to spend the winter in Patrai.

In the spring of 31 B.C. the couple moved their forces to the vicinity of the promontory of Aktion (more familiarly Actium), at the southern entrance to the Ambrakian Gulf in northwestern Greece. Again this reflected Cleopatra's primary strategy of defending Egypt because the position would allow any movement by Octavian down the Greek coast to be detected. At about the same time Octavian occupied Kerkyra

(Corfu) and coastal Epeiros, where he could disrupt his opponents' supply lines and demoralize their allies. Missing from the coalition this year were Herod and Malchos, whose long-standing animosity, allegedly stoked by Cleopatra, had ended in open warfare.[50] With great difficulty, Herod prevailed, despite the treachery of a certain Athenion, one of Cleopatra's generals seemingly in his service. Yet losing these kings' support was a serious strategic error for Cleopatra and Antonius. While the war was under way, a terrible earthquake devastated Judaea, and Herod, who may have realized that the couple were involved in a lost cause, had the excuse that he needed to stay away from Actium.

In and around Actium there were various engagements through the summer, which generally went badly for Cleopatra and Antonius. Octavian had spies in their camp, and defections became commonplace, including the long-loyal Dellius. Amyntas of Galatia and Deiotaros of Paphlagonia were the first allied kings to change sides.[51] Antonius

FIGURE 9. Aerial view of Actium, looking south. The promontory of Actium is to the right of the far end of the runway; Cleopatra's fleet was stationed just offshore. The main battle took place at a site visible in the upper right of the photograph. Courtesy of William M. Murray.

himself was almost captured. Cleopatra began to fear for the security of Egypt and suggested that she and Antonius leave some forces in place but return home with most of their troops. The usual ominous portents were reported. Milk and blood dripped from beeswax, and swallows had built their nests on her flagship, a particularly bad omen, yet probably an after-the-fact explanation to explain her actions in the battle, which seemed enigmatic to the Romans.[52] In fact, the swallow, a bird associated with Isis, was probably part of the decoration of the ship, yet it was eagerly interpreted by the Romans, always interested in bird omens, as a portent of disaster. But Cleopatra was not alone in looking for a way to avoid battle. Others suggested abandoning the naval operation and sending her away, and then withdrawing into the interior of Greece to fight on land. This did not meet with her favor, as it would have meant yielding the sea to Octavian and opening the way to Egypt, and thus she pressed for a naval engagement. The Battle of Actium was fought on 2 September 31 B.C.

The Battle of Actium has become a mythic event in world history, seen by the victors—and their extremely literate supporters—as the ultimate triumph of civilization over barbarism. Although perhaps not the great turning point that it has been made out to be, nevertheless it brought to an end whatever plans Cleopatra and Antonius had for the future.[53] The outcome was hardly ever in doubt: Octavian's better-trained forces and his spies made his victory almost certain. When the naval forces engaged, Cleopatra was in charge of 60 ships at the mouth of the Ambrakian Gulf just west of the peninsula of Actium and to the rear of the main forces, not the best place to achieve her primary goal of defending Egypt and perhaps an attempt by Antonius's officers to marginalize her. Her flagship was the *Antonias*, one of the few ships' names known from the Hellenistic period, which followed a contemporary pattern of names based on the powerful personalities of the era.[54]Antonius had given orders that the ships would engage with their sails on board—often not carried in battle because of their weight—allegedly better to pursue the enemy but perhaps also to prepare for flight.[55] Thus Cleopatra was capable of sudden swift movement, and in the middle of the battle, when the wind was favorable, she moved her ships through the zone of fighting, much to everyone's surprise, and headed for the Peloponnesos. When Antonius saw this happening he went after her and boarded her ship, easily recognized by its purple sails (she had had also used them at Tarsos).[56]A story circulated in the following months that he was forced to do this because his flagship had become immobilized by a fish known as the *echeneïs*—the "ship-detainer"—which could become entangled in the rudder cables.[57] Yet this is probably a mere excuse, although one with historic precedents.[58] Cleopatra's ships were pursued by a detachment from Octavian's forces, which captured two vessels before returning to the main battle. But the queen and Antonius escaped and three days later went into port at Tainaron at the southern end of the Peloponnesos. Although the literary tradition established by Octavian and his supporters saw these events as treachery on Cleopatra's part and love-struck stupidity on Antonius's, it is more probable that Cleopatra realized that she was in no position to defend Egypt—a failure to understand her essential needs was a constant misjudgment by the Romans—and that Antonius needed to learn what Cleopatra was doing and so boarded her ship and found himself on his way south. Yet all during the journey from Actium to Tainaron—three days—he sat alone in the prow, avoiding the queen, until at Tainaron her ladies-in-waiting Eiras and Charmion persuaded him to talk to her.[59] This is the first definitive evidence that Antonius was being overtaken by serious depression, a condition that would remain with him for the rest of his life.

The Battle of Actium continued for some time after the couple's departure, but massive defections, first by the senior officers and then by large numbers of the men themselves, decided the matter by the morning of 3 September. Octavian promptly established himself in Athens, presumably desirous of neutralizing historic Ptolemaic support there—a witness to his arrival was Plutarch's great-grandfather Nikarchos—and quickly took possession of the Greek mainland. The allied kings hastily repudiated Antonius.

From Tainaron the couple crossed to Egypt, landing at Paraitonion (modern Marsa Matruh in the western desert). Here they separated. First reports from Actium indicated that the battle was still undecided, especially on land, so Antonius wanted to go to Cyrene, perhaps because there were four legions that, oddly, were still available there and that he might mobilize to maintain a force nearer Egypt.[60] Meanwhile Cleopatra was more anxious than ever to return to Alexandria, especially fearing public reaction if news of the battle were to beat her home. She sailed into the harbor at Alexandria as if celebrating a victory and began to make plans for further operations. It was said that she killed many wealthy citizens, confiscated their holdings, and robbed temple treasures in an attempt to raise as much funding as possible. This desperate action is seemingly at odds with the reported vast sums on board the ships at Actium,[61] repeated references to her treasure in the last days of her life, and the large amounts of money that Octavian obtained after her death through gifts or outright confiscation.[62] It is difficult to determine what her financial situation was at the end of her life. A comment by Athenaios that Ptolemy XII had used up all the wealth of the Ptolemies has been used to suggest that Cleopatra was virtually bankrupt.[63] But the statement may be simply a slander against her father. Yet it does seem that the queen never gained total control of the poor financial situation that she had inherited, and her recent lavish military expenditures would have aggravated the situation. But it may merely be relative, as poverty in Egypt was wealth anywhere else. Or it may be that the executions were more to eliminate political rebellion than to gain funds, or even fabricated Augustan propaganda that made its way into the later historical tradition.[64] Cleopatra also looked for new allies and supposedly executed Artavasdes II of Armenia, still a hostage at the court, and sent his head to his rival, the king of Media Atropatene, also named Artavasdes, in the hopes of support from that region. How true these tales are cannot be determined.

Meanwhile Antonius had found no help in Cyrene. The governor, his appointee L. Pinarius Scarpus, had received information from Actium before Antonius's messengers arrived. He killed them and refused to receive Antonius, and delivered the four legions to Octavian. Antonius had to be prevented from suicide and was brought to Alexandria by his staff. He withdrew from society and built himself a beach cottage, perhaps on the island of Pharos, which he named the Timoneion in honor of the famous misanthrope Timon of Athens, and lived in isolation, receiving ever more depressing reports.[65] The worst news was the defection of Herod the Great, who, despite his absence from the battle, had continued to advise Antonius after Actium, suggesting that the only way to save himself was to eliminate Cleopatra.[66] Herod knew that he was in great danger, as next to the queen he was Antonius's most powerful ally. He went to Rhodes, where Octavian had moved from Athens, and presented himself in a speech that remains a masterpiece of rhetoric. He admitted his devotion to Antonius and was candid in noting that had he not been otherwise engaged he would have been at Actium on Antonius's side, since Herod was a man who stressed loyalty as a primary virtue. But now he was prepared to resign his kingship.

Octavian, who needed Herod as much as Antonius had and respected his loyalty, refused the offer and confirmed his position and territory. Since Octavian had already placed his own man in charge of Syria, Q. Didius, this meant that Cleopatra and Antonius had no ally left between Greece and Egypt.

In the last year of their lives, Cleopatra emerged as by far the stronger of the pair.[67] Antonius was suicidal and withdrawn much of the time and increasingly irrelevant to the course of events, although paradoxically he was an obstacle to any resolution of the differences between Cleopatra and Octavian. The queen took command of the situation and was always at the forefront of efforts to find a solution that would save her kingdom, even if she herself were dispensable. Her first attempt in this direction, in the late summer of 31 B.C., was to clear the way for her children to rule by leaving Egypt permanently, a recognition that she was the focus of Roman hostility.[68] She also realized that Antonius was a liability and began to disassociate herself from him. If all had gone as it should, Antonius would have returned from Cyrene to find her gone, for she had engineered an elaborate plan to hand over her throne to Caesarion and to drag her fleet from the Mediterranean across the isthmus and then to relaunch it on the Red Sea (or, more plausibly, to build a new fleet at her naval base of Kleopatris, modern Suez), accompanied by troops and money, and to begin a life elsewhere, perhaps even in India. Her need for new ships on the Red Sea, where there should have been an extensive fleet for the India trade, demonstrates that those vessels had been put to use at Actium. Yet she had miscalculated her proximity to the Nabataean coast and the feelings of Malchos, who had lost heavily in the war with Herod that Cleopatra was said to have instigated, and who still was offended at having been forced to give up his coastal territory in 37 B.C. Malchos, persuaded by Didius, burned her fleet, and the queen realized that her only remaining option was to stay in Egypt and negotiate with Octavian.

Eventually Antonius gave up his misanthropic life and returned to the palace.[69] To raise morale among the Egyptians, Cleopatra enrolled Caesarion among the ephebi—young men of military age—and Antonius did the same with Antyllus, his and Fulvia's son who had been living in Alexandria. This gave the Egyptians an alternative, as it is clear that Cleopatra was preparing for her son to take over the kingdom. A stele from Koptos, now in the British Museum, dated 21 September 31 B.C.— nineteen days after the Battle of Actium—prominently shows Caesarion

("Ptolemy called Caesar"); the inscription is a contract between linen manufacturers and religious officials.[70] Significantly, although Cleopatra is mentioned in the text it is only to provide the date. Caesarion, on the other hand, appears twice on the relief. Whatever the dynamics were in the weeks after Actium, Caesarion was being groomed to be sole ruler without his mother. These events were an excuse for a series of parties, in which the Inimitable Livers were dissolved and replaced with the Synapothanoumenoi, "Those Who Die Together," perhaps the title of a comedy.[71] It was said that Cleopatra was collecting a variety of poisons: Greek women had long known the Egyptian ability in such matters.[72] There is a lengthy tradition that the queen tested the poisons on condemned prisoners and even her servants,[73] all of which is unlikely but played into Roman distaste of Egyptian medical practices and the narrow line between poisoning and curing. Yet the couple were also continuing to seek possible refuges, with the lower Red Sea still a possibility as well as Gaul or Spain, the latter having a long history of harboring Romans who were at odds with the central government and which was incidentally a great source of wealth.

Cleopatra and Antonius also began to communicate with Octavian, still on Rhodes. They sent Euphronios, one of the children's tutors, to ask on behalf of Cleopatra that Egypt be handed over to the children and for Antonius that he be allowed to live in Egypt or Athens as a private citizen. Cleopatra also opened secret negotiations with Octavian and sent him a golden scepter, crown, and throne, a symbolic gesture indicating that she was willing to reconcile herself with the new regime as its friendly and allied queen, much as Herod had done a few weeks previously. She also promised large sums of money. Antonius sent to Octavian a certain Publius Turullius, one of the last surviving assassins of Caesar, who was living in Alexandria but who had cut down the sacred grove of Asklepios on Kos for ship timbers before Actium. Octavian had him executed at the spot of his sacrilege but did not reply to Antonius.[74] Antonius then sent his son Antyllus with a vast amount of money, which Octavian kept, but he returned Antyllus, again with no message. Although the sources are not clear as to the number of embassies, and on what occasions the couple acted together or separately, communications from Cleopatra regularly received a reply, whereas those from Antonius were ignored. Octavian began to worry that the pair would either escape or even withstand him, and, worse, that they might destroy their wealth in the process, something that he desperately needed to pay his troops. Cleopatra was also threatening to immolate herself and her treasure in a tomb that she was building in the palace grounds. Thus Octavian sent a trusted freedman, Thyrsos, to the queen to negotiate in person. His message was that she should eliminate Antonius. Exactly what she would receive in return is not obvious: her life, certainly, but whether she would retain her wealth or her kingdom is by no means clear. But Thyrsos spent so much time in private with the queen that Antonius became suspicious—he may have had some hint that he was becoming dispensable—and had him flogged and returned to Octavian with no agreement.

These endless negotiations, which seem to have lasted several months, essentially to the end of 31 B.C., are remarkable because they went nowhere. At the heart of the matter, as always, was Cleopatra's obsessive need to save her kingdom, even without her. Although she obviously entertained the idea of disposing of Antonius, this was a difficult choice that she probably kept postponing. There were many precedents for those on the losing side of a Roman civil struggle to go into exile or carefully guarded retirement—Lepidus being the most recent example—but Octavian obviously wanted Antonius eliminated. Moreover, should Cleopatra give up her throne, Caesarion was not acceptable to his cousin because of the conflict over who was the true heir of Caesar—something that may not have been obvious to the couple at this time—and the younger children were not old enough to rule, although there is no evidence that the queen ever suggested that her successor should be anyone but Caesarion. It is also probable that the idea of going into exile with Antonius was not particularly interesting to Cleopatra. Her identity was totally as queen, and her home was Egypt, whereas Antonius had held a variety of offices in the Roman Republic and had spent much of his career moving throughout the Mediterranean world. Cleopatra might be prepared to go into a well-funded exile if her son became king of Egypt, but not necessarily with Antonius.

By the end of 31 B.C. Octavian was receiving messages from his people in Italy that events there needed his attention. With the Egyptian negotiations going nowhere, he went to Brundisium for a month,[75] but returned to Greece early in 30 B.C. prepared to seek a military solution to the Egyptian matter. In the spring he began to move his forces south. At Phoenician Ptolemais he was met by Herod,[76] who lavishly entertained and lodged him, reviewed his troops, and supplied the army, especially providing abundant wine and water, with a personal gift of 2,000 talents to Octavian. The force then moved down the coast to the Egyptian frontier at Pelousion, which fell remarkably quickly. Its commander, who probably died in the engagement, was a certain Seleukos, the last known officer of the vaunted Ptolemaic army that had dominated the eastern Mediterranean for much of the last 275 years.[77] It was said that Cleopatra gave orders not to defend Pelousion but that Antonius put Seleukos's family to death, a fine example of the miscommunication and differing strategies of the couple's last weeks. Octavian had sent L. Cornelius Gallus to Cyrene, who took the four legions that Antonius had failed to acquire and marched east to Paraitonion. Antonius went to meet Gallus's force but was repulsed. Octavian moved toward Alexandria, and Antonius, returning quickly, engaged him near the hippodrome and won a victory over the unrested troops. The next morning, 1 August 30 B.C., Antonius sent the fleet out, which promptly deserted to Octavian; shortly afterward the cavalry did the same, and with this the famed Ptolemaic military machine came to an end. Antonius believed that both defections were the work of Cleopatra. The queen hid herself in her tomb with Eiras and Charmion, and she sent a message to Antonius that she was dead. Cleopatra knew that he had threatened suicide at least twice previously, and her note was probably meant to plant the idea again in his mind. He responded as expected, stabbing himself in the stomach. Yet with the ironies typical of his career his attendant at his suicide was a slave named Eros, and the event soon degenerated from heroism to pathos. Plutarch used imaginative language to point out that his method would not have produced a quick death.[78] In contrast to Cleopatra's search for a painless end, he had chosen a particularly violent one. The report of his attempted suicide spread quickly through the palace and soon reached Cleopatra, who gave orders that Antonius be brought to her. She was at a window in the upper story of the tomb, and, in a touching scene, another example of Plutarch's narrative depending on an eyewitness account, the three women took construction cables and struggled to raise the bleeding Antonius into the tomb while a crowd watched. He survived only a short while. In his last mistake, he told Cleopatra to trust only a certain C. Proculeius[79] among the members of Octavian's entourage, and while he was dying he gave his own eulogy, considering himself a fortunate man because he had won fame and power and had died honorably, a Roman defeated by a Roman. He was 53 years of age. Although Cleopatra seemed genuinely distraught, it is clear that she had manipulated events in such a way as to make his death inevitable, provoking his known suicidal tendencies. His death expanded her own options.[80]

Octavian, camped near the hippodrome, quickly learned what had happened and was quite upset at the death of his former colleague and brother-in-law. He too realized that this significantly changed the dynamics of the situation. But he was in an awkward position. Leaving Cleopatra alive without her kingdom seemed the obvious choice, both to gain access to the treasure and because he had a use for her in his upcoming triumph. Yet she could become a focus of resistance to the new regime that Octavian would now be able to establish, since Antonius was dead. Cleopatra had sources of power that Octavian did not: she was the mother of Julius Caesar's only known child, a major religious figure, and the living representative of the two longest surviving Greek dynasties. She was also the mother of three of Antonius's children, although the full significance of this might not as yet have been realized. Eliminating her might also create serious instability in Egypt, regardless of whether it came under Roman control, and make her orphaned children martyrs. For the moment, however, it was most important that Octavian not let events slip away from him, and thus he sent Proculeius to the queen, who reconnoitered the situation, and then, returning with Cornelius Gallus, betrayed the trust that Antonius had placed in him and gained entry to the tomb by means of a ladder, taking possession of it. They prevented an attempt at suicide and removed anything by which Cleopatra could either burn the treasures in the tomb or kill herself. Despite requests from Antonius's staff, and perhaps even from Octavia,[81] for his body, Cleopatra was allowed to embalm it—if the report is literally true it hints at an otherwise unknown talent of the queen's—and bury it in her tomb. She then moved back into the palace.

Octavian had entered into the city proper and addressed the people in the gymnasium, making a speech of reconciliation, and took up quarters of his own in or near the palace. Cleopatra now attempted to starve herself to death, but Octavian seized the three younger children as hostages, and thus the queen requested an interview. Her physician, Olympos, wrote an report of her last days,[82] which is probably more honest and believable than the romantic versions that developed later, and in fact medical terminology pervades Plutarch's account at this point. When Cleopatra received Octavian she was poorly dressed and showed the strains of the last few days, but she still exuded the charm and poise for which she was famous. They debated about her culpability, and she blamed Antonius for everything. She provided an accounting of her wealth and offered gifts to Octavia and Livia in the hope that they would intercede on her behalf. She may also have shown Octavian some of her letters and memorabilia from Caesar, perhaps an attempt to enhance her status by stressing her relationship with him, as Octavian himself had done. And she explicitly told Octavian, "I will not be led in a triumph," a rare case where her actual spoken words survive.[83] Despite her physical state, her rhetorical abilities were unaffected, and Octavian was totally seduced, eventually unable to look her in the eye. He promised that she would survive, but he said nothing about her kingdom. Yet she soon began to suspect that she was being kept alive only for the triumph, something that would be a total humiliation, for she would not have forgotten the fate of her sister Arsinoë and had no intention of being the second daughter of Ptolemy XII to appear in a Roman triumph. If she had witnessed her sister in Caesar's triumph of 46 B.C.—by no means certain—this would only have hardened her position. When she learned from a spy that in three days she and the children would be sent to Rome, she moved quickly.

She asked permission to visit Antonius's grave and made suitable libations. Plutarch's lament by the queen at this point owes more to tragedy than history and does not appear in any other source. It is not obvious whether she returned to the palace or whether the following events occurred at the tomb.[84] She bathed and had an elaborate meal, including especially fine figs that a countryman had just brought in a basket, which Cleopatra's guards had been encouraged to help themselves to. After the meal she sent a message to Octavian and locked herself away with Eiras and Charmion. When Octavian received the message, in which she requested to be buried with Antonius, he realized what was happening and quickly sent messengers to the queen, who broke open the door and found her dead, her body carefully laid out, with full royal regalia, and Eiras and Charmion near death. Shortly thereafter Octavian himself arrived, and although exceedingly angry at the turn of events, ordered that she be buried in royal fashion in her tomb next to Antonius. Eiras and Charmion also received proper interment. A bizarre tale reported by Theophilos, Antonius's agent in Corinth, that Octavia wanted Cleopatra's body sent to Rome, is highly improbable and may be an error for Antonius's body, but suggests that unknown alternatives were considered.[85] Although the negative tradition about Cleopatra came to dominate the literature of the Augustan period, some saw her suicide as an act of supreme courage. It was 10 August 30 B.C., and she was 39 years of age.[86]

Olympos's account of these events makes no mention of what became the most famous aspect of Cleopatra's death, the asp, or Egyptian cobra, and in fact gives no cause of death. Plutarch discussed the asp only afterward, when it seems that he was no longer following Olympos's report, although the matter is introduced in such a way that Plutarch expected the reader to know about it. Yet the discussion is full of reservations and alternative versions, not only about the asp itself but the manner of death, suggesting poison in some hollow implement, a more reasonable but less romantic method. The word Plutarch used for the implement, κνηστίς (*knestis*), is rare—an indication that it might be diction from an accurate version of the queen's death—and has the connotation of something scratching.[87] Dio's word is βελόνη (*belone*), a needle, which to some extent confirms Plutarch's account.[88] Dio further noted that the only marks on her body were pricks, also suggesting a needle or pin. It is not difficult to see these marks evolving into asp bites. It was also recorded that no one ever found the asp, but that Octavian and others saw minuscule puncture wounds on her arm,[89] something not incompatible with a pin or a needle. The curious basket of figs was seen as the way of introducing the asp, but without any rational explanation about its sudden appearance, and this account ignores the fact that the basket would have been very large (the Egyptian cobra is several feet in length) and that Cleopatra's guards would not likely have been asked to help themselves if an asp had been hidden in it. Yet it may be that the figs provided the nucleus for the asp story.

One must also consider the prevalence of snakes in Egyptian lore. Yet no source discusses the difficulty of bringing the asp into Cleopatra's quarters and getting it to perform exactly as wished. There would have needed to be expert snake handlers on hand. The Egyptian cobra can be fatal, but only if its venom is injected into a vital spot: otherwise the victim is more likely to make a full recovery.[90] But the effects of such a bite had been an object of study in Egypt since at least the New Kingdom, and Cleopatra allegedly did her homework on the topic. Yet all evidence is that it would be a complex method of death with little certainty of success. The earliest extant historical account, Strabo, who was in Alexandria at the time or very shortly thereafter, writing with no ideological bias, emphasized the divergent reports, suggesting either the asp or a poisonous ointment.[91] But a few years later the Augustan poets were writing about the asp—indeed the one asp has now become two—and offered no alternatives.[92] Clearly the tale quickly became more dramatic—as one might expect—with even a single asp no longer sufficient. Granted, poetry is not prone to alternative versions, but the story quickly left the area of history and entered into the world of drama, where it has remained to this day. Soon it influenced historians, although Velleius returned to the single asp.[93] Plutarch, as noted, did not even include the asp in his official account, adding it only as a secondary explanation. His contemporary Suetonius interjected a new element, that Octavian summoned the mysterious Psylloi—an African tribe expert in reviving those bitten by snakes—but Suetonius also expressed uncertainty about the entire asp tale.[94] Galen followed the snakebite story, but Dio was somewhat more nuanced, although mentioning both the asp and the Psylloi, but stressing poison as the probable means of death.[95]

Other issues may be relevant. Cleopatra was aware that Demetrios of Phaleron, advisor to Ptolemy I, had died from an asp bite. It was even said that she carried asps on her ships as weapons.[96] Almost certainly the asp story has metaphorical overtones, the ultimate victory of Egyptian ways over Rome.[97] Cleopatra herself may even have told Octavian in her suicide note—a carefully crafted document by a master communicator but mentioned only in passing by Plutarch—that she would commit suicide by an asp bite. Whatever happened, the asp story became canonical very quickly, either because Octavian believed it or because it was suitably dramatic. In his triumph the following year there was an image of Cleopatra with the asp clinging to her.[98] This is cited only by Plutarch (Dio described the effigy but did not mention the asp) and may be a misinterpretation of the snake-related royal regalia that the effigy would have worn, such as the uraeus and serpent jewelry, perhaps leading to a popular view that the queen had died by snakebite.[99] Within a decade the tale was enshrined in literature and eventually entered medical commentary.[100] But, as Plutarch wrote, "no one knows the truth."[101]

With the death of Cleopatra, the kingdom legally passed to Caesarion, who ruled for 18 days as Ptolemy XV.[102] Yet this reign was essentially a fiction created by Egyptian chronographers to close the gap between her death and official Roman control of Egypt (under the new pharoah, Octavian).[103] Caesarion in fact had been sent away, with ample funding, to Upper Egypt, perhaps with Ethiopia or India as an ultimate destination; making these arrangements for him was one of his mother's last actions. In the end, Cleopatra, who wanted the kingdom preserved but also wished to save her children, could not reconcile her roles as mother and queen.[104] While on the road Caesarion received a report he would be made king, something that Octavian deliberated at length about, but eventually he decided that it was impossible for competing heirs of Julius Caesar to survive, and Caesarion was killed as he returned to Alexandria. Octavian was advised on this by the court philosopher Areios Didymos, who astutely pointed out that there was room in the world for only one Caesar.[105] Antyllus, the son of Antonius and Fulvia, was also executed. A less famous, but significant, casualty was the 16-year-old priest of Ptah, Petubastes IV, who died on 31 July. He was a cousin of Cleopatra's, and his death conveniently removed the most prominent Egyptian claimant to the throne.[106] On 29 August 30 B.C., the Egyptian New Year, Ptolemaic rule came to an end.

Epilogue

OCTAVIAN ANNEXED EGYPT as a Roman province, dating the event from the day he had entered Alexandria, 1 August 30 B.C.[1] Cornelius Gallus was placed in charge. The Ptolemaic Empire was dismembered, its territories divided between Rome and the allied kings. The Egyptian revenue now available paid the Roman veterans of Actium, including those who had fought for Antonius.[2] His statues were destroyed, but Cleopatra's were allowed to stand, for to remove them would have unwise religious overtones, and the 2,000 talents that Octavian received from a member of her court ensured their survival.[3] A project to build a major temple to the queen was still under discussion more than 30 years after her death, but seems to have come to nothing. Yet her cult lasted until at least A.D. 373, when the scribe of the book of Isis at Philai, Petesenufe, reported that he "overlaid the figure of Cleopatra with gold."[4]

Three years later Octavian would become the emperor Augustus. He would survive until A.D. 14, restructuring Rome in such a way as to adopt many of the ideas of Hellenistic monarchy that Cleopatra had promoted, although perhaps as no surprise he banned Egyptian religious rites from within the city limits.[5] He traveled through most of the Roman world yet never returned to Egypt. But Egyptian artistic and architectural themes pervaded the new world that he built. The Temple of Apollo Palatinus, built next to the emperor's residence and dedicated on 9 October 28 B.C.,[6] was decorated with terracotta plaques showing Egyptian lotus blossoms and sculpture depicting the mythological tale of the daughters of Danaos and the sons of Aigyptos, an allegory almost banal in its obviousness.[7] Soon an obelisk from the sixth century B.C.

was brought to Rome and set up as a sundial in the Campus Martius, near Augustus's mausoleum—itself influenced by Egypt—where (after re-erection and restoration) it still stands today.[8] The most visible piece of Egyptian-inspired architecture extant in Rome is the well-known pyramidal tomb of C. Cestius, south of the Aventine, dated to around 15 B.C.[9] Paintings in Egyptian style pervaded Roman art of the next several generations.[10] Sphinxes became a common decorative element.[11] And Cleopatra herself still stood in Caesar's Temple of Venus Genetrix. To paraphrase Horace,[12] captured Egypt captivated Rome.

Octavia never remarried, and she lived in her home on the Palatine next to that of her brother. She survived until 11 B.C., participating in the Augustan building program and devoting herself to raising the large number of children that she had acquired, including all those of Antonius who survived.

Antonius's family would continue to be prominent. His granddaughter Pythodoris would rule in Pontos, and her descendants would be significant members of the royalty and aristocracy in Asia Minor until the third century A.D.[13] Antonius's children with Fulvia and Octavia would be among the leaders of the new regime in Rome for more than half a century after his death. The longest survivor was the younger Antonia, mother of the emperor Claudius, grandmother of Gaius Caligula, and great-grandmother of Nero; she died in A.D. 37. Antonius's last known descendant in Rome was Sergius Octavius Laenas, the consul of A.D. 131.[14]

Quintus Dellius retired and wrote his history of Antonius's campaigns. Like many of Antonius' companions, he never returned to the East. Domitius Ahenobarbus died just after he left Antonius, but a large number of those around the triumvir went on to distinguished careers in the new regime. Munatius Plancus was active politically for many years, proposing the name "Augustus" for Octavian in 27 B.C., holding office, and building the Temple of Saturn in Rome. Horace dedicated an ode to him.[15] Plancus led the diplomatic mission of 20 B.C. that brought lasting peace with the Parthians, and also found time to write his memoirs. When he died—the date is unknown—he was buried at Caieta (modern Gaeta), on the coast south of Rome, where his fine tomb—inspired by what he had seen in Egypt—with its eulogy that he wrote for himself are still visible. Nikolaos of Damascus ended up in the service of both Augustus and Herod and his descendants for at least the next quarter-century, and wrote his account of Herod's reign. Cleopatra's teacher Philostratos may also have gone to the court of Herod.[16]

The kings who supported Cleopatra and Antonius had mixed fates. Malchos and Herod could not both survive and bring any hope of stability to the southern Levant, and Malchos vanishes from the historical record shortly after the death of Cleopatra, either conveniently dying or being deposed by Octavian.[17] The future career of Herod is well known: he received back the territories that he had lost to Cleopatra, as well as her bodyguard to be his own, but continued to be a problematic Roman ally for the remaining quarter-century of his life. Ironically he was designated to fund and build Nikopolis, the victory city that Octavian established at Actium.[18] Archelaos of Kappadokia was the longest survivor of the network of allied kings, lasting until around A.D. 17, one of the last alive who had served with Cleopatra and Antonius. Artavasdes of Media Atropatene lived until 20 B.C., but in reduced circumstances, and he received back his daughter, Iotape, who eventually became the matriarch of the royal line of Kommagene.[19]

Three of Cleopatra's children survived to leave Alexandria. The twins Alexander Helios and Cleopatra Selene, about 11 years of age, and Ptolemy Philadelphos, about six, were sent to Rome to the care of Octavia.[20] The removal to Rome is the last time that Ptolemy Philadelphos appears in the historical record. Presumably he died in the winter of 30/29 B.C., as he did not feature in the triumph that Octavian celebrated in August of 29 B.C., commemorating his victories of the past few years. But the twins did participate, as the Sun and Moon, and there was also an effigy of their mother with the asp clinging to her.[21] This is the last mention of Alexander, and he must have died shortly thereafter since he was almost of the age when marriage plans would need to be considered, and there is no record of such efforts. There is no reason to believe that anything suspicious happened to either of the boys: child mortality was high in Rome, and the chilly damp winters would have been especially detrimental to children from Egypt.

Thus by the early 20s B.C. Cleopatra Selene was the only living descendant of Cleopatra VII. She too was close to marriageable age, and before long Octavia found a suitable candidate within her own household. For a number of years she had been raising another royal refugee, Juba II. His father, the Numidian king Juba I, had died in 46 B.C. supporting the Pompeian cause. As a result of this, Julius Caesar provincialized his kingdom, the territory south and west of Carthage, and brought Juba's infant son to Rome. Juba II was the descendant of a long line of distinguished Hellenized kings of Numidia. His ancestors included the famous Jugurtha, who had given Rome such difficulty in the latter second century B.C., and Jugurtha's grandfather Massinissa, the intimate of Ptolemy VIII. It was probably not lost on Octavia that the families of Juba II and Cleopatra Selene had already been in contact.

One of the issues facing Augustus in the early 20s B.C. was the matter of Mauretania, northwestern Africa (roughly modern Algeria and Morocco), whose last kings had died without heirs in the late 30s B.C. As unorganized territory with a substantial Italian mercantile population, it needed Roman attention. Augustus's solution was to place Juba II and Cleopatra Selene on the throne of a new allied kingdom. The royal couple were married, probably in 25 B.C., when Juba was about 22 and Cleopatra Selene 15, and sent off to Mauretania, where they turned the decayed Carthaginian trading city of Iol into a magnificent new capital that was named Caesarea (modern Cherchel in Algeria). It would become the most important city in northwest Africa.

Cleopatra Selene enlisted the remnants of her mother's circle and created her own entourage in Caesarea. She imported a vast amount of sculpture from Alexandria, probably including portraits of her mother and a member of the priestly family of Ptah—one of her cousins—and other examples of Egyptian art. Artists also came from Alexandria to Mauretania, including the gem-cutter Gnaios, who had worked for her father and would carve portraits of Diomedes, Herakles, and the queen herself.[22] Cleopatra Selene also brought the Greek language to the court, although it was located in a region far outside its historic area, and struck her coins in that language, some commemorating her mother.[23] The inevitable court circle of scholars was created, some of whom may have come from Alexandria. Juba II was a notable scholar himself, and Cleopatra Selene became an implementer of her husband's continued scholarly activities, assisting in providing the access to data from Alexandrian sources that allowed Juba to write his *Libyka*, completed by 2 B.C., the most comprehensive study of North Africa from antiquity.[24] Issues were considered that had long been at the center of Ptolemaic scholarship but demanded new analysis in the Roman world, such as the source of the Nile, elephants, and the limits and dimensions of Africa. Juba's next treatise was titled *On Arabia*, devoted to the territories farther east—Arabia was believed to begin at the east bank of the Nile—which itself emphasized a region connected to the Ptolemies. It is the major ancient source for the Arabian peninsula and its environs.[25] The well-placed connections of Cleopatra Selene were doubtless an important asset to his scholarship. Both treatises included details about Cleopatra VII not known elsewhere.

The only certain child of Cleopatra Selene and Juba was born sometime between 13 and 9 B.C.[26] Cleopatra Selene called the boy Ptolemy, making a dramatic statement about the contemporary role of the Mauretanian dynasty and her own heritage, the strongest evidence that she saw herself as the inheritor of the Ptolemaic world, her mother's legitimate heir, and thus the surviving Ptolemaic ruler. This would give her title not only to Egypt, but other territories such as Cyprus. Her father had given her the Cyrenaica, and thus she could believe that she ruled all North Africa except the small Roman territory around Carthage. Of course this ran counter to the Roman interpretation of contemporary politics, and there is no evidence that the queen sought to enforce her claims. The relationship of her kingdom with the Roman elite seems to have remained solid throughout her life. But her activities at Caesarea, creating a Ptolemaic court in exile, making Greek the official language, stocking the city with Ptolemaic art and culture, encouraging her husband to write on topics relevant to the Ptolemaic world, and naming her son Ptolemy, is impressive evidence of her thoughts on this matter. A second child, one Drusilla, is problematic, mentioned only by Tacitus as a granddaughter of Antonius and Cleopatra, which, granted, seems to provide no options other than Juba and Selene for parents. But it is possible that Drusilla was a daughter of Ptolemy of Mauretania.[27]

Cleopatra Selene essentially vanishes from the record with the birth of her son Ptolemy, a common fate for women. The only further documentation is a eulogy on her death, written by Krinagoras of Mytilene, which suggests that it occurred in 5 B.C.[28] Only 35 years of age, she was buried in the royal mausoleum that she and her husband had built, inspired by her mother's tomb and still visible today near Tipasa in Algeria, some 25 miles east of Caesarea.

Juba II lived 30 years more, to be succeeded in A.D. 23 or 24 by his son, Ptolemy.[29] The historical record has not been good to Ptolemy, perhaps inevitable given the distinction of his parents and grandparents, and even though Rome confirmed his kingship, his reign has reports of indecisiveness and overly luxuriant living. He ruled for nearly 20 years, although little is known until the very end of the reign, when he was summoned by his cousin the emperor Gaius Caligula, probably in A.D. 40.[30] Ptolemy had been issuing gold coins, something generally prohibited to the allied kings, and assuming other paraphernalia, such as triumphal regalia, reserved for the emperor. This may demonstrate Ptolemy's perception of his status—the last surviving Ptolemaic king—and a belief that he was far more distinguished than a mere Roman emperor. Whatever the original reason for the summons, Gaius had Ptolemy executed while at the imperial court. The Mauretanian population responded by revolting, and several years of Roman operations were necessary before the territory was stabilized and provincialized.[31]

The dynasty of Cleopatra VII ended with her grandson, who was truly the last of the Ptolemies, but over 200 years after his death, the famous queen of Palmyra, Zenobia, claimed to be related to Cleopatra and to possess some of her dinnerware and jewelry.[32] Zenobia called herself Cleopatra,[33] but she also said she was descended from Dido and Semiramis, so it may all be fictitious. Moreover, the source is the notoriously unreliable *Scriptores Historiae Augustae*, and the information may merely be a misunderstood conflation of previous data,[34] but it would be perfectly reasonable for the famous queen of Palmyra to feel some kinship with her Ptolemaic predecessor, demonstrating the power that Cleopatra VII still wielded 300 years after her reign.

Cleopatra transcended the collapse of her ambition. Not only was she the object of worship in Egypt until at least the fourth century A.D., she was an important role model for the formation of the Roman Empire. For obvious reasons she was hardly acknowledged in any positive sense, but her concept of monarchy and her idea of creating a powerful Greek-oriented state in the Eastern Mediterranean helped determine Roman policy for centuries. Her territory would be part of Rome—not separated from it—but Roman sensitivity to local practices, use of the Greek language, and the network of allied kings all were continuations of the queen's policies. Even in the city of Rome her influence could long be seen, in its architecture, Egyptian tastes, and even the enhanced role of the aristocratic women of the Empire. Cleopatra was a force not to be eliminated merely by death.

Appendices

1. Outline of Cleopatra's Life and Career

69 B.C.: Cleopatra is born near the beginning of the year to King Ptolemy XII of Egypt and an unknown mother, second of (eventually) five children of the king.

58 B.C.: Ptolemy XII flees Egypt; Cleopatra may have accompanied him at least as far as Athens, perhaps to Rome. Her elder sister, Berenike IV, usurps the kingdom.

55 B.C.: Ptolemy XII is restored by the Romans, including M. Antonius, whom Cleopatra meets for the first time. Berenike IV is executed by her father.

52 B.C.: Ptolemy XII writes a will naming his two older children, Cleopatra and Ptolemy XIII, as joint heirs.

51 B.C.: Ptolemy XII dies early in the year; his two older children assume power. Cleopatra travels to Hermonthis (22 March) to install the Buchis bull. She removes Ptolemy XIII from the joint rule (by 29 August). Sons of Bibulus are killed (perhaps early 50 B.C.). Brief alliance is forged between Cleopatra and Ptolemy XIV (perhaps 50 B.C.).

50 B.C.: Ptolemy XIII gains ascendancy with assistance of his father's ministers (by 27 October).

49 B.C.: Ptolemy XIII begins his regnal dating. Gnaeus Pompeius the Younger comes to Alexandria seeking help for his father; the joint monarchs send him ships and troops, but become increasingly estranged during the year. Cleopatra flees to the Thebaid (perhaps early 48 B.C.).

48 B.C.: Cleopatra leaves Egypt for Syria and raises an army. Julius Caesar defeats the elder Pompeius at Pharsalos (9 August). Pompeius arrives in Egypt and is killed by those around Ptolemy XIII. Caesar arrives thereafter and takes up residence in Alexandria. Cleopatra returns from Syria. Caesar forces a reconciliation between the monarchs, and makes the two younger siblings (Ptolemy XIV and Arsinoë IV) rulers of Cyprus. Ptolemy XIII's advisors start the Alexandrian War, which continues into spring. Arsinoë joins the side of Ptolemy XIII (perhaps early 47 B.C.).

47 B.C.: Alexandrian War settled early in year; Ptolemy XIII killed. Caesar makes Cleopatra and Ptolemy XIV joint monarchs, including rule of Cyprus. Arsinoë is removed from the succession and sent to Rome. Caesar remains in Egypt for several weeks and takes Nile cruise. In spring, Caesar leaves Alexandria and returns to Rome by way of Pontos. Cleopatra has her first child, Caesarion (23 June).

46 B.C.: Caesar celebrates his triumph, in which Arsinoë appears and is then sent into exile in Ephesos. Cleopatra and Ptolemy XIV go to Rome (late summer) and are made friendly and allied monarchs by Caesar. Statue of Cleopatra placed in Forum Julium. She returns to Alexandria by autumn.

44 B.C.: Cleopatra returns to Rome, probably to solidify her position after Caesar eliminates all opposition. Caesar assassinated (15 March). Cleopatra returns to Alexandria as Octavian arrives in Rome (April). She has Ptolemy XIV eliminated (summer).

43 B.C.: Triumvirate constituted. Cleopatra approached by Cassius for assistance and refuses, but she sends four legions left in Egypt by Caesar to Dolabella. Cleopatra sails in command of her fleet to Greece to assist triumvirs, but the fleet is damaged in a storm. Triumvirs grant official recognition of Caesarion.

42 B.C.: Battle of Philippi (autumn). Antonius remains in East to settle affairs.

41 B.C.: Antonius makes headquarters at Tarsos and summons Cleopatra (summer). He confirms her position, perhaps giving her parts of Kilikia, kills Arsinoë at her request, and joins her (late autumn) in Egypt for a vacation.

40 B.C.: Antonius leaves Egypt (spring) to settle problems in Syria and Rome. Cleopatra gives birth to Alexander Helios and Cleopatra Selene (late summer). Perusine War occurs in Italy. Antonius's wife, Fulvia, dies. Settlement between triumvirs at Brundisium (September). Antonius officially receives East as his province and marries Octavia. Herod visits Cleopatra (December).

37 B.C.: Triumvirate renewed; preparations made for Parthian War. Octavia remains in Italy as Antonius establishes headquarters at Antioch and sends for Cleopatra, who brings the three-year-old twins. Major territorial distributions to Cleopatra begin and continue into 34 B.C. Antonius's actions, exploited by Octavian, meet with public disfavor in Rome.

36 B.C.: Parthian expedition sets forth; Cleopatra travels with it as far as Zeugma. She makes a tour of new possessions and visits Herod. She bears her fourth child, Ptolemy Philadelphos (summer). Parthian expedition becomes a disaster; Antonius struggles back to coast and summons Cleopatra for aid, eventually returning to Alexandria with her.

35 B.C.: Plans made for a renewed Parthian expedition; Octavia announces her desire to join Antonius with logistical support but is stopped at Athens and returns to Rome. Antagonism between Antonius and Octavian intensifies. Antonius abandons campaigning for the year with no significant accomplishments.

34 B.C.: Parthian campaign is renewed once again but is limited to capturing the disloyal king of Armenia. Cleopatra and Antonius celebrate Parthian triumph in Alexandria and hold the ceremony known as Donations of Alexandria, codifying territorial adjustments and making their children rulers of various areas. This is met with general outrage in Rome, exploited by Octavian.

33 B.C.: Intense propaganda war develops between the two triumvirs. Triumvirate expires at end of year and is not renewed.

32 B.C.: Senators and consuls loyal to Antonius leave Rome and join him in East (February). Cleopatra and Antonius move to Ephesos and begin to constitute their forces, then move on to Samos and Athens, where she is honored by the city. Octavian seizes Antonius's will and, after a selective reading, declares war on Cleopatra. The couple summons the support of 11 allied kings. Cleopatra persuades Antonius not to attack Octavian in Italy, and the couple goes into winter quarters in Patrai.

31 B.C.: Cleopatra and Antonius move to vicinity of Actium to block any movement by Octavian toward Egypt. Forces engage on 2 September; Cleopatra withdraws fleet during battle. Antonius attempts unsuccessfully to gain support in Cyrene; Cleopatra returns to Egypt and prepares to hand over kingdom to Caesarion and flee into exile, but is thwarted by Malchos. Octavian moves to Rhodes, and negotiations begin, lasting into 30 B.C.

30 B.C.: With negotiations going nowhere, Octavian invades Egypt. After a number of military defeats and defections, Cleopatra tricks Antonius into suicide, and then kills herself (10 August). Caesarion becomes king, but in theory only, and he is promptly killed. The Ptolemaic kingdom comes to an end, and Egypt becomes a Roman province (29 August, backdated to 1 August).

2. Genealogy of the Later Ptolemies

The stemma on the following page is greatly simplified and is limited to those prominent in the text; for detailed genealogies of the Ptolemaic family see Hölbl, *History of the Ptolemaic Empire*, 364–69, and (for the last century of the dynasty) Sullivan, *Near Eastern Royalty and Rome, 100–30 B.C.*, stemma 7. Dates are all B.C. except for the few that are A.D. at the end of the stemma, and all are regnal dates unless otherwise noted.

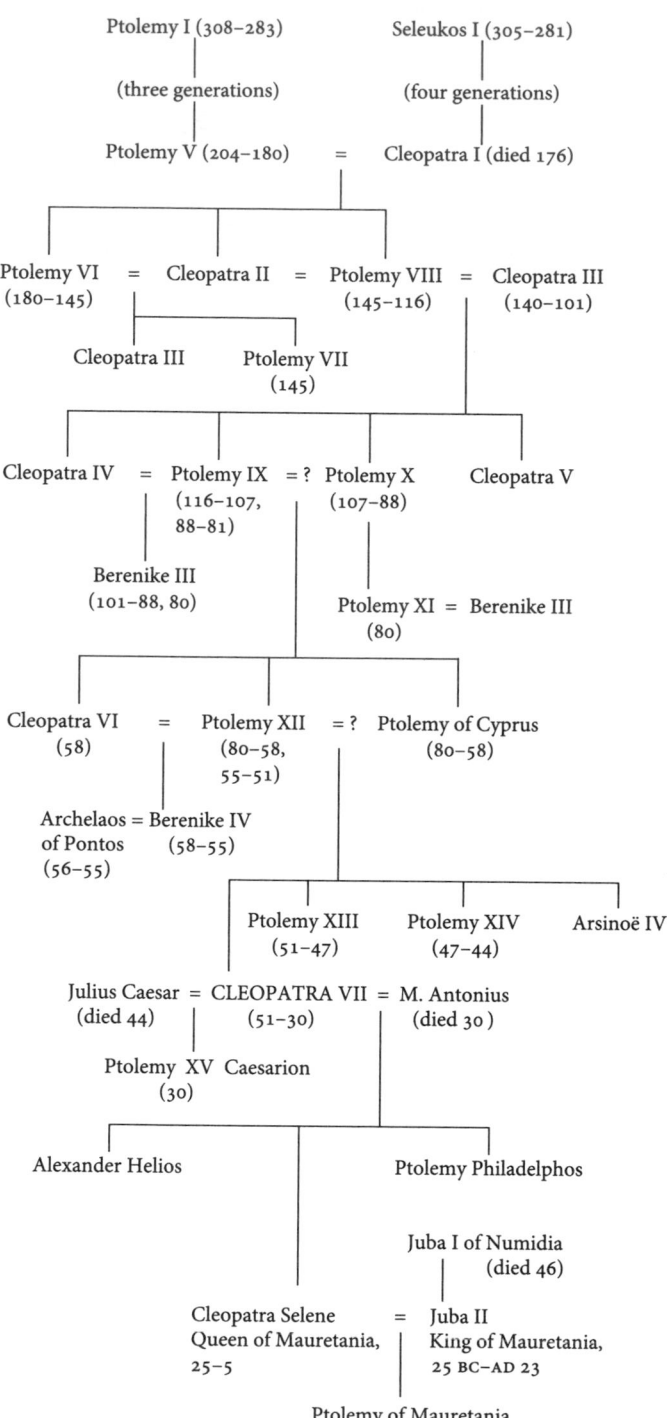

Ptolemy I (308–283)   Seleukos I (305–281)

(three generations)   (four generations)

Ptolemy V (204–180)   =   Cleopatra I (died 176)

Ptolemy VI   =   Cleopatra II   =   Ptolemy VIII   =   Cleopatra III
(180–145)   (145–116)   (140–101)

Cleopatra III   Ptolemy VII
                     (145)

Cleopatra IV   =   Ptolemy IX   = ?   Ptolemy X   Cleopatra V
                   (116–107,   (107–88)
                   88–81)

Berenike III
(101–88, 80)   Ptolemy XI = Berenike III
                                    (80)

Cleopatra VI   =   Ptolemy XII   = ?   Ptolemy of Cyprus
(58)   (80–58,   (80–58)
                   55–51)

Archelaos = Berenike IV
of Pontos   (58–55)
(56–55)

                   Ptolemy XIII   Ptolemy XIV   Arsinoë IV
                   (51–47)   (47–44)

Julius Caesar = CLEOPATRA VII = M. Antonius
(died 44) | (51–30) | (died 30)
Ptolemy XV Caesarion
(30)

Alexander Helios   Ptolemy Philadelphos

                                Juba I of Numidia
                                    | (died 46)

Cleopatra Selene   =   Juba II
Queen of Mauretania,   King of Mauretania,
25–5   25 BC–AD 23

                Ptolemy of Mauretania
                      AD 23–40

3. Cleopatra's Mother

Because the identity of the mother of Cleopatra VII is unknown, this has provided fertile ground for speculation, often more ludicrous than reasonable.[1] Although certainty is impossible, it seems clear that she was a member of the Egyptian religious elite. The legal wife of Ptolemy XII was his sister Cleopatra VI, whom he had married shortly after his accession in 80 B.C., but who fell out of favor at the court around the time of the birth of Cleopatra VII.[2] Strabo, who lived in Alexandria shortly after her death, if not before, and was well informed about the city and its culture, recorded that only the eldest of Ptolemy's three daughters, Berenike IV, was legitimate,[3] which would exclude Cleopatra VII, her younger sister Arsinoë IV, and her two brothers Ptolemy XIII and XIV from being children of Cleopatra VI. Yet no one but Strabo mentioned this, and, strangely, it is absent from the sources deriving from the Roman demonization of Cleopatra that call her all kinds of other names but never illegitimate. Thus it may be presumed that she was only technically illegitimate; in other words, she was not the daughter of Ptolemy's legal wife Cleopatra VI, yet her mother was a person of importance who was probably not Ptolemaic. Obviously she was someone that the Roman propaganda machine could not manage to condemn. If she were merely a slave or concubine, it is unlikely that Cleopatra VII would have become as powerful as she did or that the Romans would have ignored the fact. Improper parentage was repeatedly invoked in the case of her father, who was called a bastard throughout his life because of his mother, whoever she was. Yet the matter of Cleopatra VII's mother remains unresolved. Either the queen was the daughter of Cleopatra VI,[4] whose loss of favor obscured the issue, or, more probably, her mother was some other person with status at the court who could supply Cleopatra VII with a solid lineage that was more important than her failure to be a daughter of her father's legal wife. The liaisons that produced

Cleopatra VII's own offspring were similar, for the status of the parent (in this case the father) outweighed legal niceties.

Cleopatra had a great affinity for Egyptian culture, more than any of her royal predecessors, and unlike them spoke the Egyptian language: thus her early life was subject to unusual influences. A natural source for these would be her mother, therefore by necessity a non-Greek person of importance well grounded in Egyptian culture, most probably a member of the indigenous aristocracy of Egypt, a background that would provide sufficient status for a royal heir. The Egyptian religious elite had been connected to the Ptolemies since at least the late second century B.C. when Psenptais II, the high priest of Ptah, and a member of the hereditary priestly family of Petubastis,[5] married a certain Berenike, whose name demonstrates that she was a royal personage, probably the daughter of Ptolemy VIII. Psenptais's son, Petubastes III, who would have been half Ptolemaic, had enough stature to assist in implementing Ptolemy XII's claim to the throne and then to officiate at his coronation in 76 B.C.[6] On his funerary stele, Petubastes III recorded that Ptolemy XII had several wives, each of significant status to produce royal children. One of these was the mother of Cleopatra VII. It thus seems no accident that this hereditary priestly family was commemorated by Cleopatra's daughter Cleopatra Selene at her royal city of Mauretanian Caesarea,[7] thus singling out Egyptian clergy far from Egypt, a peculiar act unless they were relatives. It is impossible to fit Cleopatra VII exactly into this family, but the most likely scenario is that her mother was a daughter or granddaughter of Psenptais II and Berenike. Thus Cleopatra Selene at Caesarea was commemorating her grandmother's family, the priestly family of which she herself was a descendant.

4. Was Cleopatra a Roman Citizen?

Unlike many states in the ancient Mediterranean world, the Romans were liberal in bestowing citizenship on foreigners, as such donations created a support group among the indigenous elite that could be used in advancing Roman interests. This concept originated as Roman power spread through Italy but became more prevalent when Rome encountered the Greek states and eastern kingdoms. A prominent local person given Roman citizenship would have a reason to support Roman policy in his region, and as early as the second century B.C. Roman magistrates operating in the eastern Mediterranean regularly gave citizenship to the city leaders and royalty whom they encountered. Those who now held the privilege could also use it to their own advantage, as Herod the Great and Paul of Tarsos learned.

There is no explicit evidence that Cleopatra VII was a Roman citizen;[8] in fact the historical record is totally silent. But there is a substantial amount of circumstantial data that suggests she was one. It is clear that her daughter Cleopatra Selene was a citizen, for otherwise her marriage to Juba II would not have been legal, something that Octavia, who arranged the marriage, would hardly have allowed. But Cleopatra Selene's citizenship need not to have come from her mother, as her father Antonius could have bestowed it directly. Antonius—always generous with citizenship—could also have given it to Cleopatra VII if she did not hold it already. The references in the propaganda war of the late 30s B.C. to Antonius's marriage to a foreign queen is not a statement on Cleopatra VII's status since the issues were bigamy and xenophobia, not citizenship. In fact, these slanders stress that the marriage was illegal, which implies that there could have been a reason to consider it legal and not the mere delights of a soldier on campaign. Yet there would be no such issue unless the queen were a citizen.

Rather than receive citizenship from Antonius, however, Cleopatra likely held it from birth. There are several occasions when her ancestors might have received it: either when her great-grandfather Ptolemy VIII visited Rome and courted Cornelia, when his grandson Ptolemy XII was himself in Rome, or when the latter was restored by Gabinius and Antonius. All these were typical occasions for receiving citizenship. Even if Cleopatra did not obtain it through her ancestry, Julius Caesar or Antonius could have bestowed it, thus ensuring it for their own children. Petty dynasts and prominent people in Greek cities received it from Roman magistrates in the East, and it is hard to imagine that the Ptolemies were overlooked. If so, they would stand virtually alone among the dynasties of the late Hellenistic world.

Thus it is almost certain that Cleopatra VII was a Roman citizen, something conveniently ignored by both the propaganda wars and the Augustan recension of her career, as acknowledgment of this would substantially weaken the case against her. But it is quite probable that the Ptolemies, unlike many of the petty dynasts, did not see Roman citizenship as enhancing their status, which they felt to be far more distinguished than that of the Romans: hence the silence of the record.

5. Some Ancient Literary Descriptions of Cleopatra

Included here are four accounts of famous moments in the life of Cleopatra VII as well as the *Sibylline Oracle* that may refer to the queen. Only Horace and the oracle date from her era; the remaining three are significantly later but are based on eyewitness reports. The original sources are not known with certainty, but all, except to some extent the account from Horace, are remarkably free of the negative views of the queen popularized in her last years that continue to influence modern impressions. These are the best existing characterizations of the personality of Cleopatra.

Plutarch, *Antonius* 27.2–4. The context is the meeting with Antonius at Tarsos in 41 B.C., but the description is a general view of her demeanor and education and need not reflect that particular moment. The source is not mentioned but was presumably someone in regular contact with the queen and her court, perhaps Nikolaos of Damascus or Sokrates of Rhodes.

> Her conversation was inescapably gripping, and her appearance along with the persuasiveness of her discussion and her character, which affected those around her, was particularly incisive. There was a sweetness in the tones of her voice, and her tongue was like a many-stringed instrument, so that she could easily make use of whatever language she wished, and thus when she had discussions with barbarians she hardly ever needed an interpreter, but answered most of them without assistance, whether they were Ethiopians, Trogodytes, Hebrews, Arabians, Syrians, Medes, or Parthians. It was said that she also learned many other languages.

Plutarch, *Caesar* 49.1–2. The report of Cleopatra's first visit to Julius Caesar in late summer 48 B.C. may be based on an account by her confidant Apollodoros of Sicily, otherwise unknown, but prominent in the incident.

Taking only Apollodoros the Sicilian from her friends, she embarked in a small boat and landed at the palace when it was already becoming quite dark. Since it was otherwise difficult to escape notice, she stretched herself out in a bedsack, and Apollodoros tied up the bedsack with a rope and carried it through the doors to Caesar. It is said that by this device he was first conquered by Cleopatra, as she showed her impudence, and through the charm of further conversation with her he reconciled her with her brother as joint rulers.

Plutarch, *Antonius* 26.1–3. This vivid description of Cleopatra approaching Antonius at Tarsos in 41 B.C. is probably from Sokrates of Rhodes, who was present (Athenaios 4.147–48). Quintus Dellius, Antonius's chronicler, may also have contributed. The perspective of the source is clear: someone on the banks of the Kydnos, close enough to see Cleopatra and her entourage in her *thalamegos,* and to hear the music and smell the incense.

> She sailed up the Kydnos River in a boat with a golden stern, purple sails spread, the rowers pulling the silver oars to the sound of flutes, pipes, and strings. She herself reclined under a canopy adorned with gold, looking like a painting of Aphrodite, with boys like Erotes in paintings standing on either side and fanning her. In addition, her most beautiful serving maidens were positioned, like Nereids or Graces, at the tiller and the lines. Marvellous scents from innumerable incense offerings spread along the river banks. It was said everywhere that Aphrodite had come to celebrate with Dionysos for the good of Asia.

***Sibylline Oracle* 3.350–80.** The *Sibylline Oracles* reached their present form in late antiquity but are a complex layering of material put together over many centuries, often including Eastern thought, and with many textual uncertainties. Like most ancient oracles, their legitimacy can easily be disputed, and they served contemporary political needs. The oracle in question reflects the situation after 63 B.C. and the heavy Roman involvement in the East. Nevertheless it contains ideas of universal harmony that originated with Alexander the Great, coupled with the prophetic optimism common in the second half of the first century B.C. and familiar through contemporary literature. There is also a distinct biblical tone, which suggests that the oracle may have originated in the Levant. The identity of the woman who is cutting Rome's hair is by no means certain, but if the phrase is to be taken literally there seems no option other than Cleopatra VII. If the oracle does refer to the queen, it probably dates from the 30s B.C., and it both provides a positive view of her that is untainted by Roman thought and demonstrates that some in the contemporary Greek and Levantine world saw her as the best hope for the future, even a messianic figure.

As much tribute as Rome received from Asia, three times that amount will Asia take back from Rome, paying her back for her destructive arrogance. As many as were taken from Asia to live in Rome, 20 times that many Italians will serve in poverty in Asia, and a thousand times as many will pay. Virgin offspring of Latin Rome, rich in gold and luxury and often drunk with so many much-remembered marriages, you will be a slave bride, not a proper one, and often your mistress cuts your elegant hair, and treating you justly will cast you from the heavens to the earth, and then raise you again from the earth to the heavens. [lines 362–66 omitted as intrusive and irrelevant]

Calm peace will travel to the Asian land, and then Europe will be blessed, with the air rich in herds for many years, robust, and neither stormy nor hailing, producing all the birds and footed beasts of the earth. Blessed will be man and woman in that time, as blessed as those dwelling in the fields. All good order will come from the starry heavens to men, and justice and wise harmony, which will be totally brought forth for mortals, as well as love, friendship, and hospitality. Yet denial will then flee from men, and poverty and need, and also lawlessness, reproach, envy, anger, foolishness, murder, accursed strife, baneful wrangling, theft by night, and every kind of evil.

Plutarch, *Antonius* 85. The account of Cleopatra's death is from the report of her physician Olympos (*Antonius* 82.2), with some details added from the *Autobiography* of Augustus or perhaps the memoirs of some of his entourage. The asp does not appear in this version.

Having bathed, she reclined and had a particularly fine meal. And someone came from the country carrying a basket, and when the guards asked him what he was bringing he opened it and removed the leaves, showing a receptacle full of figs. They were amazed at their quality and size, and he smiled and invited them to take some, so they trusted him and told him to go in. After the meal Cleopatra took a tablet that she had already written on and sealed, and sent it to Caesar [i.e., Octavian], and then sending all away except her two women closed the doors. When Caesar opened the tablet and found prayers and lamentations begging that she be buried with Antonius, he immediately knew what had happened. At first he started off to give aid himself, but then sent others quickly to investigate. But the incident had happened swiftly. They arrived at a run and found that the guards had not noticed anything, and upon opening the doors found her lying dead on a golden couch, regally adorned. Regarding the two women, the one called Eiras was dying at her feet, and Charmion, already fallen and heavy in the head, was arranging the diadem around her head. Someone angrily said, "This is a fine thing, Charmion." "It is most fine," she said, "and fitting for the descendant of so many kings." She said nothing more, but fell alongside the couch.

Horace, *Ode* 1.37.21–32. Horace's poem celebrating the death of Cleopatra was written shortly after the event (no later than 23 B.C. and probably before). Thus it is one of the earliest accounts of her demise, but it already reflects the standard Roman view of a dangerous and drunken threat to Rome who was successfully eliminated. Yet at the end of his ode Horace moves to a higher level, showing true respect for the queen and her decision to die rather than to appear in Octavian's triumph. The liburnian was a fast two-banked galley modified from the pirate vessel used by the residents of Liburnia, on the Dalmatian coast. It was commonly used by Octavian in the sea battles of the 30s B.C. (Casson, *Ships and Seamanship in the Ancient World*, 141–42).

Seeking to die more nobly, she did not fear the dagger like a woman, nor did she seek a hidden shore with her swift fleet. She dared to look upon her fallen palace with a calm face, brave enough to handle the harsh snakes, so that she absorbed the black poison in her body, becoming bolder in her decision to die, unwilling to be led on hostile liburnians as a private citizen for an arrogant triumph. She would not be a humiliated woman.

6. The Iconography
of Cleopatra VII

The iconography of Cleopatra VII is elusive, although the subject of much scholarship.[9] Two excellent catalogues have appeared in the last decade, one produced by the British Museum in 2001 and the other from an exhibit in Hamburg in 2006–7.[10] The outstanding visual representations in both these books, especially the former, provide easy access to essentially the totality of the known and suggested iconography of the queen, although obviously interpretations will continue to change. Determining her extant representations remains a difficult problem, because only her coins and Egyptian reliefs and steles have inscriptions that identify her, and both these genres have their own issues of interpretation. None of the suggested portraits of the queen within the Greco-Roman tradition can be attributed on anything other than art-historical grounds, a methodology with obvious pitfalls, and although many of the conclusions are probably valid, one still lacks definitive evidence. As with the biographical details of the queen's life, the information is frustratingly limited.

Her iconography falls into four categories. There are a few pieces of Hellenistic sculpture and other artistic media, all identified by style and details. There are coins from more than a dozen cities on which the queen is identified by the legend, mostly from the Levant but as far west as Cyrene and Patrai and including a few struck by Antonius. There are a number of Egyptian portraits, sculptures, and reliefs; the latter often cite the queen by name. And finally, there is a genre of works produced immediately after her death as a parallel to the Augustan literary output, serving the same purpose of establishing the politically correct view of the queen within the new regime and the self-conception of the Augustan era. These works—whether wall paintings or three-dimensional media—have diagnostic elements that make their interpretation reasonable. Since most were produced within a generation of Cleopatra's death, they can be assumed to be accurate visual representations of her physical features, even if turned to a narrow purpose.[11]

Hellenistic-Roman portrait sculpture provides the best chance of showing the queen drawn from life and within the most familiar artistic tradition. Unfortunately the examples are few in number, and none is undisputed. Provenience is often equally uncertain. Probably the best known is a Parian marble portrait in Berlin (fig. 2),[12] by all accounts found somewhere south of Rome, although its history before being obtained by the museum in 1976— the piece seems to have been known since the early nineteenth century—is tortuous.[13] It is a fine work, well preserved, showing Cleopatra with a melon hairstyle and a royal diadem. Details, such as the hair and the prominent nose, are similar to the consistent portrait of Cleopatra on her coins. If the suggestion of an Italian provenience is correct, the Berlin head may have been produced while the queen was in Rome in the 40s B.C. Despite the vagueness, the head remains the most probable extant representation of the queen in Hellenistic-Roman art. It was carved when she was in her mid-twenties and demonstrates the dignity and resoluteness that characterized her life.

Similar to the Berlin head is one in the Vatican, discovered at a villa on the Via Appia in the late eighteenth century and recently suggested to be the most certain extant portrait of Cleopatra.[14] A striking representation in Parian

FIGURE 10. Wall painting in Room 71 of the House of M. Fabius Rufus, Pompeii, showing the statue of Cleopatra VII in the Forum Julium. Courtesy of Pietro Giovanni Guzzo, Domenico Esposito, and the Soprintendenza Archeologica di Pompei.

marble, it has the same hairstyle, royal diadem, and general features as the Berlin head. Unfortunately its nose is broken, so it does not project the same solemnity as its Berlin counterpart, but it belongs to the same tradition. A rough and irregular patch on the left cheek suggests that (at least on the original) something was attached there, perhaps the infant Caesarion perched on his mother's shoulder.[15] These portraits portray Cleopatra in her early twenties but nevertheless show a woman already of exceptionally mature bearing. Both may be versions of the famous gold statue of the queen that Caesar commissioned for his Forum Julium (see p. 72). In fact, this statue may be the archetype for many portraits of Cleopatra, and it now seems probable that a contemporary rendition of it exists as a Second Style wall painting at Pompeii, in Room 71 of the House of M. Fabius Rufus. This shows a royal woman who strongly resembles the queen as depicted in the Vatican portrait, wearing a royal diadem and holding a Cupid on her shoulder, appearing at the massive double doors of a templelike structure.[16] Although a rendering of Venus with Cupid comes immediately to mind, the diadem means that the subject is a royal person and that any divinity is only allegorical. The date of the painting is firmly fixed in the 40s B.C., the very time that Cleopatra was twice in Italy. There seems little doubt that this is a depiction of Cleopatra and Caesarion before the doors of the Temple of Venus in the Forum Julium, and, as such, it becomes the only extant contemporary painting of the queen. Interestingly, it was concealed during a major remodeling of the house in the Augustan period, perhaps not so much an objection to continued visibility of Cleopatra (who after all could be seen in the Forum Julium and probably elsewhere) but of Caesarion, whose claim to be the legitimate heir of Julius Caesar was a continuing sore point for the new regime.[17]

It has also been suggested that the Esquiline Venus is a version of Cleopatra. The statue was discovered in 1874 in Rome and is now in the Palazzo dei Conservatori.[18] A well-known piece of ancient art, it depicts a nude woman whose face is somewhat suggestive of the Berlin and Vatican Cleopatras, especially with the handling of the mouth and chin, although the face as a whole is thinner. The hairstyles are similar. At her feet is a draped base with a uraeus wrapped around it. This, and the queen's self-identification with Aphrodite or Venus, are the basis of the attribution. The piece is generally thought to be from around A.D. 50, a copy of a work perhaps from the school of Pasiteles of the first century B.C. Attribution to Cleopatra VII, first put forth in the 1950s, has been revived recently but is still very much disputed.[19] Objections generally focus on the facial differences and whether Cleopatra would have been depicted as a nude Greek goddess, and the attribution, although intriguing, remains highly speculative.

Other putative portraits are even less certain. One in Parian marble, now in a private collection but originally belonging to the Cairo collector Maurice

Nahman (1868–1948), has a striking resemblance to the Vatican and Berlin heads, but lacks a royal diadem.[20] Because it lacks a diadem, the statue most likely does not depict Cleopatra since the queen was always conscious of her royal status, indeed excessively so.[21] It may be possible that the Nahman head, probably of Egyptian origin, is from a subgenre of Cleopatran portraiture, one in which women of the court (or even private citizens) imitated her style and had themselves depicted in art but obviously could not wear the royal diadem. A Parian marble portrait in the Egyptian Museum in Cairo[22] is probably part of the same tradition, showing an important member of the court who chose to be depicted looking as much as possible as her royal mistress, although the nose hints that it might even be a portrait of the queen herself. A piece of Italian origin now in the British Museum is similar,[23] with facial features reminiscent of the Berlin and Vatican portraits but with a different hairstyle and no diadem, much like a head from Rome now in the Museo Capitolino.[24] It may even be that these last two portraits were of people in Rome in the 40s B.C. who imitated the style of the queen; not everyone could have had Cicero's abhorrence of her, and the presence of a dynamic royal personage in the city might have spawned a certain amount of adulation, as with royalty and popular figures today.

Two cameos may depict the queen. One, from perhaps 50 B.C. and in the Bibliothèque National de France,[25] shows a portrait in profile similar to the sculptural types. Another in blue glass in the British Museum,[26] of unknown provenience, portrays a woman with a hairstyle and royal diadem similar to those on the Berlin and Vatican portraits. The figure is also wearing a triple uraeus, recently and brilliantly suggested to be Cleopatra's reaction to the Roman triumvirate, an assertion of her three sons.[27] The triple uraeus appears on a number of Egyptian statues, most notably one in black basalt in the Hermitage,[28] normally identified as Arsinoë II, but now believed, based both on the uraeus and facial features, to be Cleopatra VII. Similar pieces are in the Rosicrucian Museum in San Jose, California (fig. 3),[29] and the Louvre.[30] Still Egyptian in style, but with some Greek characteristics, are pieces in the Metropolitan Museum[31] and the Brooklyn Museum.[32] All these have the triple uraeus, and although facial features vary, they bear a certain resemblance to one another.[33] The Metropolitan Museum statue is most like the Berlin and Vatican heads, and it even has a cartouche with "Cleopatra" on its upper right arm, but this is of questionable authenticity. The precise origin of these pieces is unknown, but the queen's public sculpture survived her death, since at that time a wealthy member of her court, a certain Archibios, paid Octavian the immense sum of 2,000 talents not to destroy her statues.[34]

Although Egyptian reliefs are in the ancient style of Egyptian art, they provide rare examples of unquestioned representations of the queen. Most notable is on the south wall of the Temple of Hathor at Dendera (fig. 4), where

Cleopatra is shown in profile making offerings to the gods; in front of her is the young Caesarion, who was only a teenager but has all the massive authority of a pharoah.[35] Two steles also show the queen in Egyptian manner. One from the Fayum, now in the Louvre,[36] is dated to the first year of Cleopatra Thea Philopator—who can only be Cleopatra VII—and is a dedication by one Snonais, the president of the association of Isis. The date is thus 51 B.C., and therefore it would be the earliest extant depiction of the queen. Interestingly it shows her as male. The dedication, coming exactly at the time of the death of Ptolemy XII, may originally have been intended for him, but was promptly yet incompletely reworked when his daughter came to the throne (the inscription shows evidence of recarving). Nevertheless there are precedents as early as the time of Hatshepsut for Egyptian queens being represented as male.[37] Moreover, the Bucheum stele describing the installation of the Buchis bull of 22 March 51 B.C. also describes Cleopatra first as "the king" but then as "the queen."[38] In the first months of her reign, the Egyptian aristocracy may not yet have adjusted to the idea of a female ruler—recent previous queens had ended their reigns in disaster—but this male characterization lasted to the end of her life; at her death, her maid Charmion used the masculine gender to call her a "descendant of many kings."[39] Although in popular imagination the queen became an icon of femininity, formal usage in Egypt could create a masculine Cleopatra, perhaps high praise for her status and quality of rule.[40]

Another stele of uncertain date but probably from the late 30s B.C., in a private collection in Montpellier, shows the divine triad Amen-Re, Mut, and their son Khonsu,[41] a type of family unit that was an integral part of Egyptian religion from earliest times.[42] Yet in this relief the triad is actually Julius Caesar, Cleopatra, and Caesarion, thereby placing Caesarion—who stands in the center—at the divine level, watched over by his divine parents. The format of this relief is remindful of one from Karnak now in the British Museum, perhaps from around 116 B.C., in which Cleopatra's great-grandfather Ptolemy VIII along with his wives Cleopatra II and III (who were mother and daughter) make an offering to the original divine triad.[43] Human and divine threesomes stand in opposition but are still separate; in the Montpellier stele the two groups have become one. If this stele dates from near the end of Cleopatra VII's life—the adolescent depiction of Caesarion suggests this—it probably demonstrates an attempt to put the new pharaoh into the public consciousness of the Egyptian people.

It is well known that beginning in the 30s B.C. a vast amount of Roman literature sought to define the image of Cleopatra to the Roman audience. In the years immediately after her death, this literature, often of the highest quality, was used to control the dialogue about her reputation. There are many familiar examples that need not be recounted here, culminating, perhaps, in the vivid description of the Battle of Actium in the *Aeneid*,[44] written less than a decade after the queen's death. Less familiar, perhaps, are artistic representations from the same era and continuing into the Julio-Claudian period. Some of these border on the scatological, such as a series of lamps dated to A.D. 50–75 that show a naked woman with the familiar melon hairstyle standing on a crocodile, engaged in a sexual act with a disembodied phallus.[45] The lamps were common along the northern frontier of the Roman Empire and may have been a favorite in soldiers' camps.[46] Attribution to Cleopatra is not certain but probable, and the evolution of the type before A.D. 50 is unknown.[47] Yet, in contrast, some of the best pieces of Augustan and Julio-Claudian art may be connected to Cleopatra. Most interesting is the recent suggestion that the Portland Vase in the British Museum depicts an allegory involving the queen.[48] In this compelling analysis, the main scene depicts Cleopatra drawing Antonius toward her, assisted by the serpent that rises at her legs and Eros above her. Anton, the ancestor of the Antonian family, looks on, despairing, as his descendant goes to his doom. On the other side is Octavia, in the traditional pose of an abandoned lover, with a heroic Octavian watching intently, and Venus, the ancestress of the Julian family, offering comfort from the right. Although there have been many interpretations of the scenes on the vase, there is little doubt that this is the most satisfying. The dramatic date would be after Antonius sent Octavia back to Italy, or 35–30 B.C., probably earlier in that period rather than later, although the vase itself is probably from the Augustan period.

Egyptian-influenced wall painting is a well-known aspect of early Imperial Rome: witness the Nile mosaic from the Casa del Fauno in Pompeii, the famous Nile painting from Herculaneum,[49] or the Nile mosaic at Praeneste.[50] Although many such works predate Cleopatra and have nothing to do with her personally, they show the long Roman fascination with the material culture of Egypt that would only be enhanced in her era. Yet painting would seem an obvious medium to depict the events of Cleopatra's life. At Pompeii, in addition to the painting in the House of M. Fabius Rufus already noted, which was created before the queen's death, a painting in the Casa di Giuseppe II, dated to the first quarter of the first century A.D., depicts a woman wearing a diadem in the act of committing suicide by poison, surrounded by five people.[51] Two are female, and three male; one of the males is wearing a diadem, and another appears to be in Roman dress. At the left, one of the male attendants holds the mouth of a crocodile, probably not the animal itself but the elaborate handle of a tray, the rest of which is not visible. High up on the rear wall, in an unusual position, is a set of double doors.

Conventionally this painting has been explained as the death of Sophonisba (Sophoniba), the aristocratic Carthaginian beloved by the famous Numidian king Massinissa, who late in the Second Punic War sent her poison so that she would not be captured by the Romans.[52] This romantic tale may have been popularized in a tragedy—the major extant account, by Appian, reads as such—and became a paradigm of heroic opposition to Rome. Yet the parallels to the death of Cleopatra VII are numerous, not only in the general tone and situation, but the connections between the Numidian royalty and the Ptolemies (Massinissa was a close associate of Ptolemy VIII, and his descendant Juba II would marry Cleopatra's daughter), as well as details of the painting, such as the two female attendants, the Roman bystander, the crocodile motif, and even the door enigmatically high up on the wall, suggesting the peculiar architecture of Cleopatra's tomb. No asp is shown, but many believed that Cleopatra had actually taken poison (see p. 148). The painting may well depict Sophonisba, as no royal person attended Cleopatra's death (although the artist may have suggested the presence of Caesarion), but it was created when there were people still alive who remembered the death of Cleopatra, and contemporaries viewing the painting would immediately have thought of the famous more recent suicide rather than an obscure incident that occurred more than 200 years before. However romanticized, ambiguous, and inaccurate in detail, the painting in the Casa di Giuseppe II may be the closest available to a contemporary rendition of the suicide of Cleopatra.

The Coin Portraits

Cleopatra's coinage provides the only certain visual representations of the queen within the Greco-Roman artistic tradition and in a sequence—however disputed—from throughout her reign.[53] Coins are known from more than a dozen sites, mostly in the Levant, and from essentially every regnal year. The common inscription on all her coinage is ΚΛΕΟΠΑΤΡΑΣ ΒΑΣΙΛΙΣΣΗΣ (Queen Cleopatra). Her Egyptian coin portraits consistently show a right profile, the melon hairstyle, royal diadem, and a prominent nose (fig. 11b). The portraits are remarkably similar to those of her father.[54] Although there are slight variants, with some evidence of maturation over the 20 years that she was on the throne, Cleopatra's portraits are all much alike. Her provincial coinage comes from a variety of mints. Of particular interest are silver tetradrachms from Askalon, probably from 48 B.C., when the city was not yet Ptolemaic territory and the queen was barely on the throne. These seem to represent the support of the city—and its prominent citizen, Antipatros—in her civil war with her brother Ptolemy XIII.[55] Although this should be one of the earliest extant portraits of the queen, at about age 21, it is astonishingly unattractive, with a rigid puffy face and a disproportionately large nose, perhaps a failure of the designer or mint,[56] although some of the Alexandria coins show the same characteristics.[57] A decade later, when Askalon was part of her territory, a more mature and attractive portrait appears, perhaps indicating greater control by the queen herself over the minting process.[58]

(a)

(b)

(c)

(d)

(e)

FIGURE 11. Coins of Cleopatra VII: (*a*) Bronze, probably from Cyprus, showing the queen with the infant Caesarion. Courtesy of the Trustees of the British Museum and Art Resource, New York (ART307002); (*b*) Bronze, from Alexandria. Courtesy of the Trustees of the British Museum and Art Resource, New York (ART366014); (*c*) Bronze, from Berytos. Courtesy of the American Numismatic Society (1944.100.70154); (*d*) Silver, with the queen and M. Antonius, unknown provenience, 35–33 B.C. Courtesy of the American Numismatic Society (1967.152.567); (*e*) Silver denarius with the queen and M. Antonius, probably from 32 B.C. Courtesy of the Trustees of the British Museum and Art Resource, New York (ART366016).

Much of Cleopatra's coinage reflects her territorial ambitions, especially in the early 30s B.C. Berytos (fig. 11c), Damascus, Orthosia,[59] and Tripolis, all Phoenician cities she acquired at that time, began to issue coinage with her portrait.[60] Although the artistic quality varies, the details are familiar. The coin type from Damascus, known from 37/36 and 33/32 B.C., is the only evidence that it was part of her territory other than her visit to the city in 36 B.C.[61]

An unusual bronze coinage appeared probably on Cyprus (fig. 11a).[62] The rather crude representation shows the queen wearing a crown and holding an infant, almost certainly Caesarion, suggesting that it dates to shortly after his birth in 47 B.C., which was also when the island was returned to Ptolemaic control, perhaps the reason for the rare portrait of the queen with a crown. Mother and child are a symbolic Aphrodite and Eros or Isis and Harpokrates, and the coin image parallels the sculpture that also seems to show queen and son (see p. 175). Behind the queen is a scepter, and on the reverse is a double cornucopia, imitative of coins of her distinguished ancestor Arsinoë II, who, like Cleopatra, was seen as Isis.[63] In fact Cleopatra adopted Arsinoë II regularly as her role model in art and titulature, and the two queens were the only ones to call themselves "Daughter of Geb" (the creator god).[64]

A number of Cleopatra's coins are joint issues with Antonius, including bronze ones from Chalkis in Koile Syria and Ptolemais and Dora in Phoenicia.[65] Those from Chalkis continue the style of the local rulers of the region and appear in three denominations, with the queen, in usual iconography, appearing on all. The largest denomination has Antonius on the reverse, and the smaller ones have a Nike or Athene. These seem to have been issued in 31/30 B.C. and thus are some of her latest coinage. Joint coinage is also known from an uncertain mint (fig. 11d)—often suggested without great conviction to be Antioch but more likely one of the Phoenician cities—with Cleopatra's portrait and full title (ΒΑCΙΛΙCCΑ ΚΛΕΟΠΑΤΡΑ ΘΕΑ ΝΕѠΤΕΡΑ, or Queen Cleopatra, Younger Goddess) on the obverse and the image of Antonius with his title in Greek (ΑΝΤѠΝΙΟC ΑΥΤΟΚΡΑΤѠΡ ΤΡΙΤΟΝ ΤΡΙѠΝ ΑΝΔΡѠΝ, or Antonius, Imperator For the Third Time, Triumvir) on the reverse. Instead of using the genitive, normal in Greek coinage, these issues have the nominative, reflecting Latin titulature. They must date to the period 35–33 B.C.[66] The epithet "Thea Neotera" is unknown from any other Ptolemaic queen and was seemingly used by Cleopatra only on her coins. It alludes to Cleopatra Thea, the daughter of Ptolemy VI, who married into the Seleukid family and twice was Seleukid queen as well as mother of three Seleukid kings.[67] As a Ptolemy who became prominent in the Seleukid dynasty, Cleopatra Thea was a fortuitous role model for Cleopatra VII, and by placing the epithet of the earlier queen on her coins, Cleopatra VII asserted her identity as the living representative of the Seleukids, as well as the reestablishment of Seleukid control in Syria. The image of Cleopatra on this coin is unusual, as she appears older and more stern than on most of her coin portraits, and she has a luxuriant string of pearls around her neck.[68] Other similar joint coins come from Phoenician Ptolemais, dated to 35/34 B.C., and from Dora dated to the following year.

In the last years of her life, Cleopatra's coinage moved in new directions. Joint coinage from Antonius' theoretical third consulship (31 B.C.) has only the titulature, no portraits.[69] No place of minting appears, but since this type was found only at Cyrene, presumably they were produced at this Ptolemaic outpost in the months before the Battle of Actium and the subsequent transfer of the allegiance of the city's governor, L. Pinarius Scarpus, to Octavian. Cleopatra also appeared on coinage with Latin titulature, with the oldest and sternest portrait in the repertory of the queen's coin images (fig. 11e). Antonius is on one side and the queen on the other—it becomes difficult to determine which is the obverse and which the reverse—an example of double-headed coinage that was becoming more common in the later first century B.C.[70] Whether or not one could call these coins "Roman"—even with their Latin legends and Roman weight standards—is also nebulous; indeed they are a mixture of Greek and Roman traditions that created a new numismatic style, another example of the blending of ways that characterized the era. The optimistic ARMENIA DEVICTA (Armenia Conquered) means they are after 36 B.C., but they may belong to the very end of her reign, perhaps struck in Ephesos when the couple was there in 32 B.C.[71] By the end of their lives the coin portraits of Cleopatra and Antonius look almost identical: denarii of 32 B.C. from an unknown mint have the couple looking so much alike that it is almost impossible to tell which portrait is which.[72] Antonius, in fact, has the prominent chin of the Ptolemies, suggesting that he has been assimilated.

The final place that issued new coins in the name of Cleopatra was Patrai in the northwestern Peloponnesos, where she and Antonius wintered before Actium.[73] The image is poorly preserved, but the bust of the queen appears in the standard fashion with a simple ΒΑΣΙΛΙΣΣΑ ΚΛΕΟΠΑΤΡΑ. On the reverse is the headdress of Isis. This is the last known portrait of the queen made while she was alive.[74]

Abbreviations

AHDE: *Annuario de historia del derecho español*
AJA: *American Journal of Archaeology*
AJAH: *American Journal of Ancient History*
AJP: *American Journal of Philology*
AncSoc: *Ancient Society*
AnnIsItS: *Annali dell'Istituto Italiano per gli studi storici*
ANRW: *Aufstieg und Niedergang der römischen Welt*
ANSMusN: *American Numismatic Society Museum Notes*
AntCl: *L'antiquité classique*
AntSoc: *Ancient Society*
AntW: *Antike Welt*
ArchPF: *Archiv für Papyrusforschung*
BASP: *Bulletin of the American Society of Papyrologists*
BCH: *Bulletin de correspondance hellénique*
BGU: *Ägyptische Urkunden aus den Staatlichen Museen Berlin, Griechische Urkunden* (Berlin, 1895–1983)
BiblArch: *Biblical Archaeologist*
BICS: *Bulletin of the Institute of Classical Studies*
BMC: *Catalogue of the Greek Coins in the British Museum* (London, 1873–)
BNP: *Brill's New Pauly* (Leiden, 2002–)
CAH: *Cambridge Ancient History*
CB: *The Classical Bulletin*
CBQ: *Catholic Biblical Quarterly*
CE: *Chronique d'Égypte*
CIL: *Corpus inscriptionem latinarum*
CJ: *Classical Journal*

CP: *Classical Philology*
CQ: *Classical Quarterly*
CSSH: *Comparative Studies in Society and History*
CW: *Classical World*
DSB: *Dictionary of Scientific Biography*
EANS: *The Encyclopedia of Ancient Natural Scientists* (ed. Paul T. Keyser and Georgia L. Irby-Massie, London, 2008)
ÉtPap: *Études de papyrologie*
FGrHist: F. Jacoby, *Die Fragmente der Griechischen Historiker* (Leiden, 1968–)
G&R: *Greece and Rome*
GM: *Göttinger Miszellen*
GRBS: *Greek, Roman and Byzantine Studies*
HSCP: *Harvard Studies in Classical Philology*
IG: *Inscriptiones Graecae*
IstMitt: *Istanbuler Mitteilungen*
JBM: *Jahrbuch der Berliner Museen*
JEA: *Journal of Egyptian Archaeology*
JHS: *Journal of Hellenic Studies*
JNG: *Jahrbuch für Numismatik und Geldgeschichte*
JRS: *Journal of Roman Studies*
LSJ: *A Greek-English Lexicon* (ed. Henry George Liddell, Robert Scott, and Henry Stuart Jones, 9th ed., Oxford, 1977)
MAAR: *Memoirs of the American Academy in Rome*
MusHelv: *Museum Helveticum*
OGIS: Wilhelm Dittenberger, *Orientis graeci inscriptiones selectae* (Leipzig, 1905)
ÖJh: *Jahreshefte des Osterreichischen Archäologischen Instituts in Wien*
OpRom: *Opuscula Romana*
OxyPap: *The Oxyrhynchus Papyri* (ed. Bernard P. Grenfell and Arthur S. Hunt, London, 1989–)
PACA: *Proceedings of the African Classical Associations*
PBSR: *Papers of the British School at Rome*
PECS: *Princeton Encyclopedia of Classical Sites*
PP: *La parola del passato*
RA: *Revue archéologique*
RAAN: *Rendiconti dell'Accademica di Archeologia, Napoli*
RE: Pauly-Wissowa, *Real-Encyclopädie der classischen Altertumswissenschaft*

RÉG: Revue des études grecques
RhM: Rheinisches Museum für Philologie
RINS: Revista italiana di numismatica e scienze
SchwMbll: Schweizer Münzblätter
SEG: Supplementum epigraphicum graecum
SNC: Spink Numismatic Circular
TAPA: Transactions of the American Philological Association

Notes

Introduction

1. Vergil, *Aeneid* 8.688.
2. Syme, *Roman Revolution*, 275.
3. Malalas 9.219; Plutarch, *Caesar* 49.1.
4. Plutarch, *Antonius* 27.2.
5. Plutarch, *Antonius* 83.
6. Plutarch, *Antonius* 29.

Chapter 1

1. She died at the age of 39 in August 30 B.C., and her birthday was just before Antonius's (Plutarch, *Antonius* 73.3), which was the equivalent of 14 January. Since Antonius, like Cleopatra, was born before and died after Caesar's calendar reforms of 46 B.C., exact dates can be confusing. See further, Suerbaum, "Merkwürdige Geburtstage," 327–29.

2. Strabo, *Geography* 17.1.11; Cicero, *de lege agraria* 2.42; Athenaios, *Deipnosophistai* 5.206d. On Ptolemy XII, see Sullivan, *Near Eastern Royalty and Rome, 100–30 B.C.*, 229–48.

3. Infra, pp. 165–66. It is still disputed whether the Macedonians were Greek or merely Hellenized, an argument with modern political overtones. Cleopatra's ancestry was largely Macedonian, but since the fifth century B.C. these indigenous peoples of the northern Greek peninsula had been heavily influenced by traditional Greek culture. Racial distinctions are difficult to determine in either ancient or modern times, and they have been manipulated for political ends throughout human history. There is no doubt, however, that Cleopatra and her ancestors were Greek culturally.

4. Heckel, *Who's Who*, 235–38.

5. Heckel, *Who's Who*, 246–48.

6. Livy 35.13.4; Appian, *Syrian Wars* 5; Porphyrios (*FGrHist* #260) F47. It is unlikely that Cleopatra VII was related to Alexander the Great, although it was said that Ptolemy I was a son of Philip II, Alexander's father (Pausanias 1.6.2; Quintus Curtius 9.8.22). Yet this was generally not believed, and it seems nothing more than a useful political fiction. See Errington, "Alexander in the Hellenistic World," 153–56.

7. For those named Cleopatra, see Whitehorne, *Cleopatras*.

8. Heckel, *Who's Who*, 90; Diodoros, *Bibliotheke* 16.91–95.

9. Hölbl, *History of the Ptolemaic Empire*, 78.

10. Strabo, *Geography* 17.1.11.

11. For the period, see Maehler, "Egypt under the Last Ptolemies," 1–3; Hölbl, *History of the Ptolemaic Empire*, 213–14.

12. Appian, *Civil War* 1.102; Porphyrios (*FGrHist* #260) F2.10–11.

13. Cicero, *de lege agraria* 1.1, 2.41–42. On the situation, see Crawford, *M. Tullius Cicero: The Fragmentary Speeches*, 43–56.

14. Reymond and Barns, "Alexandria and Memphis," 25–29.

15. Strabo, *Geography* 17.1.11.

16. Weill Goudchaux, "Cleopatra's Subtle Religious Strategy," 129–30.

17. Quaegebeur, "Cleopatra VII and the Cults of the Ptolemaic Queens," 51–53.

18. Seyrig, "Un petit portrait royal," *RA* for 1968, 251–56; Head, *Historia numorum*, 859–60; *BMC Ptolemies*, pl. 29, nos. 1–3.

19. Bevan, *House of Ptolemy*, 353–55.

20. The best summary of these issues is Gruen, *Last Generation of the Roman Republic*; a good general history of the period remains Scullard, *From the Gracchi to Nero*.

21. See Braund, *Rome and the Friendly King*, for the relationships between the kings and Rome.

22. Plutarch, *Crassus* 13.1; Cicero, *de lege agraria* 1.1, and *de rege Alexandrino*.

23. Lucan 2.586–87. But see Heinen, *Rom und Ägypten*, 167–75, who denied the existence of this visit.

24. Josephus, *Jewish Antiquities* 14.35; Pliny, *Natural History* 33.136–37; Appian, *Mithradatic Wars* 114.

25. The details are summarized by Rostovtzeff, *Social and Economic History*, 876–79.

26. Diodoros, *Bibliotheke* 1.83.8–9.

27. Strabo, *Geography* 17.1.8; Dio 39.12.1; Hölbl, *History of the Ptolemaic Empire*, 225.

28. Fraser, "*Prostagma* of Ptolemy Auletes from Lake Edku," 179–82. The inscription is from a village 20 miles east of Alexandria. See also Dio 39.12.1; Sullivan, *Near Eastern Royalty and Rome, 100–30 B.C.*, 231.

29. Suetonius, *Divine Julius* 54; Caesar, *Civil War* 3.107; Diodoros, *Bibliotheke* 1.83.8; Cicero, *pro C. Rabirio Postumo* 6.

30. Plutarch, *Cato the Younger* 34–36.

31. Dio 39.12; Plutarch, *Pompeius* 49; Cicero, *Pro C. Rabirio Postumo* 6.

32. Habicht, *Athens from Alexander to Antony*, 280.

33. Pausanias 1.9.3. There seems no other candidate for a memorial to Ptolemy's father.

34. "Libyan" had been used since Homer to refer to Africa, and although it has been argued (see Bennett, "Drusilla Regina," 315) that the princess was a member of the indigenous royalty of northwest Africa (Numidia or Mauretania), Cleopatra VII seems a more probable source. See Wilhelm, "Ein Grabgedicht aus Athen," 1007–20.

35. Weill Goudchaux, "Cleopatra's Subtle Religious Strategy," 131.

36. *BGU* 1762; see Maehler, "Egypt under the Last Ptolemies," 6.

37. Whitehorne, "Supposed Co-Regency of Cleopatra Tryphaena and Berenice IV (58–55 B.C.)."

38. The circumstances are summarized in a series of letters that Cicero (*ad familiares* 1.1–8) sent to Lentulus Spinther during 56 B.C.; see also his *Pro C. Rabirio Postumo* 6 and *Letters to Quintus* 2.2; Dio 39.12–16; Plutarch, *Pompeius* 49.6–7.

39. Porphyrios (*FGrHist* #260) F2.14; Strabo, *Geography* 12.3.34, 17.1.11; Dio 39.57.

40. Cicero, *Letters to Quintus* 2.3 (February 56 B.C.).

41. Cicero, *Pro Rabirio Postumo* 4, 6, 25, 38, and *ad familiares* 1.7; Plutarch, *Antonius* 3.1–2.

42. Josephus, *Jewish Antiquities* 14.98–99, and *Jewish War* 1.175; Kokkinos, *Herodian Dynasty*, 94–100.

43. Plutarch, *Antonius* 3; Appian, *Civil War* 5.8; Dio 39.58.

44. Cicero, *Letters to Quintus* 3.1–6, and *Letters to Atticus* #92–93; Fantham, "Trials of Gabinius in 54 B.C.," 425–43; Lintott, *Cicero as Evidence*, 242–49.

45. Williams, "*Rei publicae causa*," 25–38.

46. Dio 39.60.

47. Caesar, *Civil War* 3.103, 110; Strabo, *Geography* 17.1.12.

48. Cicero, *Pro Rabirio Postumo* 22–28, 37–40.

49. Sullivan, *Near Eastern Royalty and Rome, 100–30 B.C.*, 244.

50. *Bellum africanum* 8, 26.

51. The birthdate of Arsinoë is uncertain. She was younger than Cleopatra VII and was allegedly mature enough to make political decisions in 48 B.C. (Caesar, *Civil War* 3.112), unless others were acting in her name. But the implication is that she was close in age to her brothers.

52. Criscuolo, "La successione a Tolemeo Aulete," 325–39.

53. Caesar, *Civil War* 3.108.

54. *OGIS* 186; Sullivan, *Near Eastern Royalty and Rome, 100–30* B.C., 255–56.

55. Quaegebeur, "Cléopâtre VII et le temple de Dendara," 49–72.

56. Sullivan, *Near Eastern Royalty and Rome, 100–30* B.C., 235; Reymond and Barns, "Alexandria and Memphis," 1–33.

57. *OGIS* 741.

Chapter 2

1. Vermeule, *Greece in the Bronze Age*, 128.

2. Homer, *Iliad* 9.381–83, and *Odyssey* 4.351–62, 14.245–86, 17.426–44.

3. Plutarch, *On Isis and Osiris* 34. Even Homer was said to have made the trip.

4. Boardman, *Greeks Overseas*, 117–33.

5. Plutarch, *Kimon* 18.6–7; Thoukydides 1.104; Diodoros, *Bibliotheke* 11.71, 74.

6. Arrian, *Anabasis* 3.1.3–4; Hölbl, *History of the Ptolemaic Empire*, 9–10, 77–78.

7. Arrian, *Anabasis* 3.1.4–5.

8. Diodoros, *Bibliotheke* 18.21.6–9; Arrian, *Matters after Alexander* (*FGrHist* #156) F9.17–18.

9. Pausanias 1.6.3; Strabo, *Geography* 17.1.8. On the significance of Alexander's tomb, see Errington, "Alexander in the Hellenistic World," 141–45.

10. Arrian, *Anabasis* 3.1.3–4; Hölbl, *History of the Ptolemaic Empire*, 21–22.

11. Plutarch, *Antonius* 27.4.

12. Diodoros, *Bibliotheke* 20.113.1–2.

13. Hölbl, *History of the Ptolemaic Empire*, 25–26.

14. McKenzie, *Architecture of Alexandria and Egypt*, esp. 7–146.

15. Erskine, "Culture and Power in Ptolemaic Egypt," 38–48.

16. Fraser, *Ptolemaic Alexandria*, 1:305–35.

17. *FGrHist* #138. There are 35 fragments of his history extant, many quite lengthy and most from the *Anabasis* of Arrian, who used Ptolemy as one of his major sources.

18. Diogenes Laertios 5.37; Heckel, *Who's Who*, 235–38.

19. Diogenes Laertios 4.1.

20. Diogenes Laertios 5.51–53.

21. Diogenes Laertios 5.78.

22. Athenaios, *Deipnosophistai* 1.3.

23. Bulver-Thomas, "Euclid," 414–15.

24. Strabo, *Geography* 17.1.8.

25. Shenouda, "Naukratis," 609–10.

26. Strabo, *Geography* 17.1.42.

27. Heckel, *Who's Who*, 35–38.

28. Pausanias 1.6.8.

29. Hazzard, "Regnal Years of Ptolemy II Philadelphos," 140–58.

30. Pausanias 1.7.

31. Diogenes Laertios 5.78; Cicero, *pro C. Rabirio Postumo* 23; supra, p. 26.

32. Adamson, "Consanguinous [*sic*] Marriages," 85–92.

33. Hölbl, *History of the Ptolemaic Empire*, 24–25.

34. Pausanias 1.7.1; Hopkins, "Brother-Sister Marriage in Roman Egypt," 311–12; Shaw, "Explaining Incest," 267–99.

35. Adamson (in "Consanguinous [*sic*] Marriages") has catalogued 32 Egyptian, 11 Ptolemaic, eight Persian, and six Seleukid incestuous royal marriages.

36. Athenaios, *Deipnosophistai* 14.620–21.

37. Dio 43.27.3.

38. Herodotos 5.92.

39. Theokritos 17.

40. Strabo, *Geography* 17.1.6; Pliny, *Natural History* 36.83.

41. Roller, *World of Juba II*, 234–35.

42. Plutarch, *Camillus* 22.3.

43. Plutarch, *Pyrrhos* 4–11; N. G. L. Hammond, "Which Ptolemy Gave Troops and Stood as Protector of Pyrrhus' Kingdom?" 405–13.

44. Dionysios of Halikarnassos, *Roman Archaeology* 20.14.1.

45. Justin 26.3.2.

46. Hölbl, *History of the Ptolemaic Empire*, 55. On Romans who were connected to the Ptolemies at an early date, see Peremans and Dack, "Sur les rapports de Rome avec les Lagides," 660–67.

47. Polybios 9.11a; Livy 27.4.10.

48. Livy 27.30.4–12, 28.7.13–16.

49. The details are well outlined by Gruen, *Hellenistic World and the Coming of Rome*, 678–92.

50. Polybios 16.34.3, 18.1.14, 18.50.5; Livy 22.33.3, 27.30.4–12, 33.40.3; Appian, *Syrian Wars* 2–3.

51. Livy 35.13.4; Porphyrios (*FGrHist* #260) F47; Appian, *Syrian Wars* 5.

52. Porphyrios (*FGrHist* #260) F48.

53. Hölbl, *History of the Ptolemaic Empire*, 143.

54. Livy 42.6.4–5; Polybios 28.1; Diodoros, *Bibliotheke* 30.2.

55. *Tebtunis Papyrus* #33 (= *Select Papyri* [Loeb] #416).

56. Polybios 28.18–20; Livy 44.19.6–14.

57. Polybios 29.27.1.

58. Diodoros, *Bibliotheke* 31.18.2; Valerius Maximus 5.1f.

59. Polybios 31.10, 17–20.

60. *SEG* 9.7. The will survives only in this inscription, not in the literary tradition, perhaps indicating that it is of far more interest to modern scholars than to Ptolemy's contemporaries.

61. Missing from these events is Ptolemy VII, a son of Ptolemy VI and Cleopatra III who ruled briefly in 145 B.C. after his father died (and perhaps jointly with him just before) but was promptly eliminated by his uncle Ptolemy VIII; he was never crowned or generally recognized as king, which has caused difficulties for scholars ever since. Until recently it was common not to number him and to reduce the numeration of all successive Ptolemies by one, a confusing issue for the reader of older modern works.

62. Plutarch, *Tiberius Gracchus* 1.4. On Cornelia, see Dixon, *Cornelia*.

63. On Roman citizenship and the Ptolemies, see Roller, *World of Juba II*, 84–86.

64. Josephus, *Jewish Antiquities* 12.235. He was king for 54 years, from 170 to 116 B.C., although at first jointly with his siblings, then briefly alone in Alexandria, and then in Cyrene before returning to Alexandria in 145 B.C. For the fragments of his *Hypomnemata* see *FGrHist* #234.

Chapter 3

1. *OxyPap* 1241.

2. *OGIS* 172.

3. Fraser, *Ptolemaic Alexandria*, 1: 312, 361–62, 806–9. On this generally, see Marasco, "Cléopâtre et les sciences de son temps," 39–53.

4. Since Apollonios himself was from Cyprus, it is impossible to determine which king is meant. The extant treatise is a commentary to *On Limbs*, in the Hippokratic corpus. For the sources, see Fraser, *Ptolemaic Alexandria*, 1:362; Stok, "Apollonios of Kition," 113–14.

5. Celsus 5.23.2; Stok, "Zopuros of Alexandria."

6. Irby-Massie, "Khrusermos of Alexandria."

7. Strabo, *Geography* 14.1.34; Galen 1.305; Athenaios, *Deipnosophistai* 15.688–89; Irby-Massie, "Herakleides of Eruthrai," 370, and "Apollonios Mus," 111–12.

8. Plutarch, *Antonius* 82.2.

9. Cicero, *Academica*, provides much of the extant information about philosophical life in Alexandria during the reign of Ptolemy XII.

10. Plutarch, *Brutus* 2; Fraser, *Ptolemaic Alexandria*, 1:487–91.

11. Strabo, *Geography* 17.1.5; Stobaios 2.7.2.

12. Supra, p. 23. He is probably the Dion mentioned anecdotally by Plutarch (*Symposiakon* 1 [612d]) and Athenaios (*Deipnosophistai* 1.34b).

13. Suetonius, *Augustus* 89.1; Plutarch, *Antonius* 80.2; Julian, *Letter to Themistios*; Seneca, *To Marcia* 3.4.2–4.

14. *FGrHist* #88; *Suda*, "Timagenes"; Plutarch, *Antonius* 72.2; Seneca, *On Anger* 3.23.4–7.

15. Philostratos, *Lives of the Sophists* 5, implies that Cleopatra taught Philostratos, an unlikely situation but perhaps a subtle demonstration of her reputation as an educated woman; Plutarch, *Antonius* 80.3.

16. Krinagoras 20; Roller, *Building Program of Herod the Great*, 62–63.

17. Plutarch, *Antonius* 27; infra, p. 169.

18. Plutarch, *Pyrrhus* 18–21; Cicero, *de finibus* 5.89.

19. Fitzmyer, "Languages of Palestine," 504–7. The two major men in Cleopatra's life, Julius Caesar and Marcus Antonius, both used Latin in Judaea (Josephus, *Jewish Antiquities* 14.191, 319).

20. *OGIS* 129.

21. Pliny, *Natural History* 6.183; Diodoros, *Bibliotheke* 1.33; Hölbl, *History of the Ptolemaic Empire*, 56–58.

22. Plutarch, *Antonius* 69.

23. Diodoros, *Bibliotheke* 19.94; Strabo, *Geography* 16.4.4; Pliny, *Natural History* 12.56–81.

24. Fitzmyer, "Languages of Palestine," 518–28.

25. Ptolemy VIII (*FGrHist* #234) F7–8; Roller, "Note on the Berber Head in London," 144–46.

26. For the circumstances of the collapse and provincialization of the Numidian kingdom, see Roller, *World of Juba II*, 30–38.

27. The letter was paraphrased by Josephus, *Jewish Antiquities* 12.20–23.

28. Pliny, *Natural History* 30.4; Athenaios, *Deipnosophistai* 2.58f, 5.213f.

29. *FGrHist* #609.

30. Fraser, *Ptolemaic Alexandria*, 1:330; infra, p. 132.

31. Fraser, *Ptolemaic Alexandria*, 1:311.

32. Scholia to Aristophanes, *Thesmophoriazousai* 1059.

33. *FGrHist* #275.

34. *FGrHist* #236.

35. Aulus Gellius, *Noctes atticae* 1.10.4; Suetonius, *Divine Julius* 56.5–7.

36. Pliny, *Natural History* 25.5–7.

37. If one assumes that *Sibylline Oracle* 3.350–80 refers to the queen, her role as successor to Mithradates seems certain. See further, infra, pp. 170–71.

38. The title is preserved both in the singular and plural: τὸ κοσμητικόν or τὰ κοσμητικά: Galen 12.403–5, 434–35, 492–93, 13.432–34, 19.767–71; Aetios of Amida 8.6; Paulos 3.2.1; Nardis, "Kleopatra of Alexandria," 488–89. Fragments are numbered as in Plant, *Women Writers of Ancient Greece and Rome*, 136–38.

39. Plant, *Women Writers of Ancient Greece and Rome*, 135.

40. Plant, *Women Writers of Ancient Greece and Rome*, 141–42. Nero reduced the denarius to the equivalent of 3.375 gm.: see Richardson, *Numbering and Measuring in the Classical World*, 39.

41. It was known to Aristotle (*Problems* 10.27).

42. Another literary Cleopatra, who wrote on alchemy, is unlikely to have been the queen. See Irby-Massie and Keyser, *Greek Science of the Hellenistic Era*, 244.

43. Dio 42.42.4.

44. Philostratos, *Lives of the Sophists* 5.

Chapter 4

1. For the period, see Heinen, *Rom und Ägypten*.

2. Samuel, *Ptolemaic Chronology*, 156–60, is a useful guide to the chronology of the reign of Cleopatra VII.

3. Hölbl, *History of the Ptolemaic Empire*, 231; Ricketts, *Administration*, 12–21; Tarn, "Bucheum Stele," 187–89; Weill Goudchaux, "Cleopatra's Subtle Religious Strategy," 132–33. For doubt on whether she attended (based largely on chronological grounds), see Skeat, "Notes on Ptolemaic Chronology III," 101. The Augustan date of the inscription can also be used to question its accuracy.

4. Letter of M. Caelius Rufus to Cicero, 1 August 51 B.C. (*ad familiares* 8.4).

5. Plutarch, *Caesar* 48.4.

6. These issues are discussed in detail by Rostovtzeff, *Social and Economic History*, 877–914; see also Maehler, "Egypt under the Last Ptolemies," 6–7.

7. *Select Papyri* (Loeb) #209; Lenger, *Corpus des Ordonnances des Ptolémées*, #73 (see also #74–76); Thompson, "Cleopatra VII: The Queen in Egypt," 32–33.

8. *BGU* 1760.

9. Pliny, *Natural History* 5.58.

10. Cicero, *Letters to Atticus* 119 (late June of 50 B.C.); Caesar, *Civil War* 3.110; Valerius Maximus 4.1.15; Seneca, *To Marcia* 14.2; Hazzard, *Imagination of a Monarchy*, 149; Gray-Fow, "Mental Breakdown of a Roman Senator," 179–90.

11. Caesar, *Civil War* 3.6–18.

12. Thompson, *Memphis under the Ptolemies*, 124–25. Herodotos's discussion of the bull cult (2.38), from the fifth century B.C., remains one of the classic moments of Greek literature.

13. Dio 42.36.3.

14. Caesar, *Civil War* 3.108; Appian, *Civil War* 2.84.

15. Dio 42.35.5; Livy, *Summary* 112; Caesar, *Civil War* 3.108.

16. Ricketts, "Chronological Problem in the Reign of Cleopatra VII," 213–17; Heinen, *Rom und Ägypten*, 23–36.

17. Ricketts, *Administration*, 21–30. An alternative explanation is that Year 1 refers to Ptolemy XIV, but the matter is quite confused and uncertain. See further, Skeat, "Notes on Ptolemaic Chronology," 100–105.

18. Plutarch, *Antonius* 25.3; Caesar, *Civil War* 3.4, 40; Appian, *Civil War* 2.49, 71.

19. He was to be recalled by Caesar but died probably in late 49 or early 48 B.C. (Dio 42.11).

20. Supra, p. 26; Caesar, *Civil War* 3.108; Dio 42.35.4; Lucan 8.448–49.

21. Plutarch, *Antonius* 25.3 (he is described along with Caesar and Antonius as Romans influenced personally by the queen).

22. Dio 42.12. The elder Pompeius was criticized for not using his naval forces effectively: Plutarch (*Pompeius* 76) called it his greatest strategic error.

23. Lucan (5.58–64, 8.448) saw this as an especially despicable act; see Heinen, *Rom und Ägypten*, 18–20.

24. Malalas 9.217.

25. Caesar, *Civil War* 3.103, 107; Livy, *Summary* 111; Appian, *Civil War* 2.84; Strabo, *Geography* 17.1.11.

26. Supra, p. 24; Sullivan, *Near Eastern Royalty and Rome, 100–30 B.C.*, 204–5.

27. They probably lasted throughout her reign: a certain Seleukos was one of her commanders in Egypt after Actium (Plutarch, *Antonius* 74.1).

28. Caesar, *Civil War* 3.102.

29. Brett, "New Cleopatra Tetradrachm of Ascalon," 452–63; Spaer, "Royal Male Head and Cleopatra at Ascalon," 347–50; supra, p. 24.

30. Caesar, *Civil War* 3.99; Appian, *Civil War* 2.82–84; Plutarch, *Pompeius* 73–76; Dio 42.2–3. Huzar, *Mark Antony*, 56–62, has a good summary of the battle.

31. Caesar, *Civil War* 3.103–4, 110; Dio 42.3–5; Appian, *Civil War* 2.84–86; Plutarch, *Pompeius* 77–80. See also the lengthy and vivid poetical description by Lucan (8.472–712).

32. It is impossible to refine the chronology to the point of determining whether Cleopatra was still in Syria when Caesar arrived in Egypt, as Strabo implied (*Geography* 17.1.11).

33. Appian, *Civil War* 2.84.

34. Caesar, *Civil War* 3.106–7, 112; Appian, *Civil War* 2.89.

35. Caesar, *Civil War* 3.107; Suetonius, *Divine Julius* 35; Plutarch, *Caesar* 48.4.

36. Dio 42.34.3–6; see also Lucan 10.56–60, 82–84.

37. Plutarch, *Caesar* 49.1–2 (infra, pp. 169–70). The word, στρωματόδεσμος (*stromatodesmos*), is not common but appears from at least the fifth century

B.C. (see *LSJ*). The meaning is clear and it is not, as popular imagination has it, a carpet. See Whitehorne, "Cleopatra's Carpet," 1287–93.

38. Gruen, "Cleopatra in Rome," 265.

39. Appian, *Civil War* 4.40.

40. A hint by Lucan (10.67) suggests that this was one of the possibilities; see also Florus 2.13.55–57.

41. Criscuolo, "La successione a Tolemeo Aulete," 325–39.

42. Caesar, *Civil War* 3.108–10; Dio 42.36–38; Plutarch, *Caesar* 49.2–3.

43. Dio 42.38.2; Ammianus 22.16.13; Seneca, *On Tranquility* 9.5; Aulus Gellius, *Noctes atticae* 7.17.3; Orosios 6.15.31–32. It is interesting that the fire is not mentioned in *de bello alexandrino*. See also Fraser, *Ptolemaic Alexandria*, 1:334–35; Casson, *Libraries in the Ancient World*, 45–47; Robert Barnes, "Cloistered Bookworms," 70–72.

44. Caesar, *Civil War* 3.112; Plutarch, *Caesar* 49.2–3; Appian, *Civil War* 2.90; *de bello alexandrino* 4–9, 23–25; Dio 42.39–40. According to Appian, it was Caesar who killed Achillas.

45. *De bello alexandrino* 1, 26; Josephus, *Jewish War* 1.187–94, and *Jewish Antiquities* 14.127–37.

46. *De bello alexandrino* 31–33; Livy, *Summary* 112; Florus 2.13.60; Josephus, *Jewish Antiquities* 15.89; Dio 43.19.2.

47. Plutarch, *Pompeius* 80.6.

48. *De bello alexandrino* 33.

49. Dio 42.20–21.

50. Suetonius, *Divine Julius* 35.

51. *De bello alexandrino* 33; Strabo, *Geography* 17.1.11; Dio 42.44; Hölbl, *History of the Ptolemaic Empire*, 237; Criscuolo, "La successione a Tolemeo Aulete," 325–39.

52. Strabo, *Geography* 14.6.6.

53. Dio 48.40.6.

54. Appian, *Civil War* 5.9.

55. Bicknell, "Caesar, Antony, Cleopatra and Cyprus," 325–42.

56. Dio 42.45.1; Huzar, *Mark Antony*, 64–67.

57. Cicero, *Letters to Atticus* #226, 229–31. The letters run from 14 May to 5 July, when there is finally a rumor that Caesar has left.

58. Hillard, "Nile Cruise," 549–54; Lord, "Date of Julius Caesar's Departure," 19–40; Sullivan, *Near Eastern Royalty and Rome, 100–30 B.C.*, 260; but see Heinen, *Rom und Ägypten*, 148–58.

59. Lucan 10.268.

60. Suetonius, *Divine Julius* 52.1; Appian, *Civil War* 2.90.

61. Kallixeinos of Rhodes (*FGrHist* #627), *On Alexandria* F1 (= Athenaios, *Deipnosophistai* 5.204–6); for details of the *thalamegos*, see Nielsen, *Hellenistic Palaces*, 136–38 (with hypothetical deck plan); Hillard, "Nile Cruise," 549–54.

62. Strabo, *Geography* 17.1.16.

63. Caesar, *Gallic War* 6.24; Roller, *Through the Pillars of Herakles*, 116–17. In the late third century B.C., Eratosthenes had written the first systematic study of world geography, essentially inventing the discipline. Pytheas had traveled to the British Isles, Arctic, and Baltic in the latter fourth century B.C., and Poseidonios wrote a major geographical study in the early first century B.C.

64. The source of the Nile as a goal is suggested in Lucan's fictionalized account (10.189–92). Lucan's lengthy speech attributed to the priest Acoreus concerns this topic.

65. Malalas 9.217; Strabo, *Geography* 17.1.9; Sjöqvist, "Kaisareion," 86–108; Fishwick, "Temple of Caesar at Alexandria," 131–34.

66. Lord, "Date of Julius Caesar's Departure," 19–40.

67. Appian, *Civil War* 2.91, 3.78, 4.59; Plutarch, *Caesar* 49.5; *de bello alexandrino* 33; Suetonius, *Divine Julius* 76.3. By March of 43 B.C. there were four legions (letter of L. Cassius Longinus to Cicero [Cicero, *ad familiares* 12.11]).

Chapter 5

1. Plutarch, *Caesar* 49.5; Grzybek, "Pharao Caesar in einer demotischen Grabinschrift aus Memphis," 149–58; Hölbl, *History of the Ptolemaic Empire*, 238.

2. Plutarch, *Antonius* 54.4: Κλεοπάτραν ἔγκυον καταλιπόντος.

3. Cicero, *Letters to Atticus* #374, 377; Balsdon, "Ides of March," 80–94. See also Chaveau, *Cleopatra*, 32–33. The best summary of the issues—more complex than one might think—is Heinen, "Cäsar und Kaisarion," 181–203.

4. Plutarch, *Caesar* 49.5: καταλιπὼν δὲ τὴν Κλεοπάτραν βασιλεύουσαν Αἰγύπτου καὶ μικρὸν ὕστερον ἐξ αὐτοῦ τεκοῦσαν υἱόν.

5. Meiklejohn, "Alexander Helios and Caesarion," 191–95.

6. Plutarch, *Caesar* 51; Appian, *Civil War* 2.92; Dio 42.50.

7. Suetonius, *Divine Julius* 52.2.

8. Nikolaos of Damascus, *Life of Augustus* 20. See also Dio 47.31.5, which states that Cleopatra fabricated Kaisarion's parentage.

9. Ashton, "Cleopatra: Goddess, Ruler, or Regent?" 25–29. On Cleopatra as Isis, see infra pp. 114–17.

10. Dio 43.27.3; Suetonius, *Divine Julius* 52.1; Aly, "Cleopatra and Caesar at Alexandria and Rome," 49–50, suggested an arrival date of August, meaning that she would be at the triumph. See also Dack, "La date de C. Ord. Ptol. 80–83 = BGU VI 1212 et le séjour de Cléopâtre VII à Rome," 53–67.

11. Cicero, *Letters to Atticus* #301. His efforts were both unsuccessful and unnecessary, as he succeeded naturally as Ariarathes X three years later.

12. For an alternative view, see Böhn, "Wo war/Was tat Cleopatra an den Iden des März 44?" (Cicero, *ad Atticum* XV, 15, 2)," 151–55.

13. Valerius Maximus 5.1f; Diodoros, *Bibliotheke* 31.18.2.

14. Gruen, "Cleopatra in Rome," 257–74.

15. Suetonius, *Divine Julius* 52; Dio 43.27.3.

16. Plutarch, *Antonius* 58.6.

17. See Cicero, *Letters to Atticus* #393; see also #24, 26 (from 59 B.C.), for the account of his acquisition of the rare *Geographika* of Eratosthenes; for Ammonios, see Cicero, *ad familiares* 1.1.1.

18. Suetonius, *Divine Julius* 44.2. The project, like so many of Caesar's, was never implemented during his lifetime.

19. Suetonius, *Divine Julius* 44.2–3.

20. Richardson Jr., *New Topographical Dictionary*, 165–67; Dio 51.22.3; Appian, *Civil War* 2.102. On some of the problems in interpreting the two textual citations, see Kleiner, *Cleopatra and Rome*, 149–50; Gruen, "Cleopatra in Rome," 259. The statue may be represented in a Pompeian wall painting: *infra*, pp. 174–75.

21. Hölbl , *History of the Ptolemaic Empire*, 290; Dio 47.15.4.

22. Plutarch, *Antonius* 12.

23. Cicero, *Philippics* 2.85.

24. See the astute discussion of the need for two trips by Gruen, "Cleopatra in Rome," 267–73.

25. Suetonius, *Divine Julius* 52.1.

26. Cicero, *Letters to Atticus* #362, 374, 377, 381, 393–94; #362, of 16 April, refers to her departure; in #374 of 11 May there is a hint that Cleopatra had a miscarriage.

27. Ptolemy XIV is last mentioned on 26 July (*OxyPap* 1629); see also Josephus, *Jewish Antiquities* 15.89; Porphyrios (*FGrHist* #260) F2.16–17; *OGIS* 194.

28. Dio 47.31; Appian, *Civil War* 3.78, 4.59, 61, 63, 74, 5.8; letter of Cassius to Cicero of 7 March 43 B.C. (Cicero, *ad familiares* 12.11).

29. Brenk, "Antony—Osiris, Cleopatra—Isis," 159–82.

30. Huzar, *Mark Antony*, 129–47.

31. Appian, *Civil War* 5.7; Martial 11.20.

32. Plutarch, *Antonius* 10.3. The "rule of women" (γυναικοκρατία, gynaikokratia) is a concept developed by Aristotle (*Politics* 2.6.6, 5.9.6), but seen negatively, a characteristic of states such as Sparta.

33. Plutarch, *Antonius* 2–3, and *Brutus* 20.4.

34. Pelling, *Plutarch: Life of Antony*, 181–82.

35. Plutarch, *Antonius* 26.1.

36. Strabo, *Geography* 11.13.3; Seneca, *Suasoria* 1.7; Roller, *Building Program of Herod the Great*, 28.

37. Homer, *Iliad* 14.161–65.

38. Appian, *Civil War* 5.8.

39. Josephus, *Jewish War* 1.226.

40. For the *thalamegos*, supra, p. 66. The boat was capable of a sea journey if handled carefully (Appian, *Preface* 10).

41. Xenophon, *Anabasis* 1.2.23.

42. Plutarch, *Antonius* 26 (infra, p. 170); Sokrates of Rhodes (*FGrHist* #192) F1 [= Athenaios, *Deipnosophistai* 4.147–48]).

43. These scenes were one of Vergil's sources for the banquet between Dido and Aeneas (*Aeneid* 1.723–27); Pelling, *Plutarch: Life of Antony*, 190.

44. Dio 47.30.5; Appian, *Civil War* 4.62, 5.8.

45. Josephus, *Against Apion* 2.57, and *Jewish Antiquities* 15.89; Appian, *Civil War* 5.9, Dio 48.24.2. Evidence from the excavators of Ephesos suggests that the Octagon in the central part of the site may have been Arsinoë's grave (Thür, "Arsinoe IV, eine Schwester Kleopatras VII, Grabinhaberin des Oktogons von Ephesos?" 43–56, and her "Processional Way in Ephesos as a Place of Cult and Burial," 178–83).

46. Plutarch, *Antonius* 28–30; Appian, *Civil War* 5.10–11.

47. Carney, "Women and *Dunasteia* in Caria," 65–91.

48. Leon, "One Roman's Family," 61–65.

49. Hopkins, "Contraception in the Roman Empire," 124–51.

50. Plutarch, *Antonius* 28.2, repeated at 71.3: the word is not otherwise documented, although alluded to, satirically, in *OGIS* 195, an inscription of 28 December 34 B.C., where "Initimable Liver" has become "Inimitable Aphrodisian" (i.e., "Lover," ἀμίμητον Ἀφροδίσιος). See Fraser, "Mark Antony in Alexandria—A Note," 71–73; also Pelling, *Plutarch: Life of Antony*, 195. The banquet Lucan (10.136–71) had Cleopatra serve Caesar, although fictionalized, may be based on data from this period.

51. Intinsky, "Bemerkungen Ueber die Ersten Schenkungen des Antonius an Kleopatra," 2:975–79.

52. Diodoros, *Bibliotheke* 20.19.5; Theokritos 17.86–90; Hölbl, *History of the Ptolemaic Empire*, 48.

53. Strabo, *Geography* 14.5.3, 6; Michaelidou-Nicolaou, *Prosopography of Ptolemaic Cyprus*, 53; Pouilloux et al., *Salamine de Chypre* 13: *Testimonia Salaminia* 2, #97.

54. Strabo, *Geography* 14.5.10.

55. Pelling, *Plutarch: Life of Antony*, 197–98.

56. Plutarch, *Antonius* 30.2, 33.2; Dio 48.24.3–8.

57. Roller, *World of Juba II*, 77–79.

58. Plutarch, *Antonius* 36.3.

59. Appian, *Civil War* 5.32–49.

60. Pelling, *Plutarch: Life of Antony*, 197–99.

61. Appian, *Civil War* 5.7.

62. Augustus F4 (= Martial 11.20); Scott, "Political Propaganda of 44–30 B.C.," 24–25.

63. Plutarch, *Antonius* 30–31; Appian, *Civil War* 5.64–65.

64. The exact dating of this journey is uncertain. For details of the chronology followed here (late 40 B.C.), see Roller, *Building Program of Herod the Great*, 11–12, but for the suggestion that it was earlier in 40 B.C. (i.e., the late winter of 41–40 B.C.), see Kokkinos, *Herodian Dynasty*, 367–68. It is impossible to be certain, although the earlier date has more problems than the latter, given that it would require Antonius to leave Alexandria early enough for Herod himself to leave in "midwinter" and for Antonius, who was involved with Labienus as soon as he left Alexandria, to have ended up in Rome while Herod (who was in the city only briefly) was still there (Josephus, *Jewish War* 1.279–85).

65. Josephus, *Jewish War* 1.242–45, and *Jewish Antiquities* 14.324–26.

66. For further on Cleopatra and Herod, see infra, pp. 118–22.

Chapter 6

1. Plutarch, *Antonius* 33.4; Appian, *Civil War* 5.76.

2. Josephus, *Jewish War* 1.290–357, and *Jewish Antiquities* 14.394–491.

3. Plutarch, *Antonius* 36.1; Appian, *Civil War* 5.76.

4. Plutarch, *Antonius* 35; Dio 48.54.

5. Plutarch, *Antonius* 36; Meiklejohn, "Alexander Helios and Caesarion," 191–95.

6. Sullivan, *Near Eastern Royalty and Rome, 100–30 B.C.*, 171–74.

7. Sullivan, *Near Eastern Royalty and Rome, 100–30 B.C.*, 151–53.

8. Sullivan, *Near Eastern Royalty and Rome, 100–30 B.C.*, 180–85.

9. Reinhold, *From Republic to Principate*, 63.

10. Plutarch, *Antonius* 36; Dio 49.32.4–5; Josephus, *Jewish War* 1.361–63, and *Jewish Antiquities* 15.91–96; Porphyrios (*FGrHist* #260) F2.17. A thorough discussion of the evidence for the territorial gifts is by Schrapel, *Das Reich der Kleopatra*, especially pp. 17–207.

11. Kokkinos, *Herodian Dynasty*, 115–16, 131–32.

12. Infra, p. 182; Schrapel, *Das Reich der Kleopatra*, 226–28.

13. This is mentioned in a single obscure notice, Porphyrios (*FGrHist* #260) F2.17, and it is far from certain exactly where this petty kingdom was, as there are two Syrian cities in the region with the name Chalkis (see Cohen, *Hellenistic Settlements*, 143–45, 239–42).

14. It is possible that Lysanias and Lysimachos, obscure contemporaries ruling essentially contiguous territories, were the same person. But it is improbable that Cleopatra had the former eliminated to acquire his territory, as Josephus asserted (*Jewish Antiquities* 15.92).

15. Josephus, *Jewish War* 1.398–99, and *Jewish Antiquities* 15.344, 17.319; Kokkinos, *Herodian Dynasty*, 281.

16. Walker and Higgs, *Cleopatra of Egypt*, #235.

17. Heinen, "Syrian-Egyptian Wars," 440–42.

18. Strabo, *Geography* 16.2.41; Theophrastos, *Research on Plants* 9.6.

19. Cleopatra's control of the bitumen sources—important for the Egyptian mummification industry—is not specifically documented but probable (see Philip C. Hammond, "Nabataean Bitumen Industry at the Dead Sea," 47–48).

20. Sullivan, *Near Eastern Royalty and Rome, 100–30 B.C.*, 207–8.

21. Plutarch, *Antonius* 36.2; Bowersock, *Roman Arabia*, 41.

22. Diodoros, *Bibliotheke* 3.43.5; Strabo, *Geography* 16.4.18.

23. Hölbl, *History of the Ptolemaic Empire*, 42–43.

24. Pelling, "Triumviral Period," 30.

25. Dio 49.38.1; Reinhold, From Republic to Principate, 72.

26. Plutarch, *Gaius Gracchus* 4.3–4; Pliny, *Natural History* 34.31; Dixon, *Cornelia*, 29–31.

27. Flory, "Livia and the History of Public Honorific Statues for Women in Rome," 287–308.

28. Hölbl, *History of the Ptolemaic Empire*, 242.

29. Porphyrios (*FGrHist* #260) F2.17; see Sherk, *Rome and the Greek East to the Death of Augustus*, #88; Forrer, *Portraits of Royal Ladies*, #120. On the unlikely possibility that this double dating represents a regency or joint rule of Caesarion, see Samuel, "Joint Regency of Cleopatra and Caesarion," 73–79.

30. Pelling, *Plutarch: Life of Antony*, 193–94.

31. Plutarch, *Antonius* 37–51; Strabo, *Geography* 11.13.3; Livy, *Summary* 130; Pelling, "Plutarch's Method of Work in the Roman Lives," 87–88.

32. Dio 43.51.2.

33. Plutarch, *Antonius* 37.4.

34. Josephus, *Jewish Antiquities* 15.96–103.

35. Livy, *Summary* 132; Dio 49.32.5.

36. Plutarch, *Antonius* 37.3; Justin 41.2.6.

37. Plutarch, *Antonius* 50.2–3, and *Comparison of Demetrios and Antonius* 5.2.

38. Buttrey Jr., "*Thea Neotera* on Coins of Antony and Cleopatra," 95–109.

39. Dio 49.32.1.

40. Plutarch, *Antonius* 52–53; Dio 49.33.

41. Huzar, *Mark Antony*, 191.

42. Appian, *Civil War* 5.142–44.

43. Livy, *Summary* 131; Plutarch, *Antonius* 50.3–4; Velleius 2.82.3.

44. Plutarch, *Antonius* 50.4; Dio 49.40.3–4.

45. Versnel, *Triumphus*, esp. 235–54.

46. Plutarch, *Antonius* 54.3–6; Dio 49.41, 44. For Ptolemy II's ceremony, see infra, p. 116.

47. He may have received honors on Delos at this time (*CIL* 3.7232).

48. For a detailed discussion, see Kokkinos, *Antonia Augusta*, 70–86.

49. For example, see the "Aegyptia coniunx" of Vergil (*Aeneid* 8.688), Suetonius's report (*Augustus* 69.2) of an explicitly descriptive letter Antonius wrote Octavian about the relationship, or the "Romam dotalem stupri turpis" of *Elegiae in Maecenatem* 1.53–54. See also Strabo, *Geography* 17.1.11, and Reinhold, *From Republic to Principate*, 220–22. Much has been written inconclusively about the marriage. See, in particular, Huzar, *Mark Antony*, 106–11; Volterra, "Ancora sul matrimonio di Antonio con Cleopatra," 1:205–12; Ors, "Cleopatra 'uxor' de Marco Antonio?" 639–42; Kraft, "Zur Sueton, Divus Augustus 69,2," 496–99.

50. It is cited briefly by Plutarch in his *Comparison of Demetrios and Antonius* (1.3, 4.1). On the difficulties of understanding whether there was a marriage, many of which are semantic, see Syme, *Roman Revolution*, 273–75, and Pelling, *Plutarch: Life of Antony*, 219–20. The ambiguity about marriage is another characteristic of Cleopatra and Antonius transferred to Dido and Aeneas (Vergil, *Aeneid* 4.172, 338–39).

51. Ashton, "Cleopatra: Goddess, Ruler, or Regent?" 27.

52. Dio 49.41.2; see also Livy, *Summary* 131: "as if his [Antonius's] wife."

53. Baldus, "Eine Münzprägung auf das Ehepaar Mark Anton—Kleopatra VII," 5–10.

54. The title is first documented in a contract of March 35 B.C. (Thompson, "Cleopatra VII: The Queen in Egypt," 31–34; Bingen, "Cléopâtre VII Philopatris," 118–23).

55. It was used of Demosthenes (Plutarch, *Letter to Apollonios* 33) and of Lykourgos of Sparta (Plutarch, *Kleomenes* 10.5); see also Polybios 1.14.4.

56. Dio 49.41.4.

Chapter 7

1. Pliny, *Natural History* 5.58; Seneca, *Natural Questions* 4a.2.16. See Thompson, "Egypt, 146–31 B.C.," 322–26.

2. Appian, *Civil War* 4.61, 63, 108.

3. Poseidonios T113 Kidd; Marasco, "Cléopâtre et les sciences de son temps," 46.

4. *BGU* 1843 (Rostovtzeff, *Social and Economic History*, 908).

5. *BGU* 1835.

6. Josephus, *Against Apion* 2.60.

7. *OGIS* 129; Thompson, "Cleopatra VII: The Queen in Egypt," 33.

8. Maehler, "Egypt under the Last Ptolemies," 7–8.

9. Josephus, *Jewish Antiquities* 16.128.

10. Strabo, *Geography* 14.5.6.

11. Livy, *Summary* 68; Velleius 2.31; Huzar, *Mark Antony*, 13–16.

12. Theokritos 17.77–81; Josephus, *Jewish War* 2.386.

13. Plutarch, *Antonius* 59.4.

14. A full and detailed list of Ptolemaic monopolies appears in Rostovtzeff, *Social and Economic History*, 274–316.

15. Orosius 6.19.20.

16. Strabo, *Geography* 2.1.20; Pliny, *Natural History* 6.174, 183, 37.24.

17. Strabo, *Geography* 2.3.4–6, 17.1.13.

18. Kosmas Indikopleustes, *Christian Topography* 3.65. No specific Ptolemy is cited, but given that the Indian route was opened up only at the end of the second century B.C., Ptolemy XII seems the only possibility.

19. Casson, *Periplus Maris Erythraei*, 169–70.

20. Lucan 10.141–43.

21. Ricketts, *Administration*, 46–47, 139–40.

22. Strabo, *Geography* 17.1.13.

23. *BMC Ptolemies*, lxxx–lxxxi.

24. The coins are in the relevant volumes of the *BMC*, but are conveniently summarized in Forrer, *Portraits of Royal Ladies*, 31–42; many appear in Walker and Higgs, *Cleopatra of Egypt*, and in Andreae et al., *Kleopatra und die Caesaren*.

25. Walker and Higgs, *Cleopatra of Egypt*, 177–78.

26. *BMC Ptolemies*, pp. 105–6, #5–6, 20–35.

27. *BMC Ptolemies*, p. 74, #62. It is possible that Ptolemy VIII struck a few gold coins in the name of his famous ancestor Arsinoë II: see Walker and Higgs, *Cleopatra of Egypt*, #78.

28. Braund, *Rome and the Friendly King*, 123–28.

29. Roller, *World of Juba II*, 253.

30. Supra, pp. 50–51. On the weights of Kleopatra's coinage, see Reinach, "Du rapport de valeur," 170–90.

31. Grant, *Cleopatra*, 48.

32. Sutherland, *Roman Coins*, 114.

33. *BMC Cyrenaica*, p. 117, #24–26; Roller, *World of Juba II*, 80–81. Cleopatra VII was also part of the titulature on the coinage of her daughter Cleopatra Selene after the latter became queen of Mauretania in 25 B.C.: see Mazard, "Un denier inedit de Juba II et Cléopâtre-Séléne," 1–2.

34. Visonà, "Tetradrachm of Cleopatra VII from Este," 47.

35. Ricketts, *Administration*, 137–49.

36. Plutarch, *Antonius* 76.5.

37. Seneca, *Letters* 87.16; *Suda*, "Chelidon."

38. Malalas 9.218; Loukianos, *How to Write History* 62. On this, see Fraser, *Ptolemaic Alexandria*, 2:48–49.

39. Minnen, "Royal Ordinance of Cleopatra," 36.

40. The statue is in the Detroit Institute of Arts (51.83).

41. Chaveau, *Egypt in the Age of Cleopatra*, 74.

42. Plutarch, *Antonius* 67.4, 77.1, 85.4.

43. Travlos, *Pictorial Dictionary of Ancient Athens*, 233–41; Roller, *World of Juba II*, 136–37.

44. Diodoros, *Bibliotheke* 17.52.

45. *De bello alexandrino* 13, 19.

46. Plutarch, *Caesar* 49.3; Dio 42.38.2; supra, p. 63.

47. Strabo, *Geography* 17.1.10.

48. Ammianus's report (22.16.10–11) that the Rhodians possessed the island of Pharos and were paid tribute by Cleopatra seems a garbling of the close trade relations between Alexandria and Rhodes, especially in the third century B.C. (Fraser, *Ptolemaic Alexandria*, 1:162–71), and the occupation of Pharos by Euphranor, commander of a Rhodian fleet in the service of Caesar during the Alexandrian War (*de bello alexandrino* 15, 25), who was killed in the fighting. There is no evidence of a Rhodian presence after the war.

49. Strabo, *Geography* 17.1.6; Pliny, *Natural History* 36.83.

50. Ammianus 22.16.9; Malalas 9.218.

51. Josephus, *Jewish Antiquities* 12.103; Ammianus 22.16.10–11; McKenzie, *Architecture of Alexandria and Egypt*, 45–47.

52. Plutarch, *Antonius* 58.5.

53. Malalas 9.217, suggested that this was not the only building project by Caesar in Alexandria, but he provided no further details.

54. Richardson Jr., *New Topographical Dictionary*, 165–67; Malalas 9.216.

55. Suetonius, *Augustus* 17.5; Dio 51.15.5.

56. Kleiner, *Roman Sculpture*, 45–46.

57. *Suda*, ἡμίεργον; Strabo, *Geography* 17.1.9; McKenzie, *Architecture of Alexandria and Egypt*, 177–78.

58. Fishwick, "Caesareum at Alexandria Again," 65–69; McKenzie, *Architecture of Alexandria and Egypt*, 77–79; Fraser, *Ptolemaic Alexandria*, 1:96–97.

59. Philon, *Embassy to Gaius* 151. For a reconstructed view, see Pfrommer, *Alexandria im Schatten der Pyramiden*, 135.

60. Pliny, *Natural History* 36.69.

61. A temple of Hermes credited to the queen is probably a late misunderstanding; see Dunand and Zivie-Coche, *Gods and Men in Egypt*, 242–44; McKenzie, *Architecture of Alexandria and Egypt*, 406–7.

62. Suetonius, *Augustus* 18.1.

63. Plutarch, *Antonius* 74, 76–77, 86; Dio 51.10.4–15.1; Suetonius, *Augustus* 17.4; McKenzie, *Architecture of Alexandria and Egypt*, 78–79. A reconstructed view is in Pfrommer, *Alexandria im Schatten*, 142–44.

64. Arrian, *Anabasis* 3.1.5.

65. Martial 4.59.5–6.

66. Tacitus, *Annals* 2.53, 59–61.

67. Fraser, *Ptolemaic Alexandria*, 2:33–34; Bickel, "Das Mausoleum der Kleo-patra und des Antonius in lateinischer Dischtung," 191–92. See also Malalas 9.219.

68. Strabo, *Geography* 5.3.8; Roller, *Building Program of Herod the Great*, 72–73, 164–68, and *World of Juba II*, 128–30.

69. Strabo, *Geography* 17.1.8–9; Nielsen, *Hellenistic Palaces*, 130–33.

70. Diodoros, *Bibliotheke* 17.52.4.

71. McKenzie, *Architecture of Alexandria and Egypt*, 68–71; Grimm, "Kleopatras Palast?" 509–12.

72. The elaborate structure depicted on the wall of Room M of the Boscoreale villa near Pompeii now in New York (Metropolitan Museum 03.14.13) has been suggested to show the palace of the Ptolemies (see Pfrommer, *Alexandria im Schatten*, 138–40).

73. Lucan 10.111–71. Another poetic account of the palace of the Ptolemies of an earlier era—the third century B.C.—is found in Apollonios's description of the palace of Aietes in Colchis (*Argonautika* 3.210–44).

74. Kleiner, *Cleopatra and Rome*, 85–87; Quaegebeur, "Cléopâtre VII et le temple de Dendara," 49–72.

75. Ray, "Cleopatra in the Temples of Upper Egypt," 9–11.

76. Porter and Moss, *Topographical Bibliography*, 128; Walker and Higgs, *Cleopatra of Egypt*, #170; Ashton, "Cleopatra: Goddess, Ruler, or Regent?" 25–26.

77. McKenzie, *Architecture of Alexandria and Egypt*, 131; Weill Goudchaux, "Cleopatra's Subtle Religious Strategy," 136–37; for the archaeological details, see Porter and Moss, *Topographical Bibliography*, 151–57.

78. Weill Goudchaux, "Cleopatra's Subtle Religious Strategy," 136.

79. Lenger, *Corpus des Ordonnances des Ptolémées*, #67.

80. There are six sites with the name listed in Mueller, *Settlements of the Ptolemies*, 205, but not all date to the time of Cleopatra VII; see also Calderini, *Dizionario dei nomi geografici e topografici dell'Egitto greco-romano* 3, part 1, 124–26.

81. Strabo, *Geography* 16.4.23, 17.1.26. On the topographic and onomastic issues regarding this town, see Agatharchides (ed. Burstein) 134; Mayerson, "Aelius Gallus at Cleopatris (Suez) and on the Red Sea," 17–24.

82. Talbert, *Barrington Atlas*, map 77; Drew-Bear, *Le nome Hermopolite*, 141–44.

83. Herodotos 2.42, 59.

84. Arrian, *Anabasis* 3.1.5; Tarn, *Alexander the Great*, 2:49–62, 358.

85. Hölbl, *History of the Ptolemaic Empire*, 93–94.

86. Weill Goudchaux, "Cleopatra's Subtle Religious Strategy," 130–31.

87. Herodotos 2.59, 156.

88. *IG* 2.2.4994.

89. About a dozen places named Arsinoë are known: see Talbert, *Barrington Atlas*, index; Hölbl, *History of the Ptolemaic Empire*, 101–4.

90. Alfano, "Egyptian Influences in Italy," 279–85.

91. Hölbl, *History of the Ptolemaic Empire*, 286.

92. Ricketts, *Administration*, 39.

93. Plutarch, *Antonius* 54.6; Ashton, "Cleopatra: Goddess, Ruler, or Regent?" 27. For a good depiction of Isis at the time of the queen, see the bronze figurine in the British Museum (GR 1824.4–51.3 [Bronze 1467]), from the first century B.C. (Walker and Higgs, *Cleopatra of Egypt*, #338).

94. Dio 47.15.4: it was actually voted by the triumvirs in 43 B.C., but it was surely one of Caesar's plans.

95. Richardson Jr., *New Topographical Dictionary*, 211–12.

96. Dio 42.26.1–2.

97. Kallixeinos of Rhodes (*FGrHist* #627) F2 (= Athenaios, *Deipnosophistai* 5.197–200). See further, Erskine, "Culture and Power in Ptolemaic Egypt," 43–44.

98. Fraser, *Ptolemaic Alexandria*, 1:244.

99. Malalas 8.197; Nock, "Notes on Ruler Cult," 30–41.

100. Chaniotis, "Divinity of Hellenistic Rulers," 432–33.

101. Pliny, *Natural History* 8.4; Pausanias 8.46.5.

102. Appian, *Civil War* 2.144.

103. Forrer, *Portraits of Royal Ladies*, #111.

104. Plutarch, *Antonius* 24, 26.3.

105. Dio 48.39.2; Seneca, *Suasoria* 1.6–7; Plutarch, *Antonius* 60.2–3; Velleius 2.82.4; Nock, "Notes on Ruler Cult," 30–38.

106. Herodotos 2.42; Dio 50.5.3; Brenk, "Antony—Osiris, Cleopatra—Isis," 159–82.

107. Malalas 8.197.

108. Dio 50.15.2; Plutarch, *Antonius* 61.3.

109. These statues were located on the Pergamene monument (Plutarch, *Antonius* 61.3) whose base is still conspicuously visible to the left of the entrance to the Akropolis.

110. Forrer, *Portraits of Royal Ladies*, #135.

111. *OGIS* 196.

112. Plutarch, *Antonius* 75.4.

113. For many examples, see Pelling, *Plutarch: Life of Antony*, 303–4.

114. For example, see Aeschylus, *Seven against Thebes* 217–18.

115. Hölbl, *History of the Ptolemaic Empire*, 293; infra, pp. 148–49.

116. Dio 50.25.3–4.

117. Nock, "Notes on Ruler Cult," 36.

118. Strabo, *Geography* 17.1.9.

119. On the phenomenon of the allied and friendly king, see the detailed study by Braund, *Rome and the Friendly King*.

120. *FGrHist* #236.

121. For the negative portrait of Cleopatra in Josephus's works, see Simões Rodrigues, "O Judeu e a Egípcia," 217–60.

122. Josephus, *Jewish War* 1.360.

123. On Malchos, see Sullivan, *Near Eastern Royalty and Rome, 100–30 B.C.*, 211–13.

124. Josephus, *Jewish War* 1.364–65, 7.300–303.

125. Josephus, *Jewish War* 1.344, and *Jewish Antiquities* 14.407.

126. Josephus, *Jewish Antiquities* 15.9, 22.

127. Josephus, *Jewish Antiquities* 15.23–38.

128. Kokkinos, *Herodian Dynasty*, 185.

129. Josephus, *Jewish Antiquities* 15.97–103, but see Kokkinos, "Cleopatra and Herod," 17.

130. Josephus, *Jewish Antiquities* 15.254–58.

131. Josephus, *Jewish War* 1.360, 365.

Chapter 8

1. Fraser, *Ptolemaic Alexandria*, 1:361–62; Stok, "Herakleides of Alexandria," 373–74.

2. Keyser, "Antiokhis of Tlos," 95.

3. Plutarch, *Antonius* 28; Oldfather, "Friend of Plutarch's Grandfather," 177; Scarborough, "Philotas of Amphissa," 668.

4. For an exhaustive list, see Marasco, "Cléopâtre et les sciences de son temps," 39–53, although not all can be associated with Cleopatra or even her precise era.

5. Soranus, *Gynaecology* 4.12.5; Celsus, *Preface* 3, 7.14.1; Aelian, *On the Characteristics of Animals* 5.27, 6.51; Athenaios, *Deipnosophistai* 7.303b, 312e; Fraser, *Ptolemaic Alexandria*, 1:363; Zucker, "Sostratos of Alexandria," 762.

6. *Suda*, "Dioskourides." The epithet was to distinguish him from Dioskourides of Anazarbos, author of the extant *Materials of Medicine*. See also Caesar, *Civil War* 3.109; Scarborough, "Dioskourides Phakas," 272.

7. Plutarch, *Antonius* 82.2, 59.4; Irby-Massie, "Olumpos of Alexandria," 598.

8. Fraser, *Ptolemaic Alexandria*, 1:491–92.

9. *Suda*, "Didymos," and "Iobas"; Fraser, *Ptolemaic Alexandria*, 1:471–73.

10. *Suda*, "Tryphon."

11. Fraser, *Ptolemaic Alexandria*, 1:474–75.

12. *Suda*, "Habron."

13. Strabo, *Geography* 17.1.5.

14. Strabo, *Geography* 2.3.5.

15. Strabo, *Geography* 10.5.3, 13.1.30, 14.5.3, 6, 10; 17.1.11, 3.7.

16. Opsomer, "Eudoros of Alexandria," 312–13.

17. Pliny, *Natural History* 2.39–40, 18.211–12; Bickerman, *Chronology of the Ancient World*, 47; Bowen, "Sosigenes (I)," 761.

18. Lucan 10.172–331; see also Seneca, *Natural Questions* 4a.

19. *Greek Anthology* 9.752.

20. He was active in the early Augustan period, as demonstrated by *Greek Anthology* 9.59, 93, 297, etc. Use of the Ptolemaic name Arsinoë (6.174) is not certain evidence for contact with Egypt, as it could be a mythological reference.

21. On Sokrates (*FGrHist* #192), whose two extant fragments are quoted by Athenaios (*Deipnosophistai* 4.147–48), see Roller, *Scholarly Kings*, 29–30.

22. Roller, *World of Juba II*, 150–51. There was also the problematic cameo of Methe (supra, pp. 126–27).

23. Porphyrion, *Commentary on Horace, Satires* 1.2.

24. Horace, *Satires* 1.2, 3.

25. Cicero, *Letters to Atticus* #347, and *ad familiares* 7.24.

26. Plutarch, *Antonius* 72.1, 81.

27. Despite copious information about Nikolaos and his life, and many extant fragments of his works (*FGrHist* #90), this part of his career is only mentioned by Sophronios of Damascus, patriarch of Jerusalem in the seventh century, in his *Account of the Miracles of Saints Cyrus and John* (54 = Nikolaos, T2). Sophronios may have had access to local information from their mutual hometown.

Chapter 9

1. Kleiner and Buxton, "Pledges of Empire," 79–86.

2. Plutarch, *Antonius* 55; Dio 50.1–2; Scott, "Political Propaganda of 44–30 B.C.," 36–49.

3. Dio 49.41.6.

4. Pomeroy, *Goddesses, Whores, Wives, and Slaves*, 187.

5. Reinhold, *From Republic to Principate*, 222–23.

6. Murgia, "Date of the Helen Episode," 405–26.

7. Horace, *Ode* 1.37.21; Pliny, *Natural History* 21.12; Luce, "Cleopatra as *Fatale Monstrum*," 251–57.

8. Propertius 3.11.46; Ovid, *Metamorphoses* 15.825–28.

9. Plutarch, *Antonius* 58.5–6; Horace, *Ode* 1.37; Vergil, *Aeneid* 8.689–700.

10. Juba (*FGrHist* #275) F87 (= Athenaios, *Deipnosophistai* 6.229c); Thompson, "Athenaeus in His Egyptian Context," 83–84.

11. Sidonius, *Letter* 8.12.8 ("dapes Cleopatricas").

12. Lucan 10.107–71; Tucker, "Banquets of Dido and Cleopatra," 17–20; Weber, "Dionysus in Aeneas," 338–39.

13. Vergil, *Aeneid* 1.697–756.

14. Josephus, *Against Apion* 2.56–60.

15. Macrobius, *Satires* 3.17.14; Velleius 2.84; Horace, *Epode* 9.10–12; Vergil, *Aeneid* 8.685–88; Appian, *Civil War* 4.38, 5.1; Josephus, *Jewish War* 1.243; Pliny, *Natural History* 33.50; Dio 49.34.1; Florus 2.21.11.

16. Suetonius, *Augustus* 69.

17. Augustus, F4 (= Martial 11.20); Hallett, "*Perusinae glandes* and the Changing Image of Augustus," 151–71.

18. Plutarch, *Antonius* 59.3–4; Seneca, *Suasoria* 1.6–7; Russell, *Plutarch*, 135.

19. *Sibylline Oracles* 3.350–80; Tarn, "Alexander Helios and the Golden Age," 139–43; infra, pp. 170–71.

20. Plutarch, *Alexander* 27.6, and *On the Fortune or Virtue of Alexander* 8.

21. Tarn, *Alexander the Great*, 2:414–15.

22. Pliny, *Natural History* 9.119–21; Macrobius, *Satires* 3.17.14. On Plancus, see Watkins, *L. Munatius Plancus*, 100–109.

23. Ullman, "Cleopatra's Pearls," 195–96.

24. Clodius was the son of Aisopos, the most famous tragic actor of the mid-first century B.C., mentioned several times by Cicero (for references, see Bloedhorn, "Aesopus, Clodius," 261–62).

25. Horace, *Satires* 2.3.239–41; Pliny, *Natural History* 9.122; Flory, "Pearls for Venus," 498–504.

26. Velleius 2.83.2.

27. Josephus, *Jewish Antiquities* 15.90.

28. Plutarch, *Antonius* 58.5.

29. Pliny, *Natural History* 34.58; Strabo, *Geography* 13.1.30, 14.1.14.

30. See the following works by Minnen: "Official Act of Cleopatra," 29–34, "Further Thoughts on the Cleopatra Papyrus," 74–80, and "Royal Ordinance of Cleopatra," 35–42. The document is pictured in Walker and Higgs, *Cleopatra of Egypt*, #188.

31. Turner, *Greek Papyri*, 138.

32. Under the rotation system then in use, Domitius was senior consul in January and Sosius in February (Gray, "Crisis in Rome at the Beginning of 32 B.C.," 17).

33. Dio 50.2–3.

34. For the period leading up to the Battle of Actium, the primary sources are Plutarch, *Antonius* 56–68; Dio 50.2–51.5; see also Livy, *Summary* 132.

35. Velleius 2.84.2.

36. Plutarch, *Antonius* 56.2–3.

37. Kaibel, *Epigrammata graeca ex lapidibus conlecta*, #118; Lefkowitz, "Wives and Husbands," 40–41.

38. Oliver, "Attic Text Reflecting the Influence of Cleopatra," 291–94.

39. Dio 50.20.7; John Robert Johnson, "Authenticity and Validity of Antony's Will," 494–503.

40. Livy 4.20.5–11.

41. Nikolaos, *Life of Augustus* 20.

42. Dio 50.4.5; Fontana, " 'Fetialis fui,' " 69–82.

43. Augustus, *Res gestae* 25.

44. Reinhold, "Declaration of War against Cleopatra," 97–103.

45. Dio 50.26.3.

46. Braund, *Rome and the Friendly King*, esp. 98–99.

47. Dio 50.26.2, 28.5.

48. Plutarch, *Antonius* 68.4.

49. Weill Goudchaux, "Cleopatra the Seafarer Queen," 109–12.

50. Josephus, *Jewish War* 1.364–85, and *Jewish Antiquities* 15.131–32. It is possible that Antonius—acting on a suggestion by Cleopatra—encouraged Herod to go to war at this time, not wanting him as an ally (Josephus, *Jewish Antiquities* 15.110–11).

51. Plutarch, *Antonius* 63.3.

52. Plutarch, *Antonius* 60.3, and *On Isis and Osiris* 16; Dio 50.15.1–2; Minucius Felix, *Octavius* 23.1; McDonough, "Swallows on Cleopatra's Ship," 251–58.

53. Plutarch, *Antonius* 65–69; Dio 50.6–51.3; Suetonius, *Augustus* 17.3; Velleius 2.85.

54. Plutarch, *Antonius* 60.3; Casson, *Ships and Seamanship in the Ancient World*, 354–55.

55. Plutarch, *Antonius* 64.2; Grant, *Cleopatra*, 208.

56. Pliny, *Natural History* 19.22. Purple sails would eventually designate the Roman emperor's ship.

57. Pliny, *Natural History* 32.2–4; Aristotle, *History of Animals* 2.14.

58. See, for example, Aeschylus, *Agamemnon* 149.

59. Plutarch, *Antonius* 67.4.

60. Pelling, *Plutarch: Life of Antony*, 289.

61. Plutarch, *Antonius* 67.6.

62. Plutarch, *Antonius* 86.5; Dio 51.4.8.

63. Athenaios, *Deipnosophistai* 5.206c–d; Broughton, "Cleopatra and 'the Treasure of the Ptolemies,' " 115–16.

64. Weill Goudchaux, "Cleopatra's Subtle Religious Strategy," 128.

65. Plutarch, *Antonius* 69–71.

66. Josephus, *Jewish War* 1.386–400, and *Jewish Antiquities* 15.187–201.

67. W. R. Johnson, "Quean [*sic*], a Great Queen?" 387–402.

68. Plutarch, *Antonius* 69.2–3.

69. Plutarch, *Antonius* 71–77; Dio 51.6–10.

70. British Museum EA 1325; Walker and Higgs, *Cleopatra of Egypt*, #173; Andreae et al., *Kleopatra und die Caesaren*, #14.

71. Pelling, *Plutarch: Life of Antony*, 295–96.

72. Suetonius, *Augustus* 17.3. Helen, queen of Sparta, learned about poison in Egypt (Homer, *Odyssey* 4.220–32).

73. This is first described in the vivid *Carmen de bello actiaco*, probably written shortly after her death (Benario, " 'Carmen de bello Actiaco' and Early Imperial Epic," 1657–62). See also Aelian, *On the Characteristics of Animals* 9.11; Galen 14.235–36; Marasco, "Cleopatra e gli esperimenti su cavie umane," 317–25.

74. Dio 51.8.2–3; Valerius Maximus 1.1.19.

75. Suetonius, *Augustus* 17.3; Dio 51.4.3–5.2.

76. Josephus, *Jewish War* 1.394–96, and *Jewish Antiquities* 15.199–200.

77. Plutarch, *Antonius* 74.1–2.

78. οὐκ εὐθυθάνατος, the latter a unique word (Plutarch, *Antonius* 76.5).

79. Proculeius, who had been with Octavian for a number of years, continued to be a close advisor in the new regime but was a rare and notable example of one in such a position who never entered politics (Tacitus, *Annals* 4.40).

80. Plutarch, *Antonius* 78–86; Dio 51.11–15.

81. Such a request could not have reached Egypt in the interval between Antonius's death and burial but may have been a standing order should he die away from Rome.

82. *FGrHist* #198.

83. Livy F54. Her words were οὐ θριαμβεύσομαι.

84. Plutarch, *Antonius* 84–86; Dio 51.13–14. These accounts are ambiguous about the locale, but see Florus 2.21.10–11.

85. Malalas 9.219; Plutarch, *Antonius* 67.7.

86. See especially Horace, *Ode* 1.37; Dio 51.11–14; and, further, Baldwin, "Death of Cleopatra VII," 181–82. See also Skeat, "Last Days of Cleopatra," 98–101; Levi, "Cleopatra e l'aspide," 293–95.

87. Plutarch, *Antonius* 86.2. The original Homeric meaning (*Iliad* 11.640) is a food grater.

88. Dio 51.14.2.

89. Aelian, *On the Characteristics of Animals* 9.61.

90. Tronson, "Vergil, the Augustans," 33–36.

91. Strabo, *Geography* 17.1.10.

92. Vergil, *Aeneid* 8.697; Horace, *Ode* 1.37; Propertius 3.11.53.

93. Velleius 2.87.1. Livy's version is preserved only in a *Summary* (133), and it is too abbreviated to provide details of death.

94. Suetonius, *Augustus* 17.4: "putabatur."

95. Galen 14.237; Dio 51.14.

96. Malalas 9.219.

97. Hölbl, *History of the Ptolemaic Empire*, 293.

98. Plutarch, *Antonius* 86.3. Dio's description of the triumph (51.21.8) does not mention the asp.

99. Tronson, "Vergil, the Augustans," 42.

100. Galen 14.237; Pelling, *Plutarch: Life of Antony*, 296–97, 319–20.

101. Plutarch, *Antonius* 86.2.

102. Clement of Alexandria, *Stromateis* 21.129.1–2.

103. Skeat, "Last Days of Cleopatra," 99–100.

104. Plutarch, *Antonius* 81–82; Dio 51.15.5.

105. Plutarch, *Antonius* 81.2. Areios created his own word for the occasion, πολυκαισαρίη, "too many Caesars," a pun on *Iliad* 2.204.

106. Roller, *World of Juba II*, 142–43.

Epilogue

1. Dio 51.19.6.

2. Dio 51.17.7–8.

3. Plutarch, *Antonius* 86.5.

4. Quaegebeur, "Cleopatra VII and the Cults of the Ptolemaic Queens," 41–53.

5. Dio 53.2.4.

6. Richardson Jr., *New Topographical Dictionary*, 14.

7. Propertius 2.31.1–4; Kleiner, *Roman Sculpture*, 83–84.

8. Richardson Jr., *New Topographical Dictionary*, 272–73.

9. Richardson Jr., *New Topographical Dictionary*, 353–54.

10. Kleiner, *Roman Sculpture*, 116; infra, p. 178.

11. Alfano, "Egyptian Influences in Italy," 276–91.

12. Horace, *Epistle* 2.1.156.

13. Sullivan, *Near Eastern Royalty and Rome, 100–30 B.C.*, Stemma 2.

14. *CIL* 14.2610.

15. Horace, *Ode* 1.7 (see Moles, "Reconstructing Plancus," 86–109); for Plancus's career, see Watkins, *Munatius Plancus*.

16. Roller, *Building Program of Herod the Great*, 62–63.

17. Josephus, *Jewish War* 1.440.

18. Roller, *Building Program of Herod the Great*, 228–29.

19. Sullivan, *Near Eastern Royalty and Rome, 100–30 B.C.*, Stemma 5.

20. Plutarch, *Antonius* 87. For the children, see Roller, *World of Juba II*, esp. 76–90 and 244–56.

21. Dio 51.21.8; Plutarch, *Antonius* 86.3; Eusebios, *Chronicle* 2.140; Zonaras 10.31 (531).

22. For Gnaios, supra, p. 127.

23. Roller, *World of Juba II*, fig. 26; Mazard, "Un denier inedit de Juba II et Cléopâtre-Séléne," 1–2.

24. *FGrHist* #275, F5–6, 35–40, 47–54, 56–61, 67, 71, 74–77, 79, 87, 100; Roller, *Scholarly Kings*, 48–103.

25. *FGrHist* #275, F1–3, 28–34, 41, 45, 62–76, 78, 97, 107; Roller, *Scholarly Kings*, 107–66.

26. It has astutely been argued that there may have been an earlier child, born around 20 B.C., who appears on the Ara Pacis in Rome (fig. N-37) but who died shortly thereafter (Kleiner and Buxton, "Pledges of Empire," 84–86). Although speculative, this does explain some inconsistencies in the evidence for the life of Cleopatra Selene and is worthy of serious consideration.

27. Tacitus, *Histories* 5.9; Bennett, "Drusilla Regina," 315–19.

28. Krinagoras 18.

29. Tacitus, *Annals* 4.23.

30. Seneca, *On Tranquility* 11.12; Suetonius, *Gaius* 35.1–2; Dio 59.25.1.

31. Pliny, *Natural History* 5.11; Dio 60.8–9.

32. Several notices in the *Scriptores Historiae Augustae* refer to this: *Thirty Tyrants* 27, 30, 32; *Aurelian* 27; *Claudius* 1; *Probus* 9.5. See also Bussi, "Zenobia/ Cleopatra," 261–68.

33. Kallinikos of Petra (*FGrHist* #281) T1a; *Scriptores Historiae Augustae, Probus* 9.5; Barnes, "Some Persons in the Historia Augusta," 177–78.

34. Bowersock, "Review of Becher: *Der Bild der Kleopatra*," 254.

Appendices

1. Huss, "Die Herkunft," 191–203.

2. Sullivan, *Near Eastern Royalty and Rome, 100–30 B.C.*, 424n82.

3. Strabo, *Geography* 17.1.11; see also Pausanias 1.9.3.

4. Meadows, "Sins of the Fathers," 23.

5. Reymond, *From the Records of a Priestly Family from Memphis*, 1:50–55.

6. Although the family of the priests of Ptah has been studied intensively, there is still wide divergence as to details and even numeration. The relevant inscriptions are discussed—with quite different readings and conclusions—in Reymond and Barns, "Alexandria and Memphis," 1–33; Quaegebeur, "Genealogy," 43–81; and Huss, "Die Herkunft," 191–203. Despite the differences, the broad outlines are clear.

7. Fittschen, "Juba II," in 238–39; but see Quaegebeur, "Genealogy," 61–63.

8. For the issues, see Roller, *World of Juba II*, 84–86, and the bibliography cited there.

9. Most recently, see Kleiner, *Cleopatra and Rome*, 135–56; Walker, "Cleopatra's Images," 142–47; Queyrel, "Die Ikonographie Kleopatras VII," 158–63; and Stanwick, *Portraits of the Ptolemies*, 60–61, 79–80.

10. Walker and Higgs, *Cleopatra of Egypt*; and Andreae et al., *Kleopatra und die Caesaren*.

11. There is, of course, a vast post-antique repertory of art showing Cleopatra, excellently shown in Walker and Higgs's *Cleopatra of Egypt* and Andreae's *Kleopatra und die Caesaren*, as well as in Kleiner's *Cleopatra and Rome*, but these generally have no relationship to ancient art and are most often artistic interpretations of moments described in literature. They are not the concern here.

12. Staatliche Museen, Antikensammlung 1976.10; Vierneisel, "Die Berliner Kleopatra," 5–33; Walker and Higgs, *Cleopatra of Egypt*, #198; Andreae et al., *Kleopatra und die Caesaren*, #2.

13. Higgs, "Searching for Cleopatra's Image," 204–7.

14. Musei Vaticani 38511; Walker and Higgs, *Cleopatra of Egypt*, #196; Andreae et al., *Kleopatra und die Caesaren*, #3; Bianchi, Fazzini, and Quaegebeur, *Cleopatra's Egypt*, #76; Weill Goudchaux, "Was Cleopatra Beautiful?" 211.

15. Kleiner, *Cleopatra and Rome*, 152.

16. Walker, "Cleopatra in Pompeii?" 35–46.

17. In a similar way, the Eros/Caesarion of the prototype for the Berlin Cleopatra seems to have disappeared.

18. Palazzo dei Conservatori 1141; Andreae, "Kleopatra und die sogenannte *Venus vom Esquilin*," 14–47.

19. For recent rejections of the association, see Weill Goudchaux, "Die *Venus von Esquilin* is nicht Kleopatra," 138–41; Higgs, "Searching for Cleopatra's Image," 208–9.

20. Weill Goudchaux, "Kleopatra Nahman," 126–29.

21. Cicero, *Letters to Atticus* #393.

22. Egyptian Museum 43268; Walker and Higgs, *Cleopatra of Egypt*, #267.

23. British Museum GR 1879.7–12.15; Walker and Higgs, *Cleopatra of Egypt*, #210.

24. Musei Capitolini 3356; Walker and Higgs, *Cleopatra of Egypt*, #212.

25. Bibliothèque National de France CAMEE 307; Andreae et al., *Kleopatra und die Caesaren*, fig. 83.

26. British Museum GR 1923.4–1.676 (Gem 3085); Walker and Higgs, *Cleopatra of Egypt*, #153.

27. Kleiner, *Cleopatra and Rome*, 142.

28. Hermitage 3936; Walker and Higgs, *Cleopatra of Egypt*, #160; Andreae et al., *Kleopatra und die Caesaren*, #7.

29. Rosicrucian Museum 1586; Walker and Higgs, *Cleopatra of Egypt*, #161.

30. Louvre E13102; Walker and Higgs, *Cleopatra of Egypt*, #162.

31. Metropolitan Museum 89.2.660; Walker and Higgs, *Cleopatra of Egypt*, #164.

32. Brooklyn Museum 71.12; Walker and Higgs, *Cleopatra of Egypt*, #163.

33. The definitive efforts of Sally-Ann Ashton have determined the iconography of the Egyptianizing statues of Cleopatra; see her "Identifying the Egyptian-Style Ptolemaic Queens," 148–55.

34. Plutarch, *Antonius* 86.5.

35. Kleiner, *Cleopatra and Rome*, 85–88; Quaegebeur, "Cléopâtre VII et le temple de Dendara," 49–72.

36. Louvre E27113; Walker and Higgs, *Cleopatra of Egypt*, #154; Andreae et al., *Kleopatra und die Caesaren*, #13.

37. Even the inscription on the so-called birth house at Hermonthis (supra, p. 128) gives Cleopatra the title "king" but does not show her as male. See further, Ashton, "Cleopatra: Goddess, Ruler, or Regent?" 25.

38. Tarn, "Bucheum Stele," 187–89.

39. Plutarch, *Antonius* 85.4: τοσούτων ἀπογόνῳ βασιλέων. See also Pomeroy, *Women in Hellenistic Egypt from Alexander to Cleopatra*, 28. There were other precedents for seeing a woman as male: Cleopatra, and perhaps Charmion, would probably have been aware that Mithradates the Great was so impressed with the abilities of his companion, Hypsikrateia, that he called her by the male form of the name, Hypsikrates (Plutarch, *Pompeius* 23.7–8).

40. Ashton, "Cleopatra: Goddess, Ruler, or Regent?" 25–26.

41. Andreae et al., *Kleopatra und die Caesaren*, #16.

42. Dunand and Zivie-Coche, *Gods and Men in Egypt*, 30–31.

43. British Museum EA 612; Walker and Higgs, *Cleopatra of Egypt*, #58.

44. Vergil, *Aeneid* 8.671–713.

45. Examples are in the British Museum (Lamp Q900) and the Rheinisches Landesmuseum, Trier (3747d). See Andreae et al., *Kleopatra und die Caesaren*, fig. 144, and #56.

46. Walker, "Cleopatra's Images," 146–47.

47. For other examples of this type of art, see Grimm, "Kleopatra—eine Königliche Hure?" 176–83.

48. British Museum GR 1945.9–27.1; Walker, *Portland Vase*, 41–59, and "Die Portlandvase," 184–93.

49. Both are now in Naples (Museo Nationale Archeologico 9990 and 8561).

50. Represented in Strong, *Roman Art*, 72, with previous bibliography.

51. The painting is depicted in Horn and Rüger, *Die Numider*, pl. 56, with previous bibliography.

52. Livy 30.12–15; Appian, *Libyka* 10, 27–28; Diodoros, *Bibliotheke* 27.7. The suggestion that this might represent the death of Cleopatra was vaguely raised

in 1955 by Olga Elia ("La tradizione della morte di Cleopatra nella pittura pompeiana," 153–57), but with little analysis.

53. The traditional bibliography on her coinage is *BMC Ptolemies* (1883), 122–23 (skimpy and now badly out of date); and Forrer, *Portraits of Royal Ladies*, 32–42. Both are now superseded by Walker and Higgs, *Cleopatra of Egypt*, #214–46; and Weill Goudchaux, "Was Cleopatra Beautiful?" and "Die Münzbildnisse Kleopatras VII."

54. *BMC Ptolemies*, pl. 29.

55. Walker and Higgs, *Cleopatra of Egypt*, #219.

56. Seltman, *Greek Coins*, 244–45.

57. Walker and Higgs, *Cleopatra of Egypt*, #179.

58. Walker and Higgs, *Cleopatra of Egypt*, #220.

59. Baldus, "Ein Neues Spätporträt der Kleopatra aus Orthosia," 19–43.

60. Walker and Higgs, *Cleopatra of Egypt*, #225–31.

61. Josephus, *Jewish Antiquities* 15.96.

62. Walker and Higgs, *Cleopatra of Egypt*, #186.

63. *BMC Ptolemies*, 42, #1.

64. Ashton, "Cleopatra: Goddess, Ruler, or Regent?" 25–28.

65. Walker and Higgs, *Cleopatra of Egypt*, #214–18, 231; Baldus, "Eine Münzprägung auf das Ehepaar Mark Anton—Kleopatra VII," 5–10.

66. Buttrey Jr., "*Thea Neotera* on Coins of Antony and Cleopatra," 95–109.

67. Hölbl, *History of the Ptolemaic Empire*, 192–93.

68. Walker and Higgs, *Cleopatra of Egypt*, #221–22.

69. Walker and Higgs, *Cleopatra of Egypt*, #232–34.

70. Williams, "Imperial Style and the Coins of Cleopatra and Mark Antony," 87–94.

71. Sutherland, *Roman Coins*, 114.

72. Walker and Higgs, *Cleopatra of Egypt*, #246a–b; Fleischer, "Kleopatra Philantonios," 237–40.

73. Forrer, *Portraits of Royal Ladies*, #135.

74. Some seal impressions found in a hoard allegedly from Edfu in Egypt, now in Toronto, have a female head that resembles the coin portraits of Cleopatra, but little is known about their origin. See Walker and Higgs, *Cleopatra of Egypt*, #174–76.

Bibliography

Adamson, P. B. "Consanguinous [*sic*] Marriages in the Ancient World." *Folklore* 93 (1982): 85–92.

Agatharchides. *On the Erythraean Sea.* Edited by Stanley M. Burstein. London, 1989.

Alfano, Carla. "Egyptian Influences in Italy." In *Cleopatra of Egypt*, ed. Susan Walker and Peter Higgs, 276–91. London, 2001.

Aly, Abdullatif, A. "Cleopatra and Caesar at Alexandria and Rome." In *Roma e l'Egitto nell'antichità classica*, ed. Giovanni Pugliesse Carratelli et al., 47–61. Rome, 1992.

Andreae, Bernard. "Kleopatra und die sogenannte *Venus vom Esquilin*." In *Kleopatra und die Caesaren*, ed. Bernard Andreae et al., 14–47, Munich, 2006.

Andreae, Bernard et al. *Kleopatra und die Caesaren.* Munich, 2006.

Ashton, Sally-Ann. "Identifying the Egyptian-Style Ptolemaic Queens." In *Cleopatra of Egypt*, ed. Susan Walker and Peter Higgs, 148–55. London, 2001.

———. "Cleopatra: Goddess, Ruler, or Regent?" In *Cleopatra Reassessed*, ed. Susan Walker and Sally-Ann Ashton, 25–29. London, 2003.

———. *Cleopatra and Egypt.* Oxford, 2008.

Bagnall, Roger S. "Greeks and Egyptians: Ethnicity, Status, and Culture." In *Cleopatra's Egypt: Age of the Ptolemies*, by Robert S. Bianchi, Richard A. Fazzini, and Jan Quaegebeur, 21–28. Brooklyn, 1988.

Baldus, Hans Roland. "Ein Neues Spätporträt der Kleopatra aus Orthosia." *JNG* 23 (1973): 19–43.

———. "Eine Münzprägung auf das Ehepaar Mark Anton—Kleopatra VII." *SchwMbll* 33 (1983): 5–10.

Baldwin, B. "The Death of Cleopatra VII." *JEA* 50 (1964): 181–82.

Balsdon, J. P. D. V. "The Ides of March." *Historia* 7 (1958): 80–94.

Barnes, Robert. "Cloistered Bookworms in the Chicken-Coop of the Muses: The Library of Alexandria." *The Library of Alexandria*, ed. Roy MacLeod, 61–77. London, 2002.

Barnes, T. D. "Some Persons in the Historia Augusta." *Phoenix* 26 (1972): 140–82.

Benario, Herbert W. "The 'Carmen de bello Actiaco' and Early Imperial Epic." *ANRW* 20.30.3 (1983): 1657–62.

Bennett, Chris. "Drusilla Regina." *CQ* 53 (2003): 315–19.

Bevan, Edwyn R. *The House of Ptolemy: A History of Egypt under the Ptolemaic Dynasty.* Reprint, Chicago, 1985.

Bianchi, Robert S. "The Pharaonic Art of Ptolemaic Egypt." In *Cleopatra's Egypt: Age of the Ptolemies*, 55–80. Brooklyn, 1988.

Bianchi, Robert S., Richard A. Fazzini, and Jan Quaegebeur. *Cleopatra's Egypt: Age of the Ptolemies.* Brooklyn, 1988.

Bickel, E. "Das Mausoleum der Kleopatra und des Antonius in lateinischer Dichtung." *RhM* 93 (1950): 191–92.

Bickerman, E. J. *Chronology of the Ancient World.* 2nd ed. Ithaca, N.Y., 1980.

Bicknell, Peter J. "Caesar, Antony, Cleopatra, and Cyprus." *Latomus* 36 (1977): 325–42.

Bingen, Jean. "Cléopâtre VII Philopatris." *CE* 74 (1999): 118–23.

Bloedhorn, Hanswulf. "Aesopus, Clodius." *BNP* 1 (2002): 261–62.

Boardman, John. *Greek Gems and Finger Rings: Early Bronze Age to Late Classical.* New York, 1970.

———. *The Greeks Overseas.* New and enlarged edition. London, 1980.

Böhn, Richard Gregor. "Wo war/Was tat Cleopatra an den Iden des März 44? (Cicero, *ad Atticum* XV, 15, 2)." *Gerión* 3 (1985): 151–55.

Bowen, Alan C. "Sosigenes (I)." *EANS* 761.

Bowersock, Glen W. "Review of Becher: *Der Bild der Kleopatra.*" *AJP* 90 (1969): 252–54.

———. "Review of Heinen: *Rom und Ägypten von 51 bis 47 v. Chr.*" *AJP* 90 (1969): 483–84.

———. *Roman Arabia.* Cambridge, Mass., 1983.

Braund, David C. *Rome and the Friendly King: The Character of the Client Kingship.* London, 1984.

Brenk, Frederick E. "Antony—Osiris, Cleopatra—Isis: The End of Plutarch's Antony." In *Plutarch and the Historical Tradition*, ed. Philip A. Stadter, 159–82. London, 1992.

Brett, Agnes Baldwin. "A New Cleopatra Tetradrachm of Ascalon." *AJA* 41 (1937): 452–63.

Broughton, T. Robert S. "Cleopatra and 'The Treasure of the Ptolemies': A Note." *AJP* 106 (1985): 115–16.

Bulver-Thomas, Ivor. "Euclid." *DSB* 4 (1971): 414–37.

Burstein, Stanley M. *The Reign of Cleopatra.* Norman, Okla., 2007.

Bussi, Silvia. "Zenobia/Cleopatra: Immagine e propaganda." *RINS* 104 (2003): 261–68.

Buttrey, Theodore V., Jr. "*Thea Neotera* on Coins of Antony and Cleopatra." *ANSMusN* 6 (1954): 95–109.

Calderini, Aristide. *Dizionario dei nomi geografici e topografici dell'Egitto greco-romano* 3. Edited by Sergio Daris. Milan, 1966–.

Carney, E. D. "Women and *Dunasteia* in Caria." *AJP* 126 (2005): 65–91.

Casson, Lionel. *Libraries in the Ancient World*. New Haven, Conn., 2002.

———. *The Periplus Maris Erythraei*. Princeton, N.J., 1989.

———. *Ships and Seamanship in the Ancient World*. Princeton, N.J., 1971.

Chaniotis, Angelos. "The Divinity of Hellenistic Rulers." In *A Companion to the Hellenistic World*, ed. Andrew Erskine, 431–45. Oxford, 2005.

Chaveau, Michel. *Cleopatra: Beyond the Myth*. Translated by David Lorton. Ithaca, N.Y., 2002.

———. *Egypt in the Age of Cleopatra*. Translated by David Lorton. Ithaca, N.Y., 2000.

Chronologies of the Ancient World: Names, Dates, and Dynasties. BNP, supp. 1, ed. Walter Eder and Johannes Renger, trans. Wouter F. M. Henkelman. Leiden, 2007.

Cohen, Getzel M. *The Hellenistic Settlements in Syria, the Red Sea Basin, and North Africa*. Berkeley, Calif., 2006.

Crawford, Jane W. *M. Tullius Cicero: The Fragmentary Speeches*. Atlanta, 1994.

Criscuolo, Lucia. "La successione a Tolemeo Aulete ed i pretesi matrimoni di Cleopatra VII con i fratelli." In *Egitto e storia antica dall'ellenismo all'età araba*, ed. Lucia Criscuolo and Giovanni Geraci, 325–39. Bologna, 1989.

Dack, Edmond van't. "La date de C. Ord. Ptol. 80–83 = BGU VI 1212 et le séjour de Cléopâtre VII à Rome." *AncSoc* 1 (1970): 53–67.

Dixon, Suzanne. *Cornelia: Mother of the Gracchi*. London, 2007.

Drew-Bear, Marie. *Le nome Hermopolite: toponymes et sites*. Missoula, Mont., 1979.

Dunand, Françoise, and Christiane Zivie-Coche. *Gods and Men in Egypt: 3000 B.C.E. to 395 C.E.* Translated by David Lorton. Ithaca, N.Y., 2004.

Elia, Olga. "La tradizione della morte di Cleopatra nella pittura pompeiana." *RAAN* 30 (1955): 153–57.

Errington, R. M. "Alexander in the Hellenistic World." *Alexandre le Grand: image et réalité. Entretiens Hardt* 22 (1976): 137–79.

Erskine, Andrew. "Culture and Power in Ptolemaic Egypt: The Museum and Library of Alexandria." *G&R* 42 (1995): 38–48.

Fantham, Elaine. "The Trials of Gabinius in 54 B.C." *Historia* 24 (1975): 425–43.

Fishwick, Duncan. "The Caesareum at Alexandria Again." *AJAH* 12 (1987): 62–72.

———. "The Temple of Caesar at Alexandria." *AJAH* 9 (1984): 131–34.

Fittschen, Klaus. "Juba II. und seine Residenz Jol/Caesarea (Cherchel)." In *Die Numider*, ed. Heinz Günter Horn and Christoph B. Rüger, 227–42. Cologne, 1979.

Fitzmyer, Joseph A. "The Languages of Palestine in the First Century A.D." *CBQ* 32 (1970): 501–31.

Fleischer, Robert. "Kleopatra Philantonios." *IstMitt* 46 (1996): 237–40.

Flory, Marleen B. "Livia and the History of Public Honorific Statues for Women in Rome." *TAPA* 123 (1993): 287–308.

———. "Pearls for Venus." *Historia* 37 (1988): 498–504.

Fontana, Fulvia. " 'Fetialis fui'. Note sull'*indictio belli* di Ottaviano contro Cleopatra (32 a. C.)." *AnnIsItS* 1 (1989–90): 69–82.

Forrer, Leonard. *Portraits of Royal Ladies on Greek Coins.* Chicago, 1969.

Fraser, P. M. "Mark Antony in Alexandria—A Note." *JRS* 47 (1957): 71–73.

———. "A *Prostagma* of Ptolemy Auletes from Lake Edku." *JEA* 56 (1970): 179–82.

———. *Ptolemaic Alexandria.* Oxford, 1972.

Grant, Michael. *Cleopatra.* New York, 1972.

Gray, E. W. "The Crisis in Rome at the Beginning of 32 B.C." *PACA* 13 (1975): 15–29.

Gray-Fow, Michael J. G. "The Mental Breakdown of a Roman Senator: M. Calpurnius Bibulus." *G&R* 37 (1990): 179–90.

Griffiths, J. Gwyn. "The Death of Cleopatra VII." *JEA* 47 (1961): 113–18.

———. "The Death of Cleopatra VII: A Rejoinder and a Postscript." *JEA* 51 (1965): 209–11.

Grimm, Günter. *Alexandria.* Mainz, 1998.

———. "Kleopatra—eine Königliche Hure?" In *Kleopatra und die Caesaren,* ed. Bernard Andreae et al., 176–83. Munich, 2006.

———. "Kleopatras Palast?" *AntW* 27 (1996): 509–12.

Gruen, Erich S. "Cleopatra in Rome: Facts and Fantasies." In *Myth, History, and Culture in Republican Rome,* ed. David C. Braund and Christopher Gill, 257–74. Exeter, 2003.

———. *The Hellenistic World and the Coming of Rome.* Berkeley, Calif., 1986.

———. *The Last Generation of the Roman Republic.* Berkeley, Calif., 1995.

Grzybek, Erhard. "Pharao Caesar in einer demotischen Grabschrift aus Memphis." *MusHelv* 35 (1978): 149–58.

Habicht, Christian. *Athens from Alexander to Antony.* Translated by Deborah Lucas Schneider. Cambridge, Mass., 1997.

Hallett, Judith P. *Perusinae glandes* and the Changing Image of Augustus." *AJAH* 2 (1977): 151–71.

Hammond, N. G. L. "Which Ptolemy Gave Troops and Stood as Protector of Pyrrhus' Kingdom?" *Historia* 37 (1988): 405–13.

Hammond, Philip C. "The Nabataean Bitumen Industry at the Dead Sea." *BiblArch* 22 (1959): 40–48.

Hazzard, R. A. *Imagination of a Monarchy: Studies in Ptolemaic Propaganda. Phoenix,* supp. 37, 2000.

———. "The Regnal Years of Ptolemy II Philadelphos." *Phoenix* 41 (1987): 140–58.

Head, Barclay V. *Historia Numorum*. Oxford, 1911.

Heckel, Waldemar. *Who's Who in the Age of Alexander the Great*. London, 2006.

Heinen, Heinz. "Cäsar und Kaisarion." *Historia* 18 (1969): 181–203.

———. *Rom und Ägypten von 51 bis 47 v. Chr.* Tübingen, 1966.

———. "The Syrian-Egyptian Wars and the New Kingdoms of Asia Minor." *CAH* 2nd ed. 7.1: 412–15.

Higgs, Peter. "Searching for Cleopatra's Image: Classical Portraits in Stone." In *Cleopatra of Egypt*, ed. Susan Walker and Peter Higgs, 200–209. London, 2001.

Hillard, T. W. "The Nile Cruise of Cleopatra and Caesar." *CQ* 52 (2002): 549–54.

Hölbl, Günther. *A History of the Ptolemaic Empire*. Translated by Tina Saavedra. London, 2001.

Hopkins, Keith. "Brother-Sister Marriage in Roman Egypt." *CSSH* 22 (1980): 303–54.

———. "Contraception in the Roman Empire." *CSSH* 8 (1965): 124–51.

Horn, Heinz Günter, and Christoph B. Rüger, eds. *Die Numider*. Cologne, 1979.

Hultsch, Friedrich. *Griechische und Römische Metrologie*. Berlin, 1882.

Huss, Werner. "Die Herkunft der Kleopatra Philopator." *Aegyptus* 70 (1990): 191–203.

Huzar, Eleanor Goltz. *Mark Antony: A Biography*. London, 1978.

———. "Mark Antony: Marriages vs. Careers." *CJ* 81 (1985–86): 97–111.

Intinsky, H. U. "Bemerkungen Ueber die Ersten Schenkungen des Antonius an Kleopatra." In Vol. 2 of *Studies Presented to David Moore Robinson*, ed. George E. Mylonas, 975–79. St. Louis, 1951–53.

Irby-Massie, Georgia L. "Apollonios Mus." *EANS* 111–12.

———. "Herakleides of Eruthrai." *EANS* 370.

———. "Khrusermos of Alexandria." *EANS* 480.

———. "Olumpos of Alexandria." *EANS* 598.

Irby-Massie, Georgia L., and Paul T. Keyser. *Greek Science of the Hellenistic Era*. London, 2002.

Johnson, John Robert. "The Authenticity and Validity of Antony's Will." *AntCl* 47 (1978): 494–503.

Johnson, W. R. "A Quean [*sic*], a Great Queen? Cleopatra and the Politics of Misrepresentation." *Arion* 6 (1967): 387–402.

Kaibel, Georg. *Epigrammata graeca ex lapidibus conlecta*. Berlin, 1878.

Keyser, Paul T. "Antiokhis of Tlos." *EANS* 95.

Kleiner, Diana E. E. *Cleopatra and Rome*. Cambridge, Mass., 2005.

———. *Roman Sculpture*. New Haven, Conn., 1992.

Kleiner, Diana E. E., and Bridget Buxton. "Pledges of Empire: The Ara Pacis and the Donations of Rome." *AJA* 112 (2008): 57–89.

Kokkinos, Nikos. *Antonia Augusta: Portrait of a Great Roman Lady*. London, 1992.

———. "Cleopatra and Herod: A Failed Seduction." *British Museum Magazine*. Spring 2001, 17.

———. *The Herodian Dynasty: Origins, Role in Society, and Eclipse*. Sheffield, 1998.

Kraft, Konrad. "Zur Sueton, Divus Augustus 69,2: M. Anton und Kleopatra." *Hermes* 95 (1967): 496–99.

Lefkowitz, Mary R. "Wives and Husbands." *G&R* 30 (1983): 31–47.

Lenger, Marie-Thérèse. *Corpus des Ordonnances des Ptolémées*. Brussels, 1964.

Leon, Ernestine. "One Roman's Family." *CB* 35 (1958–59): 61–65.

Levi, Mario Attilio. "Cleopatra e l'aspide." *PP* 9 (1954): 293–95.

Lintott, Andrew. *Cicero as Evidence: A Historian's Companion*. New York, 2008.

Lord, Louis E. "The Date of Julius Caesar's Departure from Alexandria." *JRS* 28 (1938): 19–40.

Luce, J. V. "Cleopatra as *Fatale Monstrum* (Horace, *Carm.* 1.37.21)." *CQ* 13 (1963): 251–57.

Maehler, Herwig. "Egypt under the Last Ptolemies." *BICS* 30 (1983): 1–16.

Marasco, Gabriele. "Cleopatra e gli esperimenti su cavie umane." *Historia* 44 (1995): 317–25.

———. "Cléopâtre et les sciences de son temps." In *Sciences exactes et sciences appliquées à Alexandrie*, ed. Gilbert Argoud and J.-Y. Guillaumin, 39–53. St-Étienne, 1998.

Mayerson, Philip. "Aelius Gallus at Cleopatris (Suez) and on the Red Sea." *GRBS* 36 (1995): 17–24.

Mazard, Jean. "Un denier inedit de Juba II et Cléopâtre-Séléne." *SchwMbll* 31 (1981): 1–2.

McDonough, Christopher M. "The Swallows on Cleopatra's Ship." *CW* 96 (2002–3): 251–58.

McKenzie, Judith. *The Architecture of Alexandria and Egypt* 300 B.C. to A.D. 700. New Haven, Conn., 2007.

Meadows, Andrew. "Sins of the Fathers: The Inheritance of Cleopatra, Last Queen of Egypt." In *Cleopatra of Egypt*, ed. Susan Walker and Peter Higgs, 14–31. London, 2001.

Meiklejohn, K. W. "Alexander Helios and Caesarion." *JHS* 24 (1934): 191–95.

Michaelidou-Nicolaou, Ino. *Prosopography of Ptolemaic Cyprus*. Vol. 44 of *Studies in Mediterranean Archaeology*. Göteborg, 1976.

Minnen, Peter van. "Further Thoughts on the Cleopatra Papyrus." *ArchPF* 47 (2001): 74–80.

————. "An Official Act of Cleopatra (With a Subscription in Her Own Hand)." *AntSoc* 30 (2000): 29–34.

————. "A Royal Ordinance of Cleopatra and Related Documents." In *Cleopatra Reassessed*, ed. Susan Walker and Sally-Ann Ashton, 35–42. London, 2003.

Moles, John. "Reconstructing Plancus (Horace, *C.* 1.7)." *JRS* 92 (2002): 86–109.

Mueller, Katja. *Settlements of the Ptolemies: City Foundations and New Settlement in the Hellenistic World.* Leuven, 2006.

Murgia, Charles E. "The Date of the Helen Episode." *HSCP* 101 (2003): 405–26.

Nardis, Mauro de. "Kleopatra of Alexandria." *EANS* 488–89.

Nielsen, Inge. *Hellenistic Palaces: Tradition and Renewal.* 2nd ed. Aarhus, 1999.

Nock, A. D. "Notes on Ruler Cult, I–IV." *JHS* 48 (1928): 21–43.

Oldfather, W. A. "A Friend of Plutarch's Grandfather." *CP* 19 (1924): 177.

Oliver, James H. "Attic Text Reflecting the Influence of Cleopatra." *GRBS* 6 (1965): 291–94.

Opsomer, Jan. "Eudoros of Alexandria." *EANS* 312–13.

Ors, A. d' "Cleopatra 'uxor' de Marco Antonio?" *AHDE* 49 (1979): 639–42.

Peek, Cecilia. *She, Like a Good King: A Reconstruction of the Career of Kleopatra VII.* Ph.D. diss., University of California, 2000.

Pelling, C. B. R. *Plutarch: Life of Antony.* Cambridge, 1988.

————. "Plutarch's Method of Work in the Roman Lives." *JHS* 99 (1979): 74–96.

————. "The Triumviral Period." *CAH* 2nd ed. 10: 1–69. Cambridge, 1998.

Peremans, Willy, and Edmond van't Dack. "Sur les rapports de Rome avec les Lagides." *ANRW* 1.1 (1972): 660–67.

Pfrommer, Michael. *Alexandria im Schatten der Pyramiden.* Mainz, 1999.

Plant, I. M., ed. *Women Writers of Ancient Greece and Rome: An Anthology.* Norman, Okla., 2004.

Plantzos, Dimitris. "Female Portrait Types from the Edfu Hoard of Clay Seal Impressions." *Archives et sceaux du monde hellénistique. BCH*, supp. 29, ed. Marie-Françoise Boussac and Antonio Invernissi, 301–13. Athens, 1996.

Pomeroy, Sarah B. *Goddesses, Whores, Wives, and Slaves: Women in Classical Antiquity.* New York, 1975.

————. *Women in Hellenistic Egypt from Alexander to Cleopatra.* Detroit, 1990.

Pouilloux, Jean, et al. *Salamine de Chypre* 13: *Testimonia Salaminia* 2. Paris, 1987.

Porter, Bertha, and Rosalind L. B. Moss. *Topographical Bibliography of Ancient Egyptian Hieroglyphic Texts, Reliefs, and Paintings* 5. *Upper Egypt: Sites.* Oxford, 1937.

Quaegebeur, Jan. "Cleopatra VII and the Cults of the Ptolemaic Queens." In *Cleopatra's Egypt: Age of the Ptolemies*, 41–54. Brooklyn, 1988.

————. "Cléopâtre VII et le temple de Dendara." *GM* 120 (1991): 49–72.

————. "The Genealogy of the Memphite High Priest Family in the Hellenistic Period." In *Studies on Ptolemaic Memphis*, ed. Dorothy J. Crawford et al., 43–81. Louvain, 1980.

Queyrel, François. "Die Ikonographie Kleopatras VII." In *Kleopatra und die Caesaren*, ed. Bernard Andreae et al., 158–63. Munich, 2006.

Ray, John. "Cleopatra in the Temples of Upper Egypt: The Evidence of Dendera and Armant." In *Cleopatra Reassessed*, ed. Susan Walker and Sally-Ann Ashton, 9–11. London, 2003.

Reinach, Th. "Du rapport de valeur des métaux monétaires dans l'Égypte au temps des Ptolémées." *RÉG* 41 (1928): 121–96.

Reinhold, Meyer. "The Declaration of War against Cleopatra." *CJ* 77 (1981–82): 97–103.

————. *From Republic to Principate: An Historical Commentary on Cassius Dio's Roman History Books 49–52 (36–29 B.C.).* Atlanta, 1988.

Reymond, E. A. E. *From the Records of a Priestly Family from Memphis.* Wiesbaden, 1981.

Reymond, E. A. E., and J. W. B. Barns. "Alexandria and Memphis: Some Historical Observations." *Orientalia* 46 (1971): 1–33.

Richardson, L., Jr. *A New Topographical Dictionary of Ancient Rome.* Baltimore, 1992.

Richardson, W. F. *Numbering and Measuring in the Classical World.* Rev. ed. Bristol, 2004.

Ricketts, Linda Maurine. *The Administration of Ptolemaic Egypt under Cleopatra VII.* Ph.D. diss., University of Minnesota, 1980.

————. "A Chronological Problem in the Reign of Cleopatra VII." *BASP* 16 (1979): 213–17.

Roller, Duane W. *The Building Program of Herod the Great.* Berkeley, Calif., 1998.

————. "A Note on the Berber Head in London." *JHS* 122 (2002): 144–46.

————. *Scholarly Kings: The Writings of Juba II of Mauretania, Archelaos of Kappadokia, Herod the Great, and the Emperor Claudius.* Chicago, 2004.

————. *Through the Pillars of Herakles: Greco-Roman Exploration of the Atlantic Ocean.* London, 2006.

————. *The World of Juba II and Kleopatra Selene: Royal Scholarship on Rome's African Frontier.* London, 2003.

Rostovtzeff, M. *Social and Economic History of the Hellenistic World.* Oxford, 1941.

Russell, D. A. *Plutarch.* New York, 1973.

Samuel, Alan E. "The Joint Regency of Cleopatra and Caesarion." *ÉtPap* 9 (1971): 73–79.

————. *Ptolemaic Chronology.* Munich, 1962.

Scarborough, John. "Dioskourides Phakas." *EANS* 272.

——. "Philotas of Amphissa." *EANS* 668.

Schmidt, Manfred Gerhard. *Caesar und Cleopatra: Philologischer und historischer Kommentar zu Lucan 10.1–171.* Frankfurt, 1986.

Schrapel, Thomas. *Das Reich der Kleopatra: Quellenkritische Untersuchungen zu den "Landschenkungen" Mark Antons.* Trier, 1996.

Scott, Kenneth. "The Political Propaganda of 44–30 B.C." *MAAR* 11 (1933): 7–49.

Scullard, H. H. *From the Gracchi to Nero.* 5th ed. London, 2003.

Seltman, Charles. *Greek Coins.* 2nd ed. London, 1955.

Seyrig, Henri. "Un petit portrait royal." *RA* (1968): 251–56.

Shaw, Brent B. "Explaining Incest: Brother-Sister Marriage in Graeco-Roman Egypt." *Man,* n.s., 27 (1992): 267–99.

Shenouda, S. "Naukratis." *PECS* 609–10.

Sherk, Robert K. *Rome and the Greek East to the Death of Augustus.* Cambridge, 1984.

Simões Rodrigues, Nuno. "O Judeu e a Egípcia: o retrato de Cleópatra em Flávio Josefo." *Polis* 11 (1999): 217–60.

Sjöqvist, Erik. "Kaisareion: A Study in Architectural Iconography." *OpRom* 1 (1954): 86–108.

Skeat, T. C. "The Last Days of Cleopatra: A Chronological Problem." *JRS* 43 (1953): 98–100.

——. "Notes on Ptolemaic Chronology III: 'The First Year Which Is Also the Third,' A Date in the Reign of Cleopatra VII." *JEA* 48 (1962): 100–105.

Spaer, Arnold. "The Royal Male Head and Cleopatra at Ascalon." In *Travaux de numismatique grecque offerts à Georges Le Rider,* ed. Michel Amandry et al., 347–50. London, 1999.

Stähelin, F. "Kleopatra" (#20), *RE* 21 (1921): 750–81.

Stanwick, Paul Edmund. *Portraits of the Ptolemies.* Austin, 2002.

Stok, Fabio. "Apollonios of Kition." *EANS* 113–14.

——. "Herakleides of Alexandria." *EANS* 373–74.

——. "Zopuros of Alexandria." *EANS* 860.

Strong, Donald. *Roman Art.* 2nd ed. Harmondsworth, 1988.

Suerbaum, Werner. "Merkwürdige Geburtstage." *Chiron* 10 (1980): 327–55.

Sullivan, Richard D. *Near Eastern Royalty and Rome, 100–30 B.C.* Toronto, 1990.

Sutherland, C. H. V. *Roman Coins.* New York, 1974.

Syme, Ronald. *The Roman Revolution.* Oxford, 1960.

Talbert, Richard J. A., ed. *Barrington Atlas of the Greek and Roman World.* Princeton, N.J., 2000.

Tarn, W. W. *Alexander the Great.* Oxford, 1948.

——. "Alexander Helios and the Golden Age." *JRS* 22 (1932): 135–60.

——. "The Bucheum Stele: A Note." *JRS* 26 (1936): 187–89.

Thompson, Dorothy J. "Athenaeus in His Egyptian Context." In *Athenaeus and His World*, ed. David C. Braund and John Wilkins, 77–84. Exeter, 2000.

———. "Cleopatra VII: The Queen in Egypt." In *Cleopatra Reassessed*, ed. Susan Walker and Sally-Ann Ashton, 31–34. London, 2003.

———. "Egypt, 146–31 B.C." *CAH* 9, 2nd ed., 310–26. Cambridge, 1994.

———. *Memphis under the Ptolemies*. Princeton, N.J., 1988.

Thür, Hilke. "Arsinoe IV, eine Schwester Kleopatras VII, Grabinhaberin des Oktogons von Ephesos? Ein Vorschlag." *ÖJh* 60 (1990): 43–56.

———. "The Processional Way in Ephesos as a Place of Cult and Burial." In *Ephesos: Metropolis of Asia*, ed. Helmut Koester, 157–87. Valley Forge, Pa., 1995.

Travlos, John. *Pictorial Dictionary of Ancient Athens*. New York, 1971.

Tronson, Adrian. "Vergil, the Augustans, and the Invention of Cleopatra's Suicide—One Asp or Two." *Vergilius* 44 (1998): 31–50.

Tucker, Robert A. "The Banquets of Dido and Cleopatra." *CB* 52 (1975–76): 17–20.

Turner, E. G. *Greek Papyri: An Introduction*. Oxford, 1980.

Ullman, B. L. "Cleopatra's Pearls." *CJ* 52 (1957): 193–201.

Vermeule, Emily. *Greece in the Bronze Age*. Chicago, 1964.

Versnel, H. S. *Triumphus*. Leiden, 1970.

Vierneisel, Klaus. "Die Berliner Kleopatra." *JBM* 22 (1980): 5–33.

Visonà, P. "A Tetradrachm of Cleopatra VII from Este." *SNC* 91 (1983): 47.

Volkmann, Hans. *Cleopatra: A Study in Politics and Propaganda*. Translated by T. J. Cadoux. New York, 1958.

Volterra, Edoardo. "Ancora sul matrimonio di Antonio con Cleopatra." In Vol. 1 of *Festschrift für Werner Flume*, ed. Horst Heinrich Jakobs et al., 205–12. Cologne, 1978.

Walker, Susan. "Cleopatra in Pompeii?" *PBSR* 74 (2007): 35–46.

———. "Cleopatra's Images: Reflections of Reality." In *Cleopatra of Egypt*, ed. Susan Walker and Peter Higgs, 142–47. London, 2001.

———. *The Portland Vase*. London, 2004.

———. "Die *Portlandvase*. Ein Dokument augusteischer Propaganda gegen Kleopatra." In *Kleopatra und die Caesaren*, ed. Bernard Andreae et al., 184–93. Munich, 2006.

Walker, Susan, and Sally-Ann Ashton, eds. *Cleopatra Reassessed*. London, 2003.

Walker, Susan, and Peter Higgs, eds. *Cleopatra of Egypt: From History to Myth*. London, 2001.

Watkins, Thomas H. *L. Munatius Plancus: Serving and Surviving in the Roman Revolution*. Atlanta, 1997.

Weber, Clifford. "The Dionysus in Aeneas." *CP* 97 (2002): 322–43.

Weill Goudchaux, Guy. "Cleopatra the Seafarer Queen: Strabo and India." In *Cleopatra Reassessed*, ed. Susan Walker and Sally-Ann Ashton, 109–12. London, 2003.

———. "Cleopatra's Subtle Religious Strategy." In *Cleopatra of Egypt*, ed. Susan Walker and Peter Higgs, 128–41. London, 2001.

———. "Kleopatra Nahman." In *Kleopatra und die Caesaren*, ed. Bernard Andreae et al., 126–29. Munich, 2006.

———. "Die Münzbildnisse Kleopatras VII." In *Kleopatra und die Caesaren*, ed. Bernard Andreae et al., 130–35. Munich 2006.

———. "Die *Venus von Esquilin* is nicht Kleopatra." In *Kleopatra und die Caesaren*, ed. Bernard Andreae et al., 138–41. Munich, 2006.

———. "Was Cleopatra Beautiful? The Conflicting Answers of Numismatics." In *Cleopatra of Egypt*, ed. Susan Walker and Peter Higgs, 210–14. London, 2001.

Whitehorne, John. *Cleopatras*. London, 1994.

———. "Cleopatra's Carpet." In *Atti del XXII Congresso Internazionale di Papirologia, Firenze 1998*, 1287–93. Florence, 2001.

———. "The Supposed Co-Regency of Cleopatra Tryphaena and Berenice IV (58–55 B.C.)." In *Akten des 21. Internationalen Papyrologenkongresses, Berlin 1995*, ed. Bärbel Kramer et al., 3:1009–13. Stuttgart, 1997.

Wilhelm, Adolf. "Ein Grabgedicht aus Athen." In *Mélanges Bidez*, 1007–20. Brussels, 1934.

Williams, Jonathan, "Imperial Style and the Coins of Cleopatra and Mark Antony." In *Cleopatra Reassessed*, ed. Susan Walker and Sally-Ann Ashton, 87–94. London, 2003.

Williams, Richard F. "*Rei publica causa*: Gabinius' Defense of His Restoration of Ptolemy Auletes." *CJ* 81 (1985–86): 25–38.

Zucker, Arnaud. "Sostratos of Alexandria." *EANS* 762.

Index of Passages Cited

Italicized numbers are citations in ancient texts; romanized numbers are pages and notes in this volume.

Greek and Latin Literary Sources

Aelian, *On the Characteristics of Animals 5.27*, 209n5; *6.51*, 209n5; *9.11*, 213n73; *9.61*, 231n89

Aeschylus:
 Agamemnon 149, 212n58
 Seven Against Thebes 217–18, 208n114

Aetios of Amida *8.6*, 195n38

Ammianus Marcellinus *22.16.9*, 206n50; *22.16.13*, 198n43; *22.16.10–11*, 206n48, 206n51

Apollonios of Kition, *Commentary to On Limbs*, 194n4

Apollonios of Rhodes, *Argonautika 3.210–44*, 207n73

Appian:
 Civil War:
  Book 1: *102*, 190n12
  Book 2: *49*, 197n18; *71*, 197n18; *82–84*, 197n30; *84*, 196n14, 197n25, 197n33; *84–86*, 197n31; *89*, 197n34; *90*, 198n44, 198n60; *91*, 199n67; *92*, 199n6; *102*, 200n20; *144*, 208n102
  Book 3: *78*, 199n67, 200n28
  Book 4: *38*, 211n15; *40*, 198n39; *59*, 199n67, 200n28; *61*, 200n28, 204n2; *62*, 201n44; *63*, 200n28, 204n2; *74*, 200n28; *108*, 204n2
  Book 5: *1*, 211n15; *7*, 200n31, 201n61; *8*, 191n43, 200n28, 201n38, 201n44; *9*, 198n54, 201n45; *10–11*, 201n46; *32–49*, 201n59; *64–65*, 202n63; *76*, 202n1, 202n3; *142–44*, 203n42
 Libyka 10, 217n52; *27–28*, 217n52
 Mithradatic Wars 114, 190n24
 Preface 10, 201n40
 Syrian Wars 2–3, 193n50; *5*, 190n6, 193n51

Aristotle:
 History of Animals 2.14, 212n57
 Politics 2.6.6, 200n32; *5.9.6*, 200n32
 Problems 10.27, 196n41

Homer (*continued*)
  Odyssey 4.220–32, 213n72;
    4.351–62, 192n2; *14.245–86*,
    192n2; *17.426–44*, 192n2
Horace:
  Epistles 2.1.56, 214n12
  Epodes 9.10–12, 211n15
  Odes 1.7, 214n15; *1.37*, 172,
    210n7m, 210n9, 213n86,
    213n92
  Satires 1.2, 210n24; *1.3*, 210n24;
    2.3.239–41, 211n25

Josephus:
  Against Apion 2.56–60, 211n14;
    2.57, 201n45; *2.60*, 204n6
  Jewish Antiquities:
    Book 12: *20–23*, 195n27; *103*,
      206n51; *235*, 194n64
    Book 14: *35*, 190n24; *98–99*,
      191n42; *127–37*, 198n45; *191*,
      195n19; *319*, 195n19; *324–26*,
      202n65; *394–491*, 202n2; *407*,
      209n125
    Book 15: *9*, 209n126; *22*,
      209n126; *23–38*, 209n127; *89*,
      198n46, 200n27, 201n45; *90*,
      211n27; *91–96*, 202n10; *92*,
      202n14; *96*, 218n61; *96–103*,
      203n34; *97–103*, 209n129;
      110–11, 212n50; *131–32*,
      212n50; *187–201*, 212n66;
      199–200, 213n76; *254–58*,
      209n130; *344*, 203n15
    Book 16: *128*, 205n9
    Book 17: *319*, 203n15
  Jewish War:
    Book 1: *175*, 191n42; *187–94*,
      198n45; *226*, 201n39; *242–45*,
      202n65; *243*, 211n15; *279–85*,
      202n64; *290–357*, 202n2;
      344, 209n125; *360*, 209n122,
      209n131; *361–63*, 202n10;
      364–65, 209n124; *364–85*,
      212n50; *365*, 209n131;

386–400, 212n66; *394–96*,
  213n76; *398–99*, 203n15; *440*,
  214n17
Book 2: *386*, 204n12
Book 7: *300–303*, 209n124
Juba of Mauretania (*FGrHist #275*)
  F1–3, 215n25; *F5–6*, 215n24;
  F28–34, 215n25; *F35–40*,
  215n24; *F41*, 215n25; *F45*,
  215n25; *F47–54*, 215n24;
  F56–61, 215n24; *F62–76*,
  215n25; *F67*, 215n24; *F71*,
  215n24; *F74–77*, 215n24; *F78*,
  215n25; *F79*, 215n24; *F87*,
  211n10, 215n24; *F97*, 215n25;
  F100, 215n24; *F107*, 215n25
Julian, *Letter to Themistios*, 195n13
Justin *26.3.2*, 193n45; *41.2.6*,
  203n36

Kallinikos of Petra (*FGrHist #281*)
  T1a, 215n33
Kallixeinos of Rhodes (*FGrHist
  #627*), *On Alexandria F1*,
  198n61; *F2*, 208n97
Kosmas Indikopleustas, *Christian
  Topography 3.65*, 205n18
Krinagoras of Mytilene *18*, 215n28;
  20, 195n16

Livy:
  Book 4: *20.5–11*, 212n40
  Book 22: *33.3*, 193n50
  Book 27: *4.10*, 193n47; *30.4–12*,
    193n48, 193n50
  Book 28: *7.13–16*, 193n48
  Book 30: *12–15*, 217n52
  Book 33: *40.3*, 193n50
  Book 35: *13.4*, 190n6, 193n51
  Book 42: *6.4–5*, 193n54
  Book 44: *19.6–14*, 193n56
  F54, 213n83
  Summary 68, 205n11; *111*,
    197n25; *112*, 196n15,
    197n46; *130*, 203n31; *131*,

Sidonius, *Letters 8.12.8*, 211n11

Sokrates of Rhodes (*FGrHist* #192)
   F1, 201n42

Sophronios of Damascus, *Account of
   the Miracles of Saints Cyrus
   and John 54*, 210n27

Soranus, *Gynaecology 4.12.5*, 209n5

Stobaios *2.7.2*, 194n11

Strabo, *Geography*:
   Book 2: *1.20*, 205n16; *3.4–6*,
      205n16; *3.5*, 210n14
   Book 5: *3.8*, 207n68
   Book 10: *5.3*, 210n15
   Book 11: *13.3*, 200n36, 203n31
   Book 12: *3.34*, 191n39
   Book 13: *1.30*, 210n15, 211n29
   Book 14: *1.14*, 211n29; *1.34*,
      194n7; *5.3*, 201n53, 210n15;
      5.6, 201n53, 205n10, 210n15;
      5.10, 201n54, 210n15; *6.6*,
      198n52
   Book 16: *2.41*, 203n18; *4.4*,
      195n23; *4.18*, 203n22; *4.23*,
      207n81
   Book 17: *1.5*, 194n11, 210n13; *1.6*,
      193n40, 206n49; *1.8*, 190n27,
      192n9, 192n24; *1.8–9*,
      207n69; *1.9*, 199n65, 206n57,
      209n118; *1.10*, 206n47,
      213n91; *1.11*, 189n2, 190n10,
      190n15, 191n39, 197n25,
      197n32, 198n51, 204n49,
      210n15, 215n3; *1.12*, 191n47;
      1.13, 205n16, 205n22; *1.16*,
      199n62; *1.26*, 207n81; *1.42*,
      193n26; *3.7*, 210n15

Suda:
   Chelidon, 205n37
   Didymos, 209n9
   Dioskourides, 309n6
   Habron, 210n12
   ἡμίεργον, 206n57
   Iobas, 209n9
   Timagenes, 195n14
   Tryphon, 209n10

Suetonius:
   Augustus 17.3, 212n53, 213n72,
      213n75; *17.4*, 206n63,
      214n94; *17.5*, 206n55; *18.1*,
      206n62; *69*, 204n49, 211n16;
      89.1, 195n13
   Divine Julius 35, 197n35, 198n50;
      44, 200n18, 200n19; *52*,
      198n60, 199n7, 199n10,
      200n15, 200n25; *54*, 191n29;
      56.5–7, 195n35; *76.3*,
      199n67
   Gaius 35.1–2, 215n30

Tacitus:
   Annals 2.53, 207n66; *2.59–61*,
      207n66; *4.23*, 215n29; *4.40*,
      213n79
   Histories 5.9, 215n27

Theokritos *17*, 193n39; *17.77–81*,
   205n12; *17.86–90*, 201n52

Theophrastos, *Research on Plants 9.6*,
   203n18

Thoukydides *1.104*, 192n5

Valerius Maximus *1.1.19*, 213n74;
   4.1.5, 196n10; *5.1f*, 193n58,
   200n13

Velleius:
   Book 2: *31*, 205n11; *82*, 203n43,
      208n15; *83.2*, 211n26; *84*,
      211n15, 211n34; *85*, 212n53;
      87.1, 213n93

Vergil, *Aeneid*:
   Book 1: *697–756*, 211n13; *723–27*,
      201n43
   Book 4: *172*, 204n50; *338–39*,
      204n50
   Book 8: *671–713*, 217n44; *685–88*,
      211n15; *688*, 189n1, 204n49;
      689–700, 210n9; *697*, 213n92

Xenophon, *Anabasis 1.2.23*, 201n41

Zonaras *10.31 (531)*, 215n21

Epigraphic Sources

CIL 3.7232, 204n47; *14.2610*, 214n14
IG 2.2.4994, 208n88
Kaibel, *Epigrammata graeca 118*,
    212n37
OGIS 129, 195n20, 204n7; *172*,
    194n2; *186*, 192n54; *194*,
    200n27; *195*, 201n50; *196*,
    208n111; *741*, 192n57
Pouilloux et al., *Testimonia Salamina*
    2, #87, 201n53
SEG 9.7, 194n60

Papyrus Sources

BGU 1760, 196n8; *1762*, 191n36;
    1835, 204n5; *1843*, 204n4
Lenger, *Corpus 73–6*, 196n7
Oxyrhynchus Papyri 1241, 194n1;
    1629, 200n27
Select Papyri (Loeb) 209, 196n7; *416*,
    192n55
Tebtunis Papyri 33, 192n55

Index

The terms Cleopatra (VII), M. Antonius, Egypt, and Rome occur on most pages of the text, and the index entries are meant to isolate important points rather than to be complete.

Alexandria, city in Egypt (*continued*) 110, 117, 145–50; founding of, 15, 30–33, 115; gymnasia in, 99–100, 109; Heptastadion in, 13, 109; as intellectual center, 37, 43–46, 48, 50–51, 63, 72, 123–28, 154; Kaisareion in, 13, 110–11; population of, 18, 25–26, 30, 34, 41; Timoneion in, 13, 141. *See also* Alexandrian War, Library

Alexandrian War, 62–3, 79, 107, 108, 119, 160, 206n48

Alexandros, member of Cleopatra's court, 108

Allienus, A., Roman official, 75

Ambrakian Gulf, 137, 139

Amen–Re, Egyptian divinity, 177

"Amimetobioi." *See* Inimitable Livers

Ammon, Egyptian oracle, 29

Ammonios, member of Cleopatra's court, 72, 200n17

Amyntas of Galatia, 91–92, 137–38

Ananel, Babylonian priest, 120

Anaxikrates, Greek explorer, 47

Antigone, daughter of Berenike I, 38

Antigonos II, Hasmonean, 86, 119–20

Antioch, Syrian city, 5, 11, 39, 47, 59, 86, 90, 98, 160; Caesar in, 110; coinage of, 107, 183; foundation of, 16, 32–33

Antiochis of Tlos, Greek physician, 124

Antiochos III, Seleukid king, 39, 92

Antiochos IV, Seleukid king, 40–41

Antiochos of Askalon, Greek philosopher, 44–45

Antipatros of Asklalon, 24, 59, 63, 77, 86, 119, 179

Antipatros of Macedonia, 35

Antipatros of Thessalonike, Greek poet, 126–27

Antius, Roman official, 61

Anton, Roman mythological figure, 178

Antonia (elder), daughter of M. Antonius, 89

Antonia (younger), daughter of M. Antonius, 89, 100, 152

Antonias, Cleopatra's flagship, 139

Antonius, Iullus, son of M. Antonius, 76

Antonius, L., brother of M. Antonius, 85

Antonius, M., triumvir, 9, 20, 127, 134, 153, 164, 168, 189n1, 195n19, 195n21; and Actium, 137–40; has Arsinoë IV killed, 16, 65, 79; as avenger of Caesar, 70, 75, 116; as Caesar's aide, 59, 64, 67, 72; character of, 76; and children with Cleopatra, 81, 84, 96, 99, 127, 146, 152, 167; and children with Fulvia, 110, 124, 128, 150, 152; with Cleopatra in Alexandria, 79–84, 97, 99, 109, 132; coinage of, 100, 107, 130, 173, 181–83; and Cyprus, 65, 79, 82; death and burial of, 111–12, 136, 145–47, 171, 213n81; depression of, 140–42; descendants of, 81, 129, 152, 155; as Dionysos, 99, 114, 116–17; early years of, 24–25; and Donations of Alexandria, 99–101; Egyptian estates of, 100; and first meeting with Cleopatra, 25, 57, 77; and first visit to Egypt, 24–25, 168; and Fulvia, 76, 84–85; and Herod the Great, 86–87, 89, 119–122, 136, 141–42, 202n64, 212n50; and marriage to Cleopatra, 100–101, 130, 204n50, 204n52; military capabilities of, 76, 97; moral position of, 94–95, 137; and negotiations with Octavian, 143–45; and Octavia, 85–86, 89, 94–95, 97–98, 135, 178; Parthian campaign of, 47–48, 90, 96–99; and piracy, 104; on Portland Vase, 178; propaganda war against, 27, 70, 129–31, 133, 204n49; and reorganization of East, 47, 49, 65, 82–83, 85, 91–95,

100–101, 118, 136; sacrilege and theft charged against, 133; support of scholars by, 45, 125; at Tarsos, 76–79, 82, 86, 125, 169–70; triumph of, 99, 117, 128; becomes triumvir, 75–76, 89–90, 134; vision of future of, 99–101; will of, 135–36

Antyllus, M. Antonius, son of above, 76, 110, 124, 128, 142, 143, 150

Apameia, Syrian city, 93, 96

Aphrodite, Greek goddess, 66, 116, 170, 175, 182

Apion, Greek grammarian, 125

Apis bull, 56

Apollo, Greek and Roman god, 22, 133, 151

Apollodoros of Sicily, member of Cleopatra's court, 61, 107, 169–70

Apollonios of Kition, Greek scholar, 44, 194n4

Apollonios Mys, Greek scholar, 44, 123

Apollonios of Rhodes, Greek scholar, 37, 43, 207n73

Arabes (Arabians), Arabia, 46–47, 94, 105, 114, 154–55, 169

Arados, Phoenician city, 79

Aramaic language, 47

Aratos of Soloi, Greek scholar, 126

Archelaos of Kappadokia, 76, 91–92, 104, 118, 123, 137, 153

Archelaos of Komana, 76

Archelaos of Pontos, 24–25, 164

Archibios, member of Cleopatra's court, 176

Archimedes of Syracuse, Greek scholar, 37

Areios Didymos, Greek scholar, 45–46, 123–24, 150, 214n105

Argaios, son of Ptolemy I, 35

Ariarathes X of Kappadokia, 71, 91, 199n11

Aristarchos of Samothrake, Greek scholar, 37, 43, 128

Aristeas, Greek scholar, 48

Aristoboulos III, Hasmonean, 119–20

Ariston of Alexandria, Greek scholar, 44, 123–25

Aristophanes of Byzantion, Greek scholar, 125

Aristos of Askalon, Greek scholar, 44

Aristotle of Stageira, Greek scholar, 31, 33–34, 38, 44, 196n41, 200n32

Armenia, 96–100, 107, 129, 136, 141, 161, 183

aromatics, 47, 105–106

Arsinoë II, 2, 35–37, 107, 114, 115, 176, 182, 205n27

Arsinoë III, 36

Arsinoë IV, sister of Cleopatra, 16, 18, 26, 59–60, 62, 65, 80, 114, 164–65, 191n51; and Alexandrian War, 63–64, 159–60; in Caesar's triumph, 64, 71, 147, 160; death of, 16, 79, 160, 201n45; exile of, 64, 71, 77, 160

Arsinoë, cities so named, 114–15

Artavasdes of Media Atropatene, 141, 153

Artavasdes II of Armenia, 97, 99, 129, 141

Artemidoros of Tarsos, Greek scholar, 125

Artemisia (I) of Halikarnasos, 2, 75, 80–81

Artemisia (II) of Halikarnassos, 80–81

Askalon, Levantine city, 11, 12, 59, 92, 107, 179

asps, 7, 35, 117, 148–49, 153, 171, 179, 214n98

astronomy, at Cleopatra's court, 44, 126

Athene, Greek goddess, 117, 133, 182

Athenion, general of Cleopatra's, 138

Athens, Athenians, 7, 11, 29, 33–34, 44, 97–98, 115, 117, 140–41, 160; Antonius in, 76, 89, 135, 143, 161;

elephants, 46, 105, 154
Eleusis, Egyptian village, 40
Eleutheros, Levantine river, 92
Ephesos, Anatolian city, 11, 24, 116, 133–34, 161, 183; as refuge of Arsinoë IV, 16, 64, 75, 77, 79, 160, 201n45
Eratosthenes of Cyrene, Greek scholar, 37, 43, 66, 125, 127, 199n63, 200n17
Eros, Greek divinity, 107, 116, 178, 216n17
Eros, slave of Antonius, 145
Erythraian Sea, 27, 106
Este, site in Veneto, 107
Ethiopia, Ethiopians, 46–47, 66, 105, 113, 149, 169
Euclid, Greek scholar, 34, 43
Eudoros of Alexandria, Greek scholar, 44–45, 123–26
Eudoxos of Knidos, Greek adventurer, 105
Eunoë Maura of Mauretania, 74
Euphranor, Rhodian admiral, 206n48
Euphrates, Mesopotamian river, 96
Euphronios, royal tutor, 128, 143
Eurydike, wife of Ptolemy I, 35–36

Fayum, Egyptian district, 100, 177
Fonteius Capito, C., Roman officer, 90
Fulvia, Roman matron, 3, 76, 84–85, 110, 131, 142, 150, 152, 160
Furies, Greek divinities, 130

Gabinians, Roman garrison, 25, 54, 56, 58, 60, 62
Gabinius, Aulus, Roman officer, 24–25, 45, 54, 57, 76, 128, 168
Gaius Caligula, Roman emperor, 110, 152, 155–56
Galatia, Anatolian district, 91
Gallus, Aelius, Roman officer, 114, 126

Gallus, C. Cornelius, Roman officer, 110, 145–46, 151
Ganymedes, royal tutor, 63–64
Gaul, 58, 143
Gaza, Levantine city, 11, 12, 92, 95, 121
Geb, Egyptian divinity, 182
Germanicus, grandson of Antonius, 112
Glaphyra of Kappadokia, 76, 85, 91–92, 131
Glaukos, Greek divinity, 133
Glaukos, Greek physician, 124
Gnaios, Greek artist, 127, 154
Gracchi, Roman family, 42
Greece, 35, 56, 58–59, 126, 137–40, 144, 168; art and material culture of, 113, 176, 182–83; and Cleopatra, 51, 75, 79, 135, 142, 146, 175; culture of, 15, 19, 33, 45, 63; language of, 9, 32, 46–49, 154–56; literature of, 37–38, 48–49; political institutions of, 30–31, 34, 101; religion of, 99, 114–17; and Rome, 38–40, 72, 167
Greeks, 19, 108, 143, 156, 170, 189n3; and Egypt, 16, 29–31, 34, 36, 115; and incest, 36–37

Halikarnassos, Anatolian city, 2, 75, 80, 115
Hannibal, Carthaginian leader, 38–39, 95
Haremephis, Egyptian official, 108
Harpokrates, 114, 182. See also Horus
Hasmoneans, Judaean dynasty, 86, 91, 119–21
Hathor, Egyptian divinity, 27, 71, 113, 176
Hatshepsut, Egyptian queen, 2, 81, 177
Hebraoi (Hebrews), 46–47, 169
Helen of Sparta, 130, 213n72
Helios, Greek divinity, 84, 90

45–46, 105, 110, 117, 144–50; and
Herod the Great, 119, 141–42,
144–45, 153; interest in Egypt of,
103–104, 106; invades Egypt, 108,
135, 144–50; and negotiations
with Cleopatra and Antonius,
128, 142–47; and Perusine War,
84–85, 131; poetry of, 85, 131;
turns public sentiment against
Antonius, 94–95, 98–101, 117,
130, 133; tomb of, 112, 152; as
triumvir, 75–76, 85, 89–90; war
declared on Cleopatra by, 136–37.
See also Augustus
Odysseus, Greek hero, 29
Olbe (Ura), Anatolian state, 83
Olous, Cretan site, 94
Olympos of Alexandria, Greek
physician, 7, 44, 124, 146, 148,
171
Onesandros of Paphos, Librarian, 43
Oppius, C., Roman official, 70
Orikon (Orikuni), Illyrian city, 58
Orontes, Syrian river, 47, 93
Orthosia, Phoenician city, 107, 182
Osiris, Egyptian divinity, 115, 117
Ostrakine, Egyptian village, 46
Ovinius, Q., Roman official, 105

Pachom, Egyptian official, 108
Pachomios, Egyptian official, 108
Palestine, 75, 92
Pamenches, Egyptian official, 108
Panopolite Nome, 108
Paphos, Cypriot town, 22, 43
Paraitonion, Libyan city, 12, 140, 145
Parthia, Parthians, 5, 46–48,
83–84, 86–87, 93, 100, 152, 169;
Antonius's expedition to, 90,
95–99, 104, 117, 120, 134, 160–61;
Crassus's expedition to, 25, 56, 95,
97
Patrai, Greek city, 107, 137, 161, 173,
183
Paul of Tarsos, 167

Pelousion, Egyptian city, 12, 13, 25,
59–62, 96, 145
Pergamon, Anatolian city, 19, 33, 44,
94, 133
Peripatic school, 44–45, 127
Periplous of the Erythraian Sea, 105
Peritheban Nome, 108
Persia, Persians, 30, 31, 44, 49,
193n35; Persian Wars, 2, 80
Perusia, 85
Perusine War, 84–85, 131, 160
Petesenufe, scribe of Isis, 151
Petra, Nabataean city, 11, 12, 47
Petubastes III, Egyptian priest, 166
Petubastes IV, Egyptian priest, 150
Petubastes, family of, 166
Pharnakes, son of Mithradates VI,
67, 70
Pharos, district of Alexandria, 13, 33,
37, 48, 109, 141, 206n48
Pharsalos, Battle of, 58, 60, 64, 159
Phasael, brother of Herod, 86
Philai, Egyptian site, 117, 151
Philip II of Macedonia, 16, 35, 190n6
Philip V of Macedonia, 39
Philippi, Battle of, 4, 65, 75–76, 83,
103, 160
philology, at Cleopatra's court, 125
philosophy, at Ptolemaic court,
44–45, 124–25
Philostratos, teacher of Cleopatra,
45–46, 124, 153
Philotas of Amphissa, Greek scholar,
7, 82, 124
Phoenicia, Phoenicians, 47, 79, 92,
95, 107, 144, 182–83
Pinarius Scarpus, L., Roman official,
141, 183
pirates, 26, 104
Plancus, L. Munatius, 132–33, 135,
152
Plato, Greek scholar, 31, 33–34, 44
Po, Italian river valley, 107
Polemon of Pontos, 91–92, 137
Polybios, Greek scholar, 40, 43

Pompeii, Italian city, 174–75, 178, 207n72

Pompeius, Gn., the Great, 9, 20–26, 57–61, 64, 111, 159, 197n22

Pompeius, Gn., son of above, 57–58, 77

Pompeius, Sextus, son of Pompeius the Great, 111

Pontos, Anatolian district, 67, 91, 152, 160

Popilius Laenas, C., Roman official, 40

Portland Vase, 178

Poseidonios of Apameia, Greek scholar, 66, 93, 125, 199n63

Potheinos, Egyptian official, 56–63, 103, 107

Proculeius, C., Roman official, 145–46

Proteus, Alexandrian islet, 109

Psenptais III, Egyptian priest, 166

Psylloi, African ethnic group, 149

Ptah, Egyptian divinity, 30, 32, 59; priestly family of, 15–16, 18, 32–33, 59, 150, 154, 166

Ptolemaia, festival, 22, 100, 116

Ptolemaic dynasty, 15, 23, 61, 84, 96, 100, 111, 130, 150, 165–66; characteristics of, 32–37, 70; cultural support by, 33–34, 43–45, 123–38, 154; genealogy of, 163–64; origins of, 32–35; religious policy of, 32, 114–17; succession concerns of, 17, 35–36, 41–42, 59, 80, 92, 118. *See also* individual monarchs

Ptolemaic Empire, 21, 107–108, 123–25, 128, 140, 155–56; decline of, 16, 40, 82, 151; economic policy of, 47, 93, 104–105; extent of, 22, 31–32, 34, 62, 82–83, 92–96, 179, 183–83; foreign policy of, 27, 32, 39, 46–47, 117–22, 134; military of, 94, 114, 145; and Rome, 37–41, 104; trade policy of, 51, 105–106

Ptolemaion, tomb of Ptolemies, 111–12

Ptolemaios, member of Cleopatra's court, 108

Ptolemais, Phoenician city, 92, 107, 144, 182–83

Ptolemais Hermiou, Egyptian city, 12, 34, 114

Ptolemy I of Egypt, 3, 29–36, 38, 49, 82, 108, 115, 149, 164, 190n6

Ptolemy II of Egypt, 3, 82, 92, 94, 96, 109, 115, 127; and Ptolemaia, 100, 116; reign of, 33–38, 46–49

Ptolemy III of Egypt, 27, 38, 108

Ptolemy IV of Egypt, 36–39, 49, 66, 92, 127

Ptolemy V of Egypt, 15–16, 36–37, 39, 41, 84, 106, 164

Ptolemy VI of Egypt, 37, 40–41, 71, 108, 127, 164, 182, 194n61

Ptolemy VII of Egypt, 37, 194n61

Ptolemy VIII of Egypt, 37, 49, 54, 95, 128, 164, 166, 177, 194n61; career of, 40–42; expels intellectuals, 43, 123, 125; and Massinissa, 48, 154, 179; Roman visits of, 23, 41–42, 168

Ptolemy IX of Egypt, 17, 22, 37, 41, 43, 106, 164

Ptolemy X of Egypt, 17, 37, 41, 84, 134, 164

Ptolemy XI of Egypt, 17, 37, 84, 164

Ptolemy XII of Egypt, 3, 16, 53, 60, 62, 105–106, 147, 164, 165–66; accession of, 17–18; building program of, 27, 113; character of, 17–18, 27, 116; death of, 27, 53–54, 57, 177; debts of, 20, 23–24, 106, 141; restoration of, 24–25, 57, 80, 119; and Rome, 20–26, 61, 72, 115, 168; succession concerns of, 26–27, 53; support of scholars by, 43–46, 123–24; will of, 26–27, 58, 64

Ptolemy XIII of Egypt, 16, 18, 26, 37, 53, 56–64, 124, 164, 165, 179; lack of education of, 51; pretender takes name of, 79

Ptolemy XIV of Egypt, 16, 18, 57, 60, 62, 71, 74–75, 164, 197n17, 200n27

Ptolemy XV of Egypt. *See* Caesarion.

Ptolemy Keraunos, 36

Ptolemy of Cyprus, 17, 22, 44, 62, 164

Ptolemy of Mauretania, 106, 155–56, 164

Ptolemy Philadelphos, 96, 100, 153, 164

Pyrrhon, Greek philosopher, 125

Pyrrhos of Epeiros, 38

Pytheas of Massalia, Greek explorer, 66

Pythodoris of Pontos, 81, 91–92, 152

Punic Wars, 38, 178

queens, 2–3, 80–81, 118, 177. *See also* monarchs

Rabirius Postumus, C., Roman banker, 21–27, 35, 46

Raphia, Egyptian city, 39

Red Sea, 11, 12, 37, 46–47, 105, 114, 137, 142–43

Rhakotis, Egyptian toponym, 30

Rhodes, Greek island, 11, 22, 94, 125, 141, 143, 206n48

Rhodon, royal tutor, 128

Rhoiteion (Baba Kale), Anatolian site, 133

Rome, Romans, 11; buildings in, 67, 72, 110, 112–13, 116, 151–52; Campus Martius in, 112, 115, 152; Capitol in, 21, 99, 116, 130; and Carthaginian wars, 38, 48, 178; Eastern policy of, 38–42; Egyptian relations of, 37–42; Forum Julium in, 72–73, 95, 110, 116, 174–75; Greek scholars in, 44–45; and Isis, 72, 115–16; and Parthians, 56, 95–97

Rufio, freedman of Caesar, 67

Salome, sister of Herod, 121

Samos, Greek island, 133, 135

Saxa, L. Dicidius, Roman officer, 83

Sceptics, 124

Schedia, Egyptian dockyard, 66

sciences, at Cleopatra's court, 125–26

Selene, the Moon, 84

Seleukid dynasty, 16, 21, 32, 39–40, 61, 82, 84, 92–93, 118, 193n35; and Cleopatra, 47–48, 59, 80, 93, 182

Seleukos I, 16, 32, 93, 164

Seleukos, member of Cleopatra's court, 108

Seleukos, Ptolemaic military officer, 145, 197n27

Semiramis, Babylonian queen, 156

Septuagint, 48

Serapion, governor of Cyprus, 65, 75, 79

Sibylline oracles, 23, 25, 132, 169–71, 195n37

Sidon, Phoenician city, 92, 97

Sikyon, Greek city, 85

silk, 106

Siwa, Egyptian oasis, 29

Snonais, Egyptian religious functionary, 177

Socotra, Indian Ocean island, 105

Sokrates of Rhodes, Greek historian, 8, 78, 127, 169–70

Sophonisba, beloved of Massinissa, 178–79

Sosigenes of Alexandria, Greek scholar, 72, 126

Sosius, C., Roman official, 89, 134, 211n32

Sostratos of Alexandria, Greek scholar, 124

Sostratos of Knidos, Greek architect, 108–109

Sotades of Maroneia, Greek poet, 36–37

Spain, 20, 74, 133, 143

Split, Dalamatian city, 107

Staius Murcus, L., Roman officer, 75

Statilius Crito, T., Greek physician, 50

Stoic school, 45

Strabo of Amaseia, Greek scholar, 45, 63, 65, 109, 112, 114, 126

Straton of Lampsakos, Greek scholar, 127

Successors, 30–32, 82, 100

Suez, Egyptian city, 114, 142

Sulla, L. Cornelius, 17, 44

Syene, Egyptian toponym, 12, 66

"Synapothanoumenoi," 143

Syria, Syrians, 24–25, 32, 39, 47, 79, 83, 92, 120; and Cleopatra, 59–60, 63, 93–96, 100, 104, 107, 182; language of, 46–47, 169; as Roman province, 21, 54–56, 75, 89, 121, 132, 134, 142; and Seleukids, 16, 21, 32, 40

Tainaron, Greek toponym, 75, 140

Tarentum, Italian city, 90, 137

Tarkondimotos of Kilikia, 82–83

Tarsos, Kilikian city, 11, 65–66, 76–79, 82, 85–86, 116, 125, 139, 169–70

thalamegos, 66, 77, 170

Thales of Miletos, Greek scholar, 29

Thebes, Thebaid, Egyptian locale, 12, 34, 53, 58–59, 108, 113

Theodoros, royal tutor, 128

Theodosios II, eastern Roman emperor, 134

Theodotos of Chios, royal tutor, 57, 60, 64, 124

Theokritos of Syracuse, Greek poet, 125

Theon, Greek grammarian, 125

Theon, member of Cleopatra's court, 108

Theophilos, agent of Antonius, 147

Theophrastos of Eresos, Greek scholar, 33–34, 127

Thera, Greek island, 115

Thyrsos, freedman of Octavian, 144

Tigellius Hermogenes, M., Greek artist, 127

Timagenes of Alexandria, Greek scholar, 45, 128

Timon of Athens, 141

Tinteris, Egyptian village, 103

Tipasa, Mauretanian city, 112, 155

Trajan, Roman emperor, 50

Tripolis, Phoenician city, 107, 182

triumph, 64, 71–72, 99, 116–17, 146–47, 149, 153, 156, 172

triumvirate, 75–76, 85, 89–90, 98, 134, 176

Trogodytika, Trogodytes, 46–47, 105, 169

Trojan War, 29

Tryphon of Alexandria, Greek scholar, 125

Turullius, Publius, Roman official, 143

Tyre, Phoenician city, 29, 60, 79, 92

uraeus, 149, 175, 176

Varro, M. Terentius, Roman scholar, 72

Venus, Roman goddess, 72, 116, 132, 152, 175, 178

Vestal Virgins, 135

wills, royal, 17, 19–20, 26–27, 33, 41–42, 58, 62, 64, 70, 74; of Antonius, 135–36

wine, 93, 105, 116, 131, 134, 144

Zenobia of Palmyra, 81, 156

Zenodoros of Ituraia, 93

Zenon, Greek rhetorician, 91

Zeugma, Syrian city, 96

Zeus, Greek god, 77, 83, 133

Zopyros of Alexandria, Greek physician, 44, 50

Zoroaster, 49